AF424298

Cybernetics for the 21st Century

Vol. 1: Epistemological Reconstruction

Edited by Yuk Hui

Philosophy, Art and Technology Series

Cybernetics for the 21st Century
Vol.1 Epistemological Reconstruction

First published 2024

Hanart Press
Jia Li Hall Foundation Limited
Flat C, 2F Mai On Industrial Building
19 Kung Yip Street Kwai Chung
New Territories, Hong Kong

Editor: Yuk Hui
Associate editor: Jianru Wu
Copyeditor: Heleen Schröder
Proofreader: Alice Ladenburg

ISBN: 978-988-70268-0-8 (print)
ISBN: 978-988-70268-4-6 (e-book)

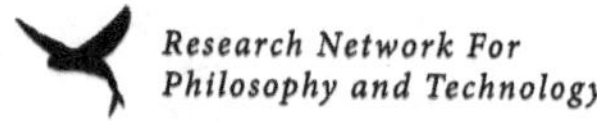

Acknowledgements

This project was initially organized by the Media Lab of the Guangdong Times Museum, the Cosmotechnics and Critical AI Project at the City University of Hong Kong, and the Research Network for Philosophy and Technology. Hanart Forum and the M Art Foundation kindly supported the continuation of the first phase of this project after the sudden closure of the Times Museum in October 2022. I would like to take this occasion to thank: all the authors for their contributions; Wu Jianru, previously curator at the Times Museum's media lab and currently curator at the Hanart Forum, for the invitation to initiate this programme and for her production (with the assistance of Guo Yun) of the video lectures and symposia that took place between autumn 2022 and spring 2023; Johnson Chang of Hanart Forum for supporting the publication of these proceedings and the second phase of this project; Heleen Schröder for her excellent copyediting; and Edwin Lo and Ashley Wong, who were essential to the operation of the Research Network for Philosophy and Technology in the past years.

Yuk Hui
Autumn 2023
Rotterdam

Table of Contents

Introduction

Why Cybernetics Now?

Yuk Hui

The title *Cybernetics for the 21st Century* may arouse an immediate question: Why cybernetics, and why now? As Katherine Hayles notes, by the 1970s the term cybernetics seemed to have disappeared from public discourse. The term 'cybernetics' was coined by Norbert Wiener in the 1940s as an outcome of his collaboration with Arturo Rosenblueth and his research group. We know that the term originates from the Greek word *kubernetes*, and in 1834, André-Marie Ampère designated the term *cybernétique* for the future art of governance. The term gained even more international fame through his seminal book his seminal *Cybernetics, or Control and Communication in Man and Animal* (1948), which was dedicated to Rosenblueth in acknowledgement of their long-term collaboration. In the following decades, cybernetics rose to a generalized science which could provide a systematic and evolutionary analysis of any given phenomenon, be that Humberto Maturana and Francesco Varela's autopoiesis or Niklas Luhmann's social system. This development, from the period of the Macy Conferences (1946–1953) to the post-Macy Conference period, is widely recognized as a shift from first-order cybernetics to second-order cybernetics. We can identify here the change of vocabulary—from feedback to recursion—which expresses itself in different tautologies: cybernetics of cybernetics,[1] society of society, observing observation, and so on. We can also find the effort to tackle the complex phenomenon of living beings, which demands neologisms such as 'structural coupling' and 'operational closure'. This introduction does not aim to recount the history of cybernetics—Hayles's *How We Became Posthuman* (1999), Mathieu Triclot's *Le moment cybernétique* (2008) as well as the Macy Conference Proceedings edited by Claus Pias (2016)[2], have been key texts for understanding different waves of cybernetics—instead it serves as an invitation to reflect on the relevance of cybernetics to our times.

1   Heinz von Foester, 'Cybernetics of Cybernetics', in *Communication and Control*, ed. K. Krippendorff (New York: Gordon and Breach, 1979), 5–8.
2   *Cybernetics The Macy Conferences 1946–1953: The Complete Transactions*, ed. Claus Pias (Chicago: University of Chicago Press, 2016).

Martin Heidegger, in his 1966 interview (published ten years later) with *Der Spiegel*, was asked what came after the end of philosophy; Heidegger answered: cybernetics.[3] In other words, he announced that cybernetics marked the end of Western philosophy. This assertion is dramatic but significant for reflecting not only on the history and future of philosophy, but also on the future of cybernetics. When speaking of cybernetics, we tend to trace its origins, as Wiener himself did, to Gottfried Wilhelm Leibniz. However, Heidegger went back even further, to Plato's metaphysics, which for him already anticipated the arrival of cybernetics. Its compatibility with philosophy also means that cybernetics has been a philosophical project since the beginning. For Heidegger, the triumph of cybernetics therefore equally means the end of philosophy—end here also means completion. In view of such an end of philosophy, Heidegger calls for a thinking to come; a thinking that is able to overcome the latest and last stage of Western philosophy: cybernetics.[4]

Cybernetics is, in this postulation, conceived as a triumph of method. That is to say, as a scientific method, cybernetics became dominant, as was the case of mechanism in the time of René Descartes. Cybernetics marked the triumph of the scientific method that rendered philosophical reflections redundant. This is also observed by Gilbert Simondon when he compares Wiener's Cybernetics with Descartes' *Discourse on Method* and considers the former as a new epistemology based on reflectivity.[5] Cybernetics is not something that arrives from somewhere outside of Western philosophy, but rather is its own realization or completion. Heidegger's assertion remains to be thought and analysed, as I have tried to show in *Recursivity and Contingency* (2019), as well as in the article titled 'Machine and Ecology' included in this volume.[6]

Ironically, philosophy has not ended, since departments of philosophy continue to survive, while the term cybernetics has slowly

---

3   Martin Heidegger, 'Nur noch ein Gott kann uns retten', *Der Spiegel*, 30 May 1976, 193–219.
4   Martin Heidegger, 'The End of Philosophy and the Task of Thinking', in *On Time and Being*, trans. Joan Stambaugh (New York: Harper & Row, 1972); see also Yuk Hui, 'Philosophy after Automation', *Philosophy Today* 65 no. 2 (2021): 217–33.
5   Gilbert Simondon, *Du mode d'existence des objets techniques* (Paris : Aubier, 2012[1958]), 147.
6   Yuk Hui, *Recursivity and Contingency* (London: Rowman and Littlefield International, 2019).

vanished from university curriculums, with the exception, surprisingly, of the National University of Australia, that recently established a
School of Cybernetics. However, the absence of cybernetics even from
engineering disciplines might also mean that it is omnipresent, like air:
we do not pay attention to it as long as we can breathe properly. Heidegger's assertion is not without significance, and in this volume, we will
see how cybernetics was applied in various domains in politics, design,
engineering and art in the twentieth century.

This anthology is dedicated to epistemological reconstruction.
Some contributors reconstruct the history of cybernetics and its significance in both the history of philosophy and the history of technology;
others discuss the reception and localization of cybernetics in Poland,
Chile, the Soviet Union, China, Japan, the USA and Britain. Different
scientific communities have attempted to localize cybernetics in order
to resolve specific socio-political problems, ranging from the Cybersyn
project in Chile to birth control policy in China. These accounts provide
the historical and cultural background of the emergence of cybernetics
in different parts of the world, and transmit the names of scientists and
thinkers, as well as some neologisms, that remain unknown to most of
us today. For example, a Polish thinker inspired by Ampère has further
elaborated on the term 'cybernetics' as the art of governance, and China's one-child policy was implicitly an application of cybernetics.

If we want to look for cybernetics for the twenty-first century, it is
necessary to take note both of the diversity of thought and imagination
that happened on other continents, and of the shortcomings of the cybernetic projects. Cybernetics does not have a single history limited to
the invention and elaboration of some American scientists, nor to that
of a few recently rediscovered French thinkers who connect cybernetics to continental philosophy, like Pierre de Latil's *Thinking by Machine:
A Study of Cybernetics* (1953), Raymond Ruyer's *La cybernétique et
l'origine de l'information* (1954) and Gilbert Simondon's *On the Mode
of Existence of Technical Objects* (1958). Slava Gerovitch's earlier work
From Newspeak to Cyberspeak: A History of Soviet Cybernetics (2004)
and Andrew Pickering's *The Cybernetic Brain: Sketches of Another Future* (2010) set good examples for us to understand cybernetics beyond
such a limited history. The richness of cybernetics is yet to be explored.
However, despite the temptation to categorize cybernetics according
to different localities, it is futile to assign a nationality to cybernetics,
because cybernetics aims to be a universal science, and as such it

cannot be pinned down to a specific nation, as Stanford Beer claimed in his lecture 'Recursion of Power', which started with an appreciation of Pierre Teilhard de Chardin's noosphere.[7] At the same time, as a universal science, it has to be 'placed', therefore subject to a 'localization', or it would remain an 'abstract universal', as Hegel would call it.

In terms of its socio-political implications, cybernetics endeavoured to introduce a 'human use of human beings' by eliminating the 'inhuman use of human beings.' Machines can take up the tasks considered as inhuman use and free the human for human use. From this aspect, early cybernetic thinking is more than relevant today, as Matthieu Triclot's analysis shows. It also introduced a new kind of technocracy, which no longer takes the top-down approach of classical mechanism, but rather offers a flexibility that welcomes contingency and irregularities. In this sense, it is also ambiguous, because cybernetics could be applied in the realization of a socialist, a communist as well as an anarcho-neoliberal management. This has to do with the fact that epistemologically, cybernetics aims to break through the opposition between mechanism and vitalism and developed a theory of organismic operation based on feedback. Its continuation in second-order cybernetics was closely linked to complex organizations in biology and neuroscience, as well as in business management. Ontologically, according to Hans Jonas, cybernetics has overcome the dualist logic pervasive since Aristotle and presents a unified logic and, according to Gotthard Günther, it has overcome the two values system of Aristotelian logic and gestures towards a three-value or multi-value logic.[8] Wiener, as we know, endeavoured to make cybernetics a universal discipline that could integrate all other disciplines. Cybernetic thinking based on feedback and information indeed provides a generalized model for understanding the dynamism of living beings and living phenomena, or more precisely, a theory of individuation based on feedback and homeostasis. Cybernetics is closer to thermodynamics and biology than to the classical mechanics and mechanism. The triumph of second-order cybernetics could also resonate with the rise of a thermodynamic

7   Stafford Beer, 'Recursion of Powers', in *Power, Autonomy, Utopia*, ed. Robert Trappl (New York: Plenum Press, 1986).
8   Hans Jonas, *The Phenomenon of Life: Toward a Philosophical Biology* (Evanston: Northwestern University Press, 2001), 111; Charles Parsons, 'Gotthard Günther', in *Gödel's Collected Works, vol. 4*, ed. Solomon Feferman and John W. Dawson (Oxford: Clarendon, 2003), 458.

ideology in the 1980s and 1990s, namely the free-market economy, neoliberalism and Francis Fukuyama's 'end of history'. Therefore, it is not surprising to read that Friedrich Hayek found in cybernetics the most adequate description of his idea of market mechanism.[9]

Cybernetics, the forgotten term in the engineering curriculum today, should be resurrected (in the context of education), in order to understand where we are at the present. This retrospective could be read as an attempt to address the current impasses concerning the division of disciplines, the superficiality of interdisciplinary methodologies, and the emptiness of art-tech enthusiasm. The history of cybernetics can reveal more than what we thought we knew—and yet we hardly know—and allows us to reflect on the possibilities of new transdisciplinary approaches.

The twenty-first century is a century of cybernetics. Many have been trying to distinguish cybernetics from artificial intelligence and artificial intelligence from machine learning. It is clear that cybernetics and today's AI belong to two different ages, but it is undeniable that cybernetics has laid an epistemological foundation for modern automation. The application of these technologies has been associated with static control via digital apparatuses, and with cybernetics's intimate relation to military research as was, and continues to be, the case in the USA and beyond. These observations are all true and important, and we must be very cautious with the application of cybernetics in politics, which has the tendency to produce police states and surveillance societies; a tendency that we must confront and resist, as Tiqqun's *The Cybernetic Hypothesis* (2020) warns. However, a more philosophically adequate understanding of cybernetics, which goes beyond the critique of surveillance capitalism, and beyond Heidegger's verdict, is urgently needed. Cybernetics is neither a technology nor an artefact, but rather, as Heidegger would say, a generalized scientific method or a completed metaphysics.[10] We have yet to critically re-examine the possibilities that cybernetics has attempted to open and its potential application for truly transdisciplinary research, and to

9   F. A. Hayek, *Law, Legislation and Liberty: A New Statement of the Liberal Principles of Justice and Political Economy* (London: Routledge, 1982), xviii.
10   Yuk Hui, 'ChatGPT, or the Eschatology of Machines," *E-flux* 137, https://www.e-flux.com/journal/137/544816/chatgpt-or-the-'eschatology-of-machines/.

explore the impasses caused by its actualization in our contemporary society. Ecological thinking (here we might want to refer to Erich Hörl's thesis on the parallel between cybernetization and ecologization),[11] artificial intelligence (the Dartmouth conference in 1956 was a response to the aftermath of the Macy Conferences), and complex theory (which is still very important today in various disciplines such as Earth system science and Cliodynamics) are continuations of the cybernetic project in this sense. Therefore, a return to the history of cybernetics is indispensable for understanding our contemporary situation.

What we are looking for here is not only a plea for the historical importance of cybernetics, but also cybernetics for the twenty-first century; that is to say, technologies and technological imaginations that exceed the framework and the ideological naivety of its twentieth-century incarnation. This naivety consists of the insistence upon the objectivity of cybernetics, and that in this sense cybernetics remains a science. We recall the claim painted on the wall outside Niklas Luhmann's house in Lüneburg, that Luhmann had invented a social theory free from ideology![12] Alas, is not a social theory free from ideology itself an ideology? It does not mean that we have to depreciate Luhmann; on the contrary, we should appreciate his innovative and systematic approach. Other than this ideological naivety, we also have to be critical of the enthusiasm to overcome the opposition between the machine and organism (which was also expressed in the notion of the cyborg in the 1990s), as Hayles and I both suggest in our contributions. Today, we remain in a state of naivety that expresses itself in the pursuit of a transhumanist future, and we are blind to our own conditions of existence, while longing for immortality and superintelligence.

In 1971 Gregory Bateson described a feedback loop that traps alcoholics: one glass of beer won't kill me; okay, I've already started, a second one should be fine; well, two already, why not three? An

11   Erich Hörl, 'A Thousand Ecologies: The Process of Cyberneticization and General Ecology', in *The Whole Earth: California and the Disappearance of the Outside*, ed. Diedrich Diederichsen and Anselm Franke (Berlin: Sternberg, 2013), 121–30.
12   The text on the wall reads: 'In dem zugehörenden Anwesen verbrachte der Soziologe Niklas Luhmann (geb. 1927) seine Kindheit und Jugend. Er entwickelte eine weltweit anerkannte, soziale Systeme übergreifend analysierende, ideologiefreie Gesellschaftstheorie.' (The sociologist Niklas Luhmann (born 1927) spent his childhood and youth in this place. He developed a globally recognized ideology-free theory of society for a comprehensive analysis of social system).

alcoholic, if they are lucky, might get out of this positive feedback loop by 'hitting bottom'; by surviving a fatal disease or a car accident, for example.[13] We moderns are like alcoholics who have failed to get out of the positive feedback of progress, like Nietzsche describes in *The Gay Science* (1882): the pursuit of the infinite leads to the realization that nothing is more frightening than the infinite.[14] A new recursive epistemology in Bateson's sense, inheriting cybernetic thinking while seeking to overcome its intoxication, is needed for our programme of re-orientation.[15] This new programme can only set off from cybernetics and it can only survive by going beyond cybernetics—an attempt that also occurs within the history of cybernetics, when Varela tried to retrieve the concept of freedom by staging an antagonism between Wiener on one side and John von Neumann and Alan Turing on the other.[16]

The anthology, dedicated to epistemological reconstruction in both the historical and geographical sense, is divided into two parts. The first focuses on the history of concepts in cybernetics. Brunella Antomarini's 'Translating Rationalism: Leibniz and Cybernetics' offers us a retrospective on the influence of Leibniz on Wiener's concept of cybernetics, and an explanation why Leibniz was referred to by the latter as the patron saint of cybernetics. My own 'Machine and Ecology' restages cybernetics in the history of philosophy, as a completion of Kant's organic condition of philosophy, imposed since the *Critique of Judgement* (1790). I suggest that cybernetics should be re-situated in a much broader context—this is also the spirit of Bateson's recursive

13   The essay 'The Cybernetics of "Self": A Theory of Alcoholism' is collected in Gregory Bateson, *Steps to an Ecology of Mind* (Northvale: Jason Aronson, 1987).
14   Friedrich Nietzsche, *The Gay Science*, ed. Bernard Williams, trans. Josefine Nauckhoff and Adrian Del Cargo (Cambridge: Cambridge University Press, 2001), 119, aphorism 124: 'We have forsaken the land and gone to sea! We have destroyed the bridge behind us—more so, we have demolished the land behind us! Now, little ship, look out! Beside you is the ocean; it is true, it does not always roar, and at times it lies there like silk and gold and dreams of goodness. But there will be hours when you realize that it is infinite and that there is nothing more awesome than infinity. Oh, the poor bird that has felt free and now strikes against the walls of this cage! Woe, when homesickness for the land overcomes you, as if there had been more *freedom* there—and there is no more "land"!'
15   One way of doing so is to think through art, as Andrew Pickering suggests in this volume, and as I have done myself in my last book; see Yuk Hui, *Art and Cosmotechnics* (Minneapolis: University of Minnesota Press, 2021).
16   Francisco Varela, 'Steps to a cybernetics of autonomy', in *Power, Autonomy, Utopia,* ed. Robert Trappl (New York: Plenum Press, 1986), 117.

epistemology—namely a locality, through a re-reading of Heidegger's seminar 'Hölderlin's Hymn "The Ister"'; and only in this sense can we talk about an ecology of machines. Mathieu Triclot's 'Ontology and the Politics of Information in the First Cybernetics' brings us back to the debate on an ontology of information, and highlights the socio-political importance of such an ontology, illustrated by Wiener's effort to eliminate the 'inhuman use of human being'—a thesis that is becoming more and more important in view of the contemporary paranoia about robotic domination and mass unemployment. Kathrine Hayles's 'Detoxifying Cybernetics: From Homeostasis to Autopoiesis and Beyond' suggests detoxifying cybernetics by revisiting the first and second wave of cybernetics—especially their effort to realize a machine-organism—and the collaboration between Lynn Margulis and James Lovelock. Hayles proposes a new framework that does not prioritize the living being and its environment, but rather a 'technosymbiosis' consisting of a cognitive assemblage constituted by humans, living non-human organisms and computational media. Finally, we have a special contribution, 'James Lovelock, Gaia, and the Remembering of Biological Being', from Dorion Sagan, who pays homage to James Lovelock and recounts the encounter between Lovelock and his mother, Lynn Margulis. Sagan's account is not only personal witness, it also lays down a scientifically informed philosophical foundation of the Gaia theory. This special contribution was originally commissioned by the Research Network for Philosophy and Technology after the death of Lovelock.

The second part is dedicated to the development and implication of cybernetics in different regions around the world. Andrew Pickering outlines a trajectory of British cybernetics, with its relation to the brain, and beyond the brain into art and society; he reconnects the cybernetic imagination with my own cosmotechnics. Slava Gerovitch challenges the universality of AI and cybernetics by demonstrating how the scientists in the Soviet Union rejected American cybernetics and developed different models conditioned by their own socio-economic and political constrains. Michał Krzykawski offers us a history of cybernetics in the Polish People's Republic as a dialogue between cybernetics and historical materialism. He also introduces the work of Bronisław Trentowski, who, under the influence of André-Marie Ampère, published *The Relation of Philosophy to Cybernetics as the Art of Governing a Nation* in 1843. Dylan Levi King recounts a little-known history of cybernetics in China around the figure of the nuclear scientist Qian Xuesen, and outlines some of its startling implications for the one-child policy and planned economy. David Maulén de los Reyes provides us with a historical survey of the introduction and application of cybernetics in Latin America, before and after the Cybersyn project in Chile. Maulén de los Reyes presents a much broader picture of the pan-Latin American cybernetics movements far beyond Cybernsyn in Chile (for example, Mexico, Colombia, and Uruguay) and its relation to the intellectual exchanges in the USA and Europe. Daisuke Harashima describes the reception of cybernetics, especially second-order cybernetics in Japan, which was later developed into what is called neo-cybernetics, made popular by the work of Nomi Ohi and Toru Nishigaki. Harashima conceives a cybernetics that allows us to maintain peace and return to life. He introduces what he calls cybernetics of the heart (*kokoro*) (distinguished from a 'cybernetics of the soul'), a subject that could bring significant contributions to an intercultural understanding of cybernetics.

This volume is the first anthology of the research project 'Cybernetics for the 21st century'. It attempts to enlarge the cartography of cybernetics, but it is still far too limited to cover the whole range of cybernetic thinking that emerged in the twentieth century. Neither can it sufficiently cover the relation between cybernetics and today's biotechnology, neuroscience, military technology and space technology. However, as we know that all futures are unthinkable without revisiting the past, I hope that this historical-epistemological project can provide inspiration for researchers who are interested in the history and aftermath of cybernetics. The second phase of the project will be dedicated to the future of cybernetics, and in this regard, we are envisioning *Cybernetics for the 21st Century Vol. 2*.

Reference

Bateson, Gregory. *Steps to an Ecology of Mind.* Northvale: Jason
    Aronson, 1987.
Beer, Stafford. 'Recursion of Powers', in *Power, Autonomy, Utopia*, ed.
    Robert Trappl. New York: Plenum Press, 1986.
Foester, Heiz von. 'Cybernetics of Cybernetics', in *Communication and
    Control*. Edited by K. Krippendorff, 5–8. New York: Gordon and
    Breach, 1979.
Gerovitch, Slava. *From Newspeak to Cyberspeak: A History of Soviet
    Cybernetics* (Cambridge, MA: MIT Press, 2004)
Hayek, F. A. *Law, Legislation and Liberty: A New Statement of the Liberal
    Principles of Justice and Political Economy*. London: Routledge, 1982.
Hayles, N. Katherine. *How We Became Posthuman Virtual Bodies in
    Cybernetics, Literature, and Informatics*. Chicago: University of
    Chicago Press, 1999.
Heidegger, Martin. 'Nur noch ein Gott kann uns retten', *Der Spiegel*, 30
    May 1976, 193–219.
———. 'The End of Philosophy and the Task of Thinking', in *On Time and
    Being*. Translated by Joan Stambaugh. New York: Harper & Row, 1972.
Hui, Yuk. *Art and Cosmotechnics*. Minneapolis: University of Minessota
    Press, 2021.
———. 'ChatGPT, or the Eschatology of Machines," *E-flux* 137, https://
    www.e-flux.com/journal/137/544816/chatgpt-or-the-eschatolo-
    gy-of-machines/.
———. 'Philosophy after Automation', *Philosophy Today* 65, no. 2 (2021): 217–33.
———. *Recursivity and Contingency*. London: Rowman and Littlefield
    International, 2019.
Hörl, Erich. 'A Thousand Ecologies: The Process of Cyberneticization
    and General Ecology', in *The Whole Earth: California and the
    Disappearance of the Outside*. Edited by Diedrich Diederichsen and
    Anselm Franke, 121–30. Berlin: Sternberg, 2013.

Jonas, Hans. *The Phenomenon of Life: Toward a Philosophical Biology*.
    Evanston: Northwestern University Press, 2001.
Latil, Pierre de, *Thinking by Machine: A Study of Cybernetics*. Translated
    by Y. M. Golla. Boston: Houghton Mifflin, 1957.
Nietzsche, Friedrich. *The Gay Science*. Edited by Bernard Williams.
    Translated by Josefine Nauckhoff and Adrian Del Cargo. Cambridge:
    Cambridge University Press, 2001.
Triclot, Mathieu. *Le moment cybernétique : La constitution de la notion
    d'information*. Ceyzérieu : *Chap Vallon* 2008.
Parsons, Charles. 'Gotthard Günther', in *Gödel's Collected Works, vol.
    4*. Edited by Solomon Feferman and John W. Dawson. Oxford:
    Clarendon, 2003.
Pias, Claus (ed). *Cybernetics The Macy Conferences 1946–1953: The
    Complete Transactions*. Chicago: University of Chicago Press, 2016.
Pickering, Andrew. *The Cybernetic Brain: Sketches of Another Future*.
    Chicago: Chicago University Press, 2010.
Ruyer, Raymond. *La cybernétique et l'origine de l'information*. Paris:
    Flammarion, 1954.
Simondon, Gilbert. *Du mode d'existence des objets techniques*. Paris :
    Aubier, 2012 [1958].
Tiqqun, *The Cybernetic Hypothesis*. Translated by Robert Hurley.
    Cambridge, MA: Semiotext(e), 2020 [2001].
Varela, Francisco. 'Steps to a Cybernetics of Autonomy', in *Power, Autonomy,
    Utopia*. Edited by Robert Trappl. New York: Plenum Press, 1986.

Part I: Maps

Translating Rationalism:
Leibniz and Cybernetics

Brunella Antomarini

The need to give philosophical depth to the current debate on AI gives a renewed importance to cybernetics. In fact, the history of cybernetics still offers a great opportunity to focus on the dynamics that has allowed AI to develop. We can even reconsider and reconfigure the Western history of philosophy in the light of a cybernetic perspective. My research on Gottfried Wilhelm Leibniz is an attempt to do so.

Why Leibniz in particular? Because Norbert Wiener, the founder of cybernetics, considered him the first philosopher of cybernetics. My intent is to investigate what, for Wiener, was a crucial source of inspiration, and to turn Leibniz from being a rationalist or a vitalist into a philosopher of process, of auto-poiesis or organology. It is interesting that Leibniz and Wiener had similar destinies: they were both successful for a while, and both saw their success decline for similar reasons. Leibniz's readers were caught up with Cartesianism and its divide between mechanicism and vitalism, and as a consequence of that distinction, they classified Leibniz as a vitalist. In the case of Wiener, his idea of finding in nature a technique that could explain the internal force that governs matter was taken as an obsession with control typical of postwar and the cold war anxieties. It would be interesting to see how we can use both inspirations and expand or backdate the perspective and impact of cybernetics. Wiener constantly goes back to Leibniz in his most philosophical writings, famously saying that he chose Leibniz as a patron saint of cybernetics.[1] Elsewhere he stated:

> Leibnitz, dominated by ideas of communication, is, in more than one way, the intellectual ancestor of the ideas of this book, for he was also interested in machine computation and in automata. My views in this book are very

---

1   Norbert Wiener, *Cybernetics, Or Control and Communication in the Animal and the Machine* (Cambridge, MA: MIT Press 1985), 12.

far from being Leibnitzian, but the problems with which I am concerned are most certainly Leibnitzian.[2]

Whether he finds Leibniz close to his research or tries to distance himself from him, what is it that makes Wiener think this way? The issue is how it is possible for a machine to possess sense organs, that is, to receive messages from outside, that guide its behaviour from the environment. If machines have sense organs, are they information machines? If there can be information machines, is it possible to find these dynamics in nature? Let us take a more detailed look at what this means, starting by asking what cybernetics means in terms of dynamics: What is a cybernetic system? It is a system that is able to govern itself. This system is not just the effect of a cause, but it is a system with an internal orientation, an automatic telos. Whether living or artificial, a cybernetic system does not move by virtue of an external action, but it moves itself. It is able to regulate itself. How? The conquest of the internal dynamics that make a system move is an ancient dream, from Hero of Alexandria to Leonardo da Vinci. They both dreamt of a system capable of perpetual motion. By way of example, Hero invented the Aeolipile, a playful spherical structure capable of motion through steam.[3] Da Vinci drew several models of a perpetuum mobile consisting of wheels containing balls that, pulled by gravity, move the wheel down and then upward due to the very momentum they gain from their fall.[4]

These two, among many other examples, show how there is a natural energy capable of sustaining motion and the reproduction of energy itself, through a constant exchange of 'information': the balls and wheel pass information to one another about the amount of energy needed and provided by returning in a circular way, retro-acting on the possible slow-down or inertia and generating the necessary speed to continue the motion. This is how the scientific writer Pierre de Latil (the first to disseminate cybernetics in Europe) visualizes the process (Fig. 1)[5]

2   Norbert Wiener, *The Human Use of Human Beings: Cybernetics and Society* (London: Free Association Books, 1989), 19.
3   Brunella Antomarini, 'L'eolipila di Erone alessandrino: L'intelligenza dimenticata dell'inventore', in *Sensibilia 6*, ed. Monica Rotili and Marco Tedeschini (Milan: Mimesis, 2013), 27–42.
4   An animation visualizing the machine is available on the Youtube channel Perpetual Useless, https://www.youtube.com/watch?v=fxe55EtbR8Y.
5   Pierre de Latil, *Thinking by Machine: A Study of Cybernetics*, trans. Y. M. Golla (Boston: Houghton Mifflin, 1957).

Fig. 1: This is how Pierre de Latil visualizes the mechanism of feedback; image redrawn.

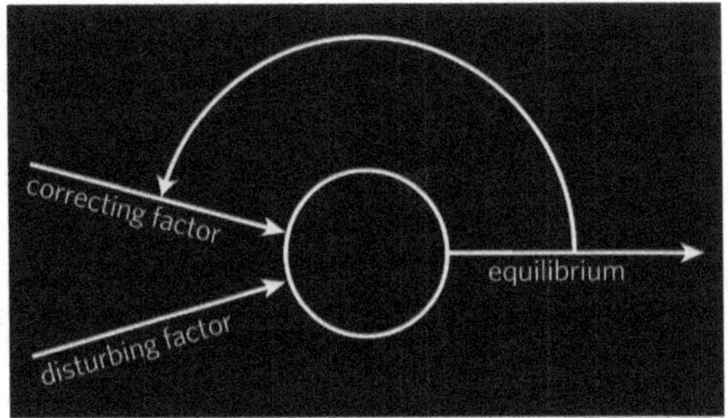

The system (at the centre) reaches its state of equilibrium without any external intervention, on condition that its very motion retroacts on the energy that has set it in motion and gives it the needed decrease (negative feedback) or increase (positive feedback) of energy. The system adjusts its condition by intervening on the information it gets from the previous condition.

This self-reproduction implies a circular direction, an impulse to go back, a constant recursivity, that turns the effect into a cause, or, in cybernetic terms, into an effector. Whereas the cause is external to the effect, the effector is internal, as it acts upon an internal cause. This is what makes the system autonomous with respect to any external factor.

At the end of the 1940s, Wiener made an electronic perpetuum mobile; an electronically rudimentary device that he called 'Palomilla,' a phototropic animaloid whose motion depends on the voltage provided by light: its two sensors make it go toward or away from the source of light. The result is a goal-seeking behaviour.[6] Its 'software' modifies its path according to the outside information; a random motion produces a variation in light and its 'perception'. As if it had sense organs, Palomilla continues to modify its 'choices', as if it were alive. Whether perception and choice are metaphoric or not, Palomilla moves independently of its creator. This is an update of the ancient dream of the perpetuum mobile.

6   'Wiener's Moth "Palomilla"—Wiener/Wiesner/Singleton', blogpost on the website *Cybernetic Zoo*, 19 September 2009, https://cyberneticzoo.com/cyberneticanimals/1949-wieners-moth-wiener-wiesner-singleton/.

Let us go back to Leibniz: a typical Renaissance man—or, as Wiener calls him, a universal genius—Leibniz is moved by different inspirations. The first is Ramon Llull's *Ars Magna* (1501), which he translates into *De arte combinatoria* and later *Ars characteristica*: an attempt to turn all possible information into symbols. In Leibniz's speculative vision, combinations of symbols would guarantee the universality of knowledge and universality of information. Again, we have an automatic device that could replace human agency, an automaton that does not need anything external to accomplish a task. Second, when Leibniz went to Paris, he became, together with Denis Papin, a pupil of Christiaan Huygens. Together, Leibniz and Papin made a steam engine; an automatic device in which a piston is powered by steam. It was one of the first steam engines; of course it did not work very well, but this shows Leibniz' interest in the new technologies of his time, and his flair for a philosophy of transformation and process. Third, Leibniz made a reckoner that he called the Calculus Ratiocinator, which is usually considered the first computer: though completely mechanical, it was a machine that made calculations independently of any human operation. He wanted to write on it 'Superior to Man', envisioning the possibility of future computers.[7] It works through a row of nine cylinders that are moved by a wheel. The wheel passes across cogs and it is either hit by the cogs (in which case it adds one number to an addition) or it is not (in which case nothing is added); the final addition results from on/off states, the presence or absence of the cogs. The reckoner converts data into sequences of on/off states. This proto-computer is quite efficient; it can make additions and multiplications, even of three-digit numbers. It was the first attempt to turn numbers into binary logic. Infinite combinations of on/off states is what makes information possible. Fourth, in the early 1700s, Father Bouvet, one of the Jesuits who established the first European contact with the Chinese culture, gave Leibniz a chart of the divination text *I Ching* as a gift. Leibniz immediately saw the similarity with his reckoner; the use of different combinations of Yin and Yang, broken lines and full lines, result in many possible numbers and therefore many possible meanings. Information

7   'The Leibniz Step Reckoner and Curta Calculators', entry on the website of the Computer History Museum, https://www.computerhistory.org/revolution/calculators/1/49.

is the result of an automatic combination of signals, of on/off states, and mathematical language that appeared to him as a way to calculate the positions of the stars and planets.[8]

Let me now retrieve from these interconnected inventions and conceptual frames the three main principles of Leibniz's philosophy: sufficient reason; the indiscernibles; and pre-established harmony.

1   Sufficient reason: Every actual event, or matter of fact, has its own particular unique reason to occur. On the contrary, Cartesian and Newtonian mechanics considered the 'reason' or 'final cause' or 'aim' to be obsolete or inessential notions; according to mechanics all material structures need some external and universal causes to move. Matter has no reason, no *telos*, and no purpose.

2   The indiscernibles: If two entities are indiscernible, they are the same entity. Here Leibniz is responding to Spinoza. In their dialogues in Amsterdam, they had to solve the Cartesian dualism. Whereas Spinoza's solution is the uniqueness of substance (distinct in itself in at least two attributes and many modes), Leibniz concludes that there must be many substances; only their plurality could explain the variety of matters of fact that can neither be conceived as illusions, nor can be reduced to effects of one or a few universal causes. If matters of fact exist, they exist because there are many of them.

3   Pre-established harmony: This is the most controversial of the three principles, because it could be considered a *deus ex machina*, that is, when Leibniz is unable to make sense of teleology to solve the conundrum of everything having a purpose or sufficient reason, he refers to God, who pre-establishes the harmony, the order of the universe. However, Leibniz is quite aware that this is impossible. It cannot be that

8   An animated illustration can be found at https://it.wikipedia.org/wiki/
Stepped_Reckoner#/media/File:Cylindre_de_Leibniz_anim%C3%A9.gif; Yuen-
Ting Lai, 'Leibniz's Studies of Chinese and Perennial Philosophy', *Il cannocchiale*
(January–April 1999): 101.

the world is a creature of a creator, neither in the theocentric sense, nor in an anthropocentric view in which the human is a privileged agent of action and the rational artificer of knowledge. We will see how this principle is better explained in its relationship with the other two.

We start with sufficient reason. Leibniz said (in *Discourse on Metaphysics*, the paramount argument through which he distances himself from Cartesianism): 'This force is something different from size, shape and motion, and from that we can see that not everything that we can conceive in bodies is a matter of extension and its modifications, as our moderns persuade themselves'.[9] If we reduce matter to motion and body, something is left out from the explanation; how these bodies come together, how they can be transformed. If the concept of force is reduced to geometric cause, it leaves the actual behaviour of matters of facts unexplained. In fact, the same effect can be the result of different causes, the way a square can be produced by two rectangles or two triangles, as Leibniz says in *Summa rerum*.[10] Therefore an actual effect has its own cause, which must be found out from a number of possible equivalent causes. If we remove the final cause from the description of the world, we fall into a contradiction or an absurdity. Expelling the final cause would be as if, in explaining a great prince's victory in a successful siege, a historian was to say:

> It was because the small particles of gunpowder, released by the touch of a spark, shot off fast enough to impel a hard, heavy body against the walls of the place, while the particles making up the strands of copper in the cannon were so densely interwoven that they were not pulled apart by that speed.[11]

What had really happened in the war could not be the mechanical product of general causes, which can explain any kind of event as effect, but

9   Leibniz, *Discourse on Metaphysics*, in *Philosophical Texts*, ed. R. Woolhouse and R. Francks (New York: Oxford University Press, 1998), § 18, 71.
10   Leibniz, *De summa rerum*, trans. G. H. R. Parkinson (New Haven: Yale University Press, 1992), 51.
11   Leibniz, *Discourse*, 1998, § 19, 73.

does not explain the singularity of the effect; that is, the moment that the effect *becomes* an effector, a cause guided by an anticipation of future events. There is a teleological behaviour that, though automatic, is not mechanical.

Here we have to solve the issue of vitalism, because this is exactly why Leibniz seems to align with the opponents of mechanicism; as the old dispute goes, if you are against mechanics, you must be a vitalist. Wiener himself was aware of this possible misunderstanding when, in his article *Quantum Mechanics, Leibniz and Haldane*, he recognized Leibniz 'as a basis for Quantum Mechanics'.[12] Wiener saw in this *force vive* an anticipation of electronic power, saying: 'It is traditional to represent Leibniz' theory of monads as a pluralistic spiritualism, or vitalism', and he adds that if Leibniz's language were 'divested' of its 'protective layer of orthodox Christian phraseology', the misunderstanding would probably be overcome and revealed as the legacy of theology. On the contrary: 'We shall see that it might as well be called a pluralistic materialism'.[13] In other places Wiener deconstructs the distinction between vitalism and materialism as an imaginative difference between living, non-living, vital and mechanical; a divide that is purely 'a badly posed question', or even a mere 'semantic choice'.[14] We simply *choose* to make a distinction between what is living and what is inanimate or simply material. The living and non-living systems cannot exist separately, because if that were the case, the transition from the one to the other would remain obscure. In a few words, we still need to understand the emergence of life. Not everything in a living system is alive, and vice versa, not everything inanimate is devoid of an intrinsic energy (that we may choose to call 'life'). As Wiener states: 'Even living systems are not (in all probability) living below the molecular level'.[15] Curiously, Leibniz asked the German linguist Andreas Mueller, who studied Chinese, whether it was a language that expressed inanimate objects in terms of the animate.[16]

Actually, no inanimate being is completely inert if it can sustain itself as a cybernetic machine (think of the surface tension of a

---

12   Norbert Wiener, 'Quantum Mechanics, Haldane, and Leibniz', *Philosophy of Science* 1, no. 4 (October 1934): 479.

13   Ibid.

14   Wiener, *Cybernetics*, 44; Wiener, *The Human Use of Human Beings*, 34.

15   Norbert Wiener, *God and Golem* (Cambridge, MA: MIT Press, 1964), 46.

16   Lai, 'Leibniz's Studies of Chinese', 113.

waterdrop, or the earth keeping its temperature stable; or, to go back to Wiener, if there can be cybernetic machines that have sense organs). Conversely, we know that more than fifty minerals are produced by living cells.[17] The continuity of all systems turns the world into a super-organism that sustains itself through a global mutual resonance, in which each part reconfigures the whole.

The organicist view of nature is expressed in an interesting passage from the fragment *Tentamen Anagogicum*, in which Leibniz uses the example of a ray of light. He takes it from the phenomenon of refraction: according to a Newtonian paradigm, the path of light is a straight line, that is, the shortest path. This is the geometric paradigm. According to Leibniz, the path of light does not take the shortest path, but the easiest, because Leibniz considers that the concrete occurrence of light, its being a matter of fact, is not a geometric, theoretical entity, but an auto-poietic system following 'the most determined or unique path, even in relation to curves'.[18] So, it can even curve if there is an obstacle that compels the light to change its direction. It simply depends on certain step-by-step information; the light changes direction if needed, which means that even a ray of light has a teleological direction. It cannot just be a mental reconstruction of a reversible geometric figure; it is a real system that has a direction and an irreversible destination meant to be reached. A ray of light is launched in space, and this launch means that it must go in a certain direction and must defend this direction, resisting any possible obstacles. Here Cartesian geometric objects are turned into what Deleuze would call "objectiles". As Jeffrey McDonough states: 'A ray of light will travel along the path which is unique with respect to ease; where "ease" is understood as the quantity obtained by multiplying the distance of the path by the resistance of the medium(s)'.[19] Distance, surface of reflection, and medium are circumstances imposed on a system insofar as it is able to show elasticity, responsiveness and continuity. Rather than a thinker of the metaphysical structure of thought, we find Leibniz to be an empiricist, as McDonough himself notes.[20]

17   Lynn Margulis and Dorion Sagan, *What is Life?* (Berkeley: University of California Press, 1995), 26.
18   Leibniz's *Tentamen Anagogicum* (1696) is quoted by Jeffrey McDonough, 'Leibniz on Natural Teleology and the Laws of Optics', *Philosophy and Phenomenological Research* 78, no. 3 (May 2009): 512.
19   Ibid., 512.
20   Ibid., 520.

So, what do all of these phenomena have in common? The reckoner, the steam engine, the automatic combinations of symbols, events that are singular, that is: matters of fact? They all share the same natural strategy: an internal or living force. This is the way to defend Leibniz from vitalism. If living means self-organized, if the ray of light, the reckoner, and so on, organize themselves to defend their direction, taking information from outside, and if force means the ability of a system to transform itself, we can say that for a teleological automaton, its sufficient reason to exist is not a vitalistic *élan*, nor an ultimate purpose of the universe, or a form of pan-psychism, but a force that is at work—in different ways—in all matter.

Within this perspective, the human rational agent is not the origin or the cause of understanding and knowledge, the one who makes sense of matter, or even the one who projects their behaviour on things; they are just one part of wider wholes. The reckoner or the *I Ching* make human mental effort irrelevant; the steam engine makes muscular effort unnecessary, and the human is possible only to the extent that it follows cybernetic automation present in its very structure, which is at the same time living and non-living, natural and technological, as we will now see. Human agency (so central in rationalism) is the cause and effect of its own nature; it identifies itself through a constant confrontation and adjustment to the environment. These circular feedback loops replace the rationalistic ideal of a linear transition from cause to effect, which, if heterogeneous, implies an action at a distance and a discontinuity that would make a relationship mysterious or magical. Circular transition, instead, from effector to effector, implies continuity and no distance, because things placed in immediate contact with each other are touching each other without interruption. What comes to mind is the swarm intelligence, in which each element has to anticipate the motion of the other in order that the whole super-organism or super-system governs itself.

We move on to the argument of the indiscernibles. In *Discourse*, Leibniz says that it is never true that 'two substances are entirely alike and differ only in number'.[21] A plurality of substances explains the variety of reasons for each existence that, as we have seen, cannot be the inert effects of general causes. However, substances in continuous contact, in a relationship of contiguity, as partes *extra partes*, must

21   Leibniz, *Discourse*, §9, 60.

at the same time, be *partes intra partes*, if contiguity must be transformed into a continuity (radical discontinuity would imply, as I said, an action at a distance). In Leibniz's words, however plural, the 'number of substances remains the same, although substances are often transformed'.[22] We have to understand how each substance can at the same time keep its own unique identity and the identity of the whole they contribute to. As philosopher Federico Leoni puts it, very clearly: 'A man who builds a clock is one of many nodes in which nature divides itself, through folds and not cuts'.[23] The machines of nature are forms in constant topological transition, phenomena that produce themselves ad infinitum: if whatever exists in nature is a machine, or an automatic system, living machines have a specific property; they are machines in their smallest parts ad infinitum.[24] Later, he says: 'We see that there is a world of created things, living beings, animals, entelechies, souls, in the minutest particle of matter. The minutest particle of matter has the same *force vive* (or in Latin *vis vive*, means living force) as human beings'.[25] An organism, unlike a reckoner, is composed of an infinite number of systems in mutual continuity and with infinite combinations—and therefore never fully detectable—within a finite amount of possibilities (as I will clarify later).

Let us now compare how Wiener retrieves Leibniz' *Monadology*, in *Quantum Mechanics*:

> Nevertheless, Leibniz' great principle of the identity of indiscernibles is retained in the modern view. Since we may permute two electrons in such a way that they will be indiscernible from each other, we now say that two electrons cannot have complete separable individualities, but must be no more than two aspects of a complex containing two or more electrons. It is retained, we cannot deny Leibniz' principle of the indiscernibles.[26]

22   Ibid.
23   Federico Leoni, *L'automa* (Milan: Mimesis, 2019), 33.
24   Leibniz, *Monadology*, in *Philosophical Texts*, ed. and trans. R. S. Woolhouse
and Richard Francks (New York: Oxford University Press), §64, 277.
25   Ibid., §66.
26   Wiener, *Quantum Mechanics*, 1934, 481.

Wiener's doubt depends on quantum nonlocality; yet, here 'indiscernible' does not mean that electrons are exactly the same, and that there can therefore be a unique substance on the ground of apparent differences. Rather, it means that the identity of a single electron is constantly exchanged through the transition of energy, and though this may sound non-Leibnizian (some indiscernibility does exist) its identity can be 'retained': substances are plural, but also continuous, as there is no empty space between them. Wiener simply considers this definition as the result of a technological experiment that Leibniz did not have: 'The modern philosopher is more subtle than Leibniz' (author's italics). [27]

Now, the issue of nonlocality or indeterminacy needs to be solved, because here Leibniz appears to be a determinist. In *Monadology* he says that the universe is regulated in a perfectly orderly manner, and based on this 'pluralistic materialism', every monad is a mirror of the universe in its own way.[28]

I will try to show that Leibniz offers a solution to Wiener's doubt, because if every monad is a mirror to the other monads or to the environment, it is at the same time continuous and discernible. It is a continuity given by communication through mirroring; it establishes an immediate information with and about the other monads, and at the same time, it is discontinuous, because each mirror is placed in a different perspective. This complex view resonates with Wiener's statement that communication is a 'subtle consequence of optical interaction'.[29] Why optical? Because a mirror is optical, but at the same time, it is automatic, and exists in mutual tactile relationship. This optic does not concern the human eye so much as it considers the human eye one possible way to accomplish the automation of interaction among substances, through light, its refraction, and touch.

We find another answer to Wiener's doubt in *Discourse*: Leibniz says that these many substances must keep themselves together in their place, and they keep their identities though constantly transforming themselves, by obstructing or limiting one another. This is how the energy, the *force vive* works in them or among them:

27   Ibid.
28   Leibniz, *Monadology*, 1998, §63, 277.
29   Wiener, *Human Use of Human Being*, 18.

> In this way therefore, we can understand how substances obstruct or limit one another; and consequently we can say that in this sense they act on one another, and are obliged to adjust themselves to one another, so to speak. For it can happen that a change which enhances the expression of one diminishes that of another.[30]

Given that monads exist only in their mutual reflections, they are 'individual' in the sense of their variety, rather than in the sense of their substantiality. If we have an increase of energy in one, a decrease of energy must occur in the other. Of course, this is intuitive, because we cannot fully detect these mutual limitations that matters of fact, monads, or systems, exert on one another, as they actually occur in nature and are hardly measurable from outside.

Now, not speaking metaphorically, what are these mirrors? I would like to consider them as pervasive observers. In reference to second-order cybernetics, here we have to understand reflexivity. The question now is: if a system receives information, does it not imply the presence of an observer? This issue, which led first-order cybernetics to expand the scope if its research to complex systems, can be traced back in monads; a mirror is a kind of automatic observer. The seeming contradiction between discrete and continuous, automatic and reflexive, can be resolved by the constant *internal* detection that *all* systems have with one another. This can be related to what, in second-order cybernetics, and particularly in the sense of Niklas Luhmann, is called 'double contingency'.[31] That is, every system is contingent upon the other system or upon the environment, and it is this double contingency that causes or compels systems to adjust to one another. It might be argued that if the monads are closed in themselves and cannot retain a representation of the external environment, how can they detect the other monads and adjust to them? To that, a possible solution is that each monad just needs to identify its next feedback; it does not need to have knowledge of something outside. The operational closure that monads show overcomes the traditional deterministic or rationalistic illusion of 'knowledge', which might be solved in these terms: in the

30   Leibniz, *Discourse*, 1998, §14, 67.
31   Niklas Luhmann, *Social Systems*, trans. John Bednarz (Stanford: Stanford University Press, 1995),

traditional model a subject (rational structure) knows an external object (matter); in cybernetics 'knowledge' is replaced by combinations of networks automatically adjusting to one another through a retroactive force. A mirror is a metaphor of the purely relational. Again, we can explain monads in terms of the emergence of more complex monads from basic ones, or from elementary monads which move only through attraction or repulsion.[32] Here, of course, living force shows a close similarity to the electron, in which 'force' is a pure resistance and resistance is retroaction—that is, an *active* resistance—because if resistance were just passive or inert, we would not have any effector.[33] But retroaction is the ability of every system to gain new energy. From these elementary phases, we can understand the increasing complexity in the form of a greater number of monadic relationships, until we arrive at the human level, in which this energy can be called freedom. At each level of complexity, every new strategy (or technology) represents a constant retroaction as a form of negentropy.

This last argument leads us to the third and last principle, pre-established harmony. In the *Summa Rerum*, Leibniz states:

> Assuming, then, that in a plenum one body cannot be expanded without another being contracted, and that one body cannot be contracted without another being expanded, and also that another expansion cannot be understood except by the aid of motion—assuming all this, it follows that for the same quantity of motion always to be conserved is the same as for the same quantity of matter always to be conserved.[34]

This vision of matter and nature is a vision of constant transformation and motion, in which there cannot be any void, that is, no action at a distance. In this plenum, all monads interact with one another by

32   Wiener, 'Back to Leibniz! Physics Reoccupies an Abandoned Position',
Technology Review 34 (1932): 203; Yuk Hui, *Recursivity and Contingency* (London:
Rowman and Littlefiled, 2019), 119.
33   George Gale, 'The Role of Leibniz and Haldane in Wiener's Cybernetics', in
the *Proceedings of the Norbert Wiener Centenary Congress on Norbert Wiener,
1994, ed.* Vidyadhar Mandrekar and Pesi Rustom Masani (Providence: American
Mathematical Society, 1997), 252.
34   Leibniz, *De Summa Rerum*, 19.

immediate contact. Now, in the all-process that nature is, how is the conservation of energy possible? How can we explain the empirical systems (matters of fact) as open but at the same time stable? We can say, following Leibniz, that the conservation of energy is allowed by the constant self-correction of the amount of energy. Here Leibniz shows at his best his continuism as neither vitalistic, nor metaphysical:

> Everything is full, which means that all matter is inter-linked. In such a plenum, any movement must have an effect on distant bodies which are in contact with it, and in some way or other it feels the effects of everything that happens to them... . As a result, every body feels the effects of everything that happens in the universe.[35]

If everything is full, it means that all matter is interlinked. The continuum is explained by innumerable networks and their intertwining. In such a plenum, any movement must have an effect on distant bodies through intermediate bodies that are in mutual contact and indirectly reach out to all. All things touch one another by reflecting (retroacting) on one another.

Leibniz is in perfect tune with Wiener's machines having sense organs—if 'sense organs' means the ability to detect, or resonate with, the external environment, and to retroact accordingly. It is in this respect that Wiener defines Leibniz as the forerunner of field theory. If there can be no action at a distance, the world must be a plenum. A monad can only mirror a distant monad through the intervention of intermediate monads,[36] or intermediate effectors that simply destroy the idea of original and external causes.

How then to translate the *deus ex machina* of pre-established harmony? We have to liberate Leibniz from this misunderstanding. The overall harmony, which is the actual keeping-itself-together in the constant transition, is not due to an external organization of the universe, but it is what happens step by step within each system when it tries to keep accord with the other systems and for the whole super-system to remain in equilibrium. What does 'organic' mean? It means

---

35   Leibniz, *Monadology*, §61, 276.
36   Wiener, *Quantum Mechanics*, 482

self-organized and correlated, a mutual correlation that Yuk Hui calls 'organizing inorganic'.[37] This is how we can talk today about the monad.

Now a final issue: how can we translate contingency in Leibniz's system, traditionally seen as deterministic? Wiener himself appears to argue against Leibniz: a living organism, he argues, is not like the "clockwork monad with its pre-established harmony, but actually seeks a new equilibrium with the universe and its future contingencies. Its present is unlike its past and its future unlike its present. In the living organism as in the universe itself, exact repetition is absolutely impossible." [38]

Wiener takes the term 'pre-established' to mean 'predetermined', whether it is such by God or by a human rational agent who is able to know things through perfectly corresponding causes and effects. Contingency seems to be jeopardized here, but I think that Leibniz has an answer to that too. Leibniz says that, though it is true that pre-established harmony seems to destroy the difference between contingent and necessary truths, 'we have to make a distinction between what is assured but is not necessary'.[39] What is assured is necessary 'only ex hypothesi—and so to speak, accidentally; this is contingent in itself'.[40] There are two ways to necessity: one is theoretical, the other concrete and empirical. In the case of the latter, there can be only assurance. Whether it was assured—that is, rational—for Caesar to cross the Rubicon, it was not necessary, in the sense that that action was not inherent in the subject, meaning that the contrary would not imply a contradiction.[41] We can only be assured of what will happen tomorrow, because there is no necessity in what has not occurred yet. He repeats, in the summary, that 'it is true that there are always reasons for their choices, but those reasons incline without necessitating'.[42] A fact or a decision occurs 'among a number of equally possible things'.[43] Again, reasons for the occurrence of matters of fact cannot be related to the principle of contradiction.

Empirical events are governed by propensity, inclination, direction, a teleological impulse that is not vitalistic but *automatic*. A

37   Hui, *Recursivity and Contingency*, 185 ff.
38   Wiener, *Human Use of Human Beings*, 48
39   Leibniz, *Discourse*, §13, 64
40   Ibid.
41   Ibid.
42   Ibid., 63.
43   Ibid.

beautiful example is Leibniz's vision of the origin of the earth in *Theodicy*. He describes the emergence of the earth from a globe on fire, leaving rocks filled with metal and minerals, a kind of 'natural furnace' (to which he curiously adds that the human furnaces are imitations of the natural ones).[44] Fire and minerals make an ocean of oil (*oleum per deliquium*), until the cooling of the heat leaves moisture in the air that falls down on the surface, absorbing the salt in the ashes and filling up the holes on its surface, turning it into salt water.[45] The constant re-shaping of matter, however, being the effects of causes, leaves no room for any external pre-established cause. In fact, he adds that after the fire has gone, earth and water, having reached an equilibrium, keep making 'ravages no less'.[46]

Once a homeostatic condition is reached, there will be another disequilibrium to solve. All homeostatic conditions are only temporary and have to be anticipated to be protected from successive threats, through effectors retroacting on causes, or in other words, through recursive constant mutual re-adjustments. This is a kind of recursivity that is not 'exact repetition', as Wiener argues, if teleological systems find their persistence in their own empirical (not necessary) auto-poiesis. It means that not all possibles may be realized, but only those that circumstances allow, thanks to exploratory re-combinations of the same material factors and elements. By reading 'possible' in terms of energy, we can say that energy must produce, sooner or later, the *same* actualities—the same in the sense of systems following the same laws of feedback loops, recursive combinatory calculations; certainly not the same matters of fact (not another Caesar crossing the Rubicon). To Leibniz, things are not products of matter, rather the result of their activity, or entelechies, which can operate without God's intervention.[47]

The fact that what occurs does not occur out of infinite possibilities can explain the famous ultimate question: 'Why something rather than nothing?', and it can explain the fact that nothing is absolutely universal or fixed. That this is 'the best of possible worlds' may mean

---

44 Leibniz, *Theodicy*, ed. A. Farrell (LaSalle, IL: Open Court, 1996), §244, 278.
45 Ibid.
46 Ibid.
47 Leibniz, Réfutation inédite de Spinoza, ed. Foucher de Careil, Paris, 1854, in *8 oeuvres de Leibniz* (e-artnow, 2013), 60.

that this is the best result out of the world's finite potentialities: more than that it is not possible. In *Réfutation de Spinoza*, Leibniz argues against Spinoza that extension cannot just be the indefinite repetition of things, rather, 'as numbers presuppose numerable things, accidents proper to each thing make actual the mere potential'.[48] Redefining Aristotle, we can say that 'potential' means teleological, and 'actual' means homeostatic; the final cause is retrieved at the intersection of the contingent transitions from potential to actual (conceived in Aristotle as necessary).

To summarize:

1   The principle of sufficient reason is translated into the internal automatic inclination, or *force vive*, as effector that provides itself the preservation of motion and existence, as active resistance or retroaction (feedback loops). Organic here means organized.

2   The principle of the indiscernibles is translated into the necessary plurality of substances, which can explain the automatic and autonomous force governing all things, by virtue of systemic relationships, or mutual adjustment and perception (optical and haptic), in a condition of double contingency. Organic here means coordinated.

3   The principle of pre-established harmony is translated into the activity of anticipating the effects that may accomplish the looked-for homeostatic condition. Whatever persists owes its persistence to its recursively going back to causes. Organic here means anticipating.

In conclusion, every effector establishes the next move. In order to do so, it has to anticipate what makes it survive and avoid what would destroy it. Again, there is a constant self-observation of systems-monads that appears to belong to all levels of matter.

48   Leibniz, ibid., 59.

I would like to add a note in which Leibniz confirms his trust in material culture and technological practice, in opposition to abstract 'rational' thinking:

> And it is the main flaw of many learned people that they only amuse themselves in vague speeches and refutations, while there is such a beautiful field to exercise their minds in solid and real objects to the public benefit. The hunters, the fishermen, the sailors, the merchants, the travellers and even games provide for an increase in useful sciences. There is even in children's exercises that which could surpass the greatest Mathematician.[49]

49   Leibniz, 'Discours touchant la methode de la certitude et l'art d'inventer pour finir les disputes et pour faire en peu de temps des grands progrès', in Leibniz, *Die philosophischen Schriften vol. 7*, ed. Carl I. Gerhardt (Berlin: Weidmannsche Buchhandlung, 1965 [1885]), 181.

Reference

Antomarini, Brunella. 'L'eolipila di Erone Alessandrino: L'intelligenza dimenticata dell'inventore'. In *Sensibilia 6*. Edited by Manrica Rotili and Marco Tedeschini, 27–42. Milan: Mimesis, 2013.

———. *Thinking Through Error*. Lanham: Lexington Edition, 2012.

De Latil, Pierre. *Thinking by Machine: A Study of Cybernetics*. Translated by Y. M. Golla. Boston: Houghton Mifflin, 1957.

Forman, David. 'Leibniz on Human Finitude, Progress, and Eternal Recurrence: The Argument of the 'Apokatastasis' Essay Drafts and Related Texts'. In *Oxford Studies in Early Modern Philosophy, Volume 8*. Edited by Daniel Garber and Donald Rutherford, 225–70. Oxford: Oxford University Press, 2019.

Gale, George. 'The Role of Leibniz and Haldane in Wiener's Cybernetics'. In the *Proceedings of the Norbert Wiener Centenary Congress on Norbert Wiener, 1994*. Edited by Vidyadhar Mandrekar and Pesi Rustom Masani, 247–61. Providence: American Mathematical Society, 1997.

Gray, Jonathan. '"Let's Calculate!" Leibniz, Llull, and the Computational Imagination'. The Public Domain Review, 10 November 2016, https://publicdomainreview.org/essay/let-us-calculate-leibniz-llull-and-the-computational-imagination.

Hui, Yuk. *Recursivity and Contingency*. London: Rowman and Littlefiled, 2019.

Lai, Yuen-Ting. 'Leibniz's Studies of Chinese and Perennial Philosophy'. *Il cannocchiale* (January–April 1999): 101–146.

Leibniz, Gottfried Wilhelm. *De summa rerum*. Translated by G. H. R. Parkinson. New Haven: Yale University Press, 1992.

———. *Discourse on Metaphysics*, in *Philosophical Texts*. Edited and translated by R. S. Woolhouse and Richard Francks. New York: Oxford University Press, 1998.

———. 'Discours touchant la methode de la certitude et l'art d'inventer pour finir les disputes et pour faire en peu de temps des grands progrès'. In Gottfried Wilhelm Leibniz, *Die philosophischen Schriften*. Edited by Carl I. Gerhardt, Volume 7, 174–83. Berlin, Weidmannsche Buchhandlung, 1965 [1885].

———. *Monadology*, in *Philosophical Texts*. Edited and translated by R. S. Woolhouse and Richard Francks. New York: Oxford University Press, 1998.

———. *Réfutation inédite de Spinoza*. Edited by Foucher de Careil, ed., Paris, 1854, in *8 oeuvres de Leibniz*. e-artnow 2013.

———. *Theodicy*. Edited by A. Farrell. LaSalle, IL : Open Court, 1996.

———. *Writings on China*. Edited and translated by Daniel Cook and Henry Rosemont jr. LaSalle, IL: Open Court, 1994.

Leoni, Federico. *L'automa*. Milan: Mimesis, 2019.

Luhmann, Niklas. *Social Systems*. Translated by John Bednarz. Stanford: Stanford University Press, 1995.

Margulis, Lynn and Sagan, Dorion. *What is Life?* Berkeley: University of California Press, 1995.

McDonough, Jeffrey. 'Leibniz on Natural Teleology and the Laws of Optics'. *Philosophy and Phenomenological Research* 78, no. 3 (May 2009): 505–44.

Rey, Anne-Lise. 'The Controversy between Leibniz and Papin: From the Public Debate to the Correspondence'. In *The Practise of Reason: Leibniz and His Controversies*. Edited by Marcelo Dascal, 75–100. Amsterdam: John Benjamins Publishing Company, 2010.

Rossi, Paolo. *Clavis Universalis: Arti mnemoniche e logica combinatoria da Lullo a Leibniz*. Bologna: Il Mulino, 1983[1960].

———. *I filosofi e le macchine* 1400–1700. *Milan: Feltrinelli*, 2007 [1962].

Sypniewski, Bernard Paul. 'China and Universals: Leibniz, Binary Mathematics and the Yijing Hexagrams'. *Monumenta Serica* 53 (2005): 287–314, https://www.jstor.org/stable/40727465.

Uchii, Soshichi. 'Leibniz's Ultimate Theory'. *PhilSci Archive* (2017), http://philsci-archive.pitt.edu/12787/.

Wiener, Norbert. 'Back to Leibniz! Physics Reoccupies an Abandoned Position'. *Technology Review* 34 (1932): 201–3; 222–24.

———. *Cybernetics, Or Control and Communication in the Animal and the Machine*. Cambridge, MA: MIT Press 1985.

———. *God and Golem*. Cambridge, MA: MIT Press, 1964.

———. *The Human Use of Human Beings: Cybernetics and Society*. London: Free Association Books, 1989.

———. 'Quantum Mechanics, Haldane, and Leibniz'. *Philosophy of Science* 1, no. 4 (October 1934): 479–82.

Machine and Ecology

Yuk Hui

In this article I hope to investigate the relation between machine and ecology, and the philosophical and historical questions concealed in these two seemingly incompatible terms through a repositioning of cybernetics in the history of thought. First of all, I want to problematize these two ambiguous terms, 'machine' and 'ecology', as a preparation to de-familiarize and de-romanticize certain ideas about techno-ecology, and to suggest a political ecology of machines, which will centre around what I term 'technodiversity'. This quest for technodiversity belongs to a systematic inquiry of my thesis on cosmotechnics in *The Question Concerning Technology in China* (2016), which argues against certain traditions of philosophy, anthropology and history of technology, and suggests that instead of taking for granted an anthropologically universal concept of technics, we should conceive a multiplicity of technics, characterized by different dynamics between the cosmic, the moral and the technical.

Conventionally, we tend to think that machines and ecology are opposed to one another, because machines are artificial and mechanical while ecology is natural and organic. We may call this a dualism of critique (instead of a critique of dualism), since its mode of critique is based on the setting up of binaries, which it fails to go beyond, like the unhappy consciousness. This opposition has resulted from some stereotypes concerning the status of machines. Even today when people talk about machines, they tend to think of mechanistic machines based on linear causality, for example, the digesting duck designed by the technician Jacques de Vaucanson, or the mechanical Turk by Wolfgang von Kempelen, (both in the eighteenth century), and when they talk about ecology they tend to think of nature as a self-regulating system, which gives everything and takes everything back.

After the overcoming of dualism

The above-mentioned notions of machine and ecology undermine both the history of technology and the history of philosophy, therefore they also ignore the technical reality which conditions the validity of such a criticism. Criticism based on dualism fails to understand itself historically and critically. The mechanistic view of machines was already completely surpassed and rendered obsolete by cybernetics in the mid-twentieth century; instead, we have witnessed the emergence of a *mechano-organicism*. Today cybernetics has become the modus operandi in machines ranging from smartphones to robots and spacecraft. The rise of cybernetics was one of the major events in the twentieth century. Different from mechanism, which is based on linear causality (i.e. A–B–C), it rests on a circular causality (i.e. A–B–C–A'), meaning that it is reflective in the basic sense that it is able to determine itself in the form of a recursive structure. By recursion I mean a non-linear reflective movement which progressively moves towards its telos, be it predefined or auto-posited. Cybernetics belongs to a larger paradigm in the sciences, namely, organicism, which originated from the criticism against mechanism as a fundamental ontological understanding. Organicism also has to be distinguished from vitalism, which often relies on a mysterious (separate, immaterial) 'vital force' to explain the existence of a living being; instead, organicism finds its foundation in mathematics. Cybernetics, as one form of organicism, mobilizes two key concepts, feedback and information, to analyse the behaviour of all beings, both animate (living) and inanimate (lifeless), and both nature and society. In the first chapter of *Cybernetics: Or Control and Communication in the Animal and the Machine* (1948), the founder of cybernetics, Norbert Wiener, first reiterates an opposition between Newtonian time and Bergsonian time.[1] Newtonian motion is mechanistic, and time-symmetric, hence reversible, while Bergsonian time is organic, biological, creative and irreversible. It is not until the Second Law of Thermodynamics, proposed by the French physicist Sadi Carnot in 1824 (almost a century after Newton's death in 1727), that we recognize the 'arrow of time' in being and the fact that the so-called entropy of a system increases with time and is irreversible. Already in his first book, *Essai sur les données immédiates de la conscience* (1889), Bergson launched a fierce attack on the way in which time was conceptualized in Western science and philosophy.[2] Time is here understood in terms

1   Norbert Wiener, *Cybernetics: Or Control and Communication in the Animal and the Machine.* Cambridge, MA: MIT Press, 1985), Chapter 1.
2   Henri Bergson, *Essai sur les données immédiates de la conscience* (Paris: PUF, 2013).

of space, for example, in terms of intervals which can be represented in space. Therefore, the time thus conceptualized is actually timeless, according to Bergson. It is also homogeneous, like the intervals marked on a clock. Instead, organic time or *durée*, Bergson suggests, cannot be fully understood as extension ordered in spatial terms; rather it contains heterogeneity or qualitative multiplicity in organic forms. Time is a force that is singular in every instant, like Heraclitus's river; it does not repeat itself twice like a mechanical clock. Indeed, mechanical or linear causality is not compatible with the concept of duration. Bergsonian 'organic' time also provides a new way to understand human consciousness and experience.

Wiener proposed that such opposition was already surpassed by the discovery of statistical mechanics in physics. For example, considering a container of particles, from the point of view of statistical mechanics it is possible to communicate between the macrostates and microstates, and therefore, control the behaviour of the system. In other words, cybernetics endeavours to eliminate dualism; it wants to create a connection between different orders of magnitude—macro and micro, mind and body—akin to what Hans Jonas describes in *Phenomenon of Life*, regarding cybernetics as 'an overcoming of the dualism which classical materials had left in possession by default: for the first time since Aristotelianism we would have a unified doctrine, or at least a unified conceptual scheme, for the representation of reality'.[3] The same observation is made in Gilbert Simondon's *On the Mode of Existence of Technical Objects* (1958), where he considers the reflexive thinking of cybernetics (characterized by feedback and information) as key to the resolution of the dualism intrinsic in culture; traditional and modern, rural and urban, major (adult) and minor (child) modes of technology education, and so on.[4] In *Recursivity and Contingency*, I put feedback under a more general category: recursivity. Recursion in general designates a non-linear operation which constantly returns to itself in order to know and determine itself.[5] There are different modalities of recursions, but they all share the overcoming of dualism. Information is the measurement of the degree of organization; feedback

3   Hans Jonas, *The Phenomenon of Life: Toward a Philosophical Biology*
(Evanston: Northwestern University Press, 2001), 111.
4   Gilbert Simondon, *On the Mode of Existence of Technical Objects*, trans.
Cecile Malaspina and John Rogove (Minneapolis: Univocal, 2017).
5   Yuk Hui, Recursivity and Contingency (London: Rowman and Littlefield, 2019).

is a recursive or circular causality that allows auto-regulation to take place. For example, when reaching out with my arm to grasp a bottle of water, many feedback processes are taking place, which allows me to adjust the attention of my eyes and the muscles of my arms until I reach the destination, or the telos. Therefore, towards the end of Chapter 1 of *Cybernetics*, Wiener was able to claim that

> modern automation exists in the same sort of Bergsonian time as the living organism, and hence there is no reason in Bergson's considerations why the essential mode of functioning of the living organism should not be the same as that of the automation of this type… In fact, the whole mechanist–vitalist controversy has been relegated to the limbo of badly posed questions.[6]

Whether Wiener's claim can be completely justified has to be scrutinized under the light of history. However, it remains significant for us to reconceptualize what is happening today regarding the relation between machine and organism, human and environment, technology and nature, departing from Wiener's cybernetics. Wiener's bold statement suggests a radical revaluation of the humanist values that oppose the organic and the inorganic, and it also renders the humanist critique ineffective. Different from what, for example, André Leroi-Gourhan and Bernard Stiegler might call 'organized inorganic', Wiener's focus is not the man-machine or man-tool hybrid, but rather the possibility of assimilating both the organic and the inorganic by cybernetic machines. Modern machines are all cybernetic machines: they all employ circular causality as their principle of operation. In this sense, a cybernetic machine is no longer merely mechanistic, but rather assimilates certain behaviours of organisms. It is important to bear in mind that resemblance does not mean equivalence, and it is this misunderstanding that dominates our contemporary politics of machines today.

 Ecology is similarly a concept charged with ambiguity. If ecology is rooted in an attempt to understand the relation between the living being and its milieu—as it is in the case of Ernst Haeckel in the

6 Wiener, *Cybernetics*, 44.

nineteenth century and is continued in the early twentieth century by Jakob von Uexküll—we have to bear in mind that this discourse remains important but insufficient to understand the complexity that belongs to human societies. Von Uexküll has furthered Haeckel's concept of ecology to show that the environment is not only that which selects according to its physicality (in this respect Haeckel remains a Darwinian), but also that which is selected and internalized by the living being. The first type of selection may be called *adaptation*, meaning that the living being has to adapt itself to the milieu according to the available resources and physical conditions. The second type of selection may be called *adoption*, meaning that the living being has to select and construct contexts from what is available to it as means of survival. The tick, an arachnid without eyes, remains inactive in its position on a tree, and only by detecting wind, warmth, and the smell of butyric acid (sweat)—which signify the approach of a mammal—it falls down in order to attach to the animal's body, to reach the skin and then to suck its blood. There is a semiotics in the process of selection of information, based on the *Bauplan* (literally building plan or blueprint), the sensorium and the central nervous system of the animal, which in turn defines its *Umwelt* (literally surrounding world).[7] However, human beings are not ticks, they invent tools and change the environment. They are beings talented not only with adapting to the external environment, but also with changing and adopting that environment itself through technical means. In these processes of adaptation and adoption, we see that there is a reciprocity between the living being and its environment, which we can also call its organicity, namely, the fact that they do not only exchange information, energy and matter but also constitute a *community*. A human community is far beyond the sum of the human actors that constitute it; it also includes their environment and other non-human beings.

The intervention of human beings in the environment defines the process of hominization; the evolutionary and historical becoming of human and its politics. It is beyond my capacity to outline this process, but human civilization could be seen as an intimate and complicit relation between humans and their environment, which gives rise to what

7   Jakob von Uexküll, *A Foray into the Worlds of Animals and Humans: With a Theory of Meaning* (Minneapolis: University of Minnesota Press, 2010), 50–51.

has been called mesology since Plato (according to Augustin Berque's historiography).[8] However, to return the subject at hand, let us turn to a provocative claim from Marshall McLuhan:

> Sputnik created a new environment for the planet. For the first time the natural world was completely enclosed in a man-made container. At the moment that the Earth went inside this new artifact, Nature ended and Ecology was born. 'Ecological' thinking became inevitable as soon as the planet moved up into the status of a work of art.[9]

This statement has to be analysed further. The 1957 launch of Sputnik by the Soviet Union is the first time that human beings were able to ponder the earth from the outside, and in this respect, the earth is now principally viewed as an artifact with the aid of space technology. In *The Human Condition*, Hannah Arendt also describes the 1957 launch of Sputnik as 'second in importance to no other, not even to the splitting of the atom', because it suggests, as Konstantin Tsiolkovsky said in a phrase quoted by Arendt, that 'mankind will not remain bound to the earth forever'.[10] This liberation from the earth directly confronts humankind with the infinite universe and prepares for a cosmic nihilism. It is the moment nature ended and ecology was born. In contrast to the meaning Haeckel gave to the term ecology towards the end of the nineteenth century, meaning the totality of relations between a living being and its environment,[11] and to Uexküll's definition of ecology as the selection process from the *Umgebung* (physical environment) to the *Umwelt* (the 'interpretation' of the world by the living being), what McLuhan means by ecology is no longer a biological concept. According to McLuhan, the earth is considered to be a cybernetic system

8   Augustin Berque, *Poétique de la Terre: Histoire naturelle et histoire humaine, essai de mésologie* (Paris, Belin, 2014).
9   Marshall McLuhan, 'At the Moment of Sputnik the Planet Became a Global Theatre in which There Are No Spectators but Only Actors', *Journal of Communication* 24, no. 1 (1974): 49.
10   Hannah Arendt, *The Human Condition* (Chicago: Chicago University Press, 1998 [1958]), 1.
11   Ernst Haeckel, *Generelle Morphologie der Organismen* (Berlin: Georg Reimer, 1866), Vol. 2: 286–87; see also: Robert J. Richards, *The Tragic Sense of Life: Ernst Haeckel and the Struggle over Evolutionary Thought* (Chicago: University of Chicago Press, 2009), 8.

monitored and governed by the machines upon it and in outer space. What we are witnessing is the disappearance of the earth, since it is continuously absorbed into a plane of immanence constructed by the recursive thinking of cybernetics.

The hybridism between the natural environment and machines constitutes a gigantic system, and it is in this conceptualization that nature ended and ecology began. Ecology, beyond its strict use in biology, is not a concept of nature but rather a concept of cybernetics.[12] This is more evident when we refer to the notion of Gaia coined by James Lovelock to describe the ecological system of the earth as 'a cybernetic system with homeostatic tendencies as detected by chemical anomalies in the Earth's atmosphere'.[13] So we quickly arrived here, at the position that the modern machine is no longer mechanistic and ecology is nothing natural; in fact, modern machines and ecology are two discourses adhering to the same principle, namely, cybernetics. The difference being, if we insist, that we have moved from individual machines—for example, the automatic machines in the factories of nineteenth-century Manchester described by Marx—to technical systems that connect different machines and establish recursivity between them. These systems can take different scales, from a local network, to a planetary system such as the earth's technosphere. Now I want to ask what the implications of this redefinition of (the relation between) machine and ecology could be.

Technological becoming of geophilosophy

We are more than ever in an epoch of cybernetics, since cybernetics was not a discipline parallel to other disciplines such as philosophy and psychology, but rather it aimed to be a universal discipline, able to unite all others—therefore, we could say, a universal mode of thinking par excellence. Cybernetics as universal reflexive thinking has displaced philosophy from the position it used to occupy. This displacement is not a

12   Note that many biologists use the term ecology, and it is generally considered to be a biological discipline studying relationships of biotic and abiotic elements.
13   James Lovelock, *Gaia: A New Look at Life on Earth* (Oxford: Oxford University Press, 2000 [1979]), 142.

rejection of philosophy, but rather, in the parlance of Martin Heidegger, the completion or end of philosophy (the German word *Ende* signifies both completion and end). What does this end mean? Does it mean that Western philosophy no longer has any role to play in the technological age, since it is already completed in technology as destiny? Or does it mean that philosophy will have to reinvent itself in order to survive, namely, become a post-European (or postmetaphysical, post-ontological) philosophy, and that this also goes for Europe itself? I do not want to open a Pandora's box here, but simply to point out that cybernetic thinking as an alleged universal and ecological thinking is that which sublates, or at least pretends to sublate, the traditional metaphysical dualisms in ontology and epistemology, and it is in this respect that it calls forth a new condition of philosophizing, and therefore a new inquiry into the question of ecology.

Here is the postulation: maybe it is no longer a dualism that is the source of danger in our epoch, but rather a non-dualistic totalizing power present in modern technology, which ironically resonates with the anti-dualist ideology (for example, the rejection of any comparison between the East and the West). Ironically, because the anti-dualist ideology still believes that the main danger is dualism, without realizing that this duality is no longer the foundation of modern science and technology. In other words, without having examined this intimate relation between philosophy and technology, it will be difficult, if not impossible, to develop a philosophical thinking adequate to our contemporary situation.

Now, let us bring our skepticism to the fore and pursue the argument further: Will cybernetics be the solution to the ecological problems that we face today? Will the organismic model at the heart of cybernetics be able to escape the shadow that European modernity has cast for centuries? If the early moderns provide us a mechanistic view of the world through geometrization (Kepler, Galileo, Newton and Descartes, among others) and experimental science (Bacon and Boyle), now with cybernetics as the realization and concretization of organismic thought which started dominating since the end of the eighteenth century, can we finally terminate modernity with cybernetics? Do we not already find in cybernetics, and its planetary version, the Gaia theory, a generic logic that rests on the recognition of the relation between the living being and its milieu, as the philosopher and orientalist Augustin Berque has emphasized in many places?

> To overcome the modern alternative is to recognize
> that the structural moment of our existence—our *medi-*
> *ance*—is such that each of us is split: 'half' (from the Latin
> medietas) in one's individual animal body, while the other
> 'half' consists of the eco-technical-symbolic system that
> is our life milieu.[14]

Berque proposes a non-binary thinking that he found in Japanese thought, or Eastern thought in general, and opposes it to the dualism of which Descartes is the modern spokesperson. However, let us not rush to an answer, because we may fall victim to the dualism of critique discussed above. Instead, let us consider a comment from Heidegger's *Black Notebook* concerning the relation between organism and technology: 'It might very well still take a considerable time to recognize that the "organism" and the "organic" present themselves as the mechanistic-*technological* "triumph" of modernity over the domain of growth, "nature".'[15] Heidegger saw that this becoming organic, or becoming ecological, is no more than the mechanistic-technological triumph of modernity over nature. This statement has to be assessed beyond the cynical impression that one may have at first glance. Heidegger's critique of cybernetics deserves our reflection today, since he does not celebrate the overcoming of dualism, but rather calls for prudence (*phronesis*) and for warding off illusions and false analysis. Because at first glance, one may be able to claim that cybernetics has fulfilled an anti-dualistic critique of modernity. I would like to suggest, rather provocatively, that with the rise of cybernetics and its organismic model, we may need a new agenda for mesology. We will have to understand this by rethinking the relation between technology and the environment. Instead of seeing technology as a result of the determination by the geographical milieu, or concluding that the natural milieu is destroyed by technology, we cannot neglect how the technology–environment complex constitutes its own genesis and autonomy, and how such genesis could be rethought or resituated in a cosmic reality which is proper to the milieu or *fûdo* (風土) in the sense of the Japanese

14   Augustin Berque, *Thinking Through Landscape*, trans. Anne-Marie Feenberg-Dibon (London: Routledge, 2014), 60.
15   Martin Heidegger, *Ponderings XII–XV: Black Notebooks 1939–1941*, trans. Richard Rojcewicz (Indianapolis: Indiana University Press, 2017), 143.

philosopher Tetsurō Watsuji. I will elaborate on this point towards the end of the article.

To be brief—and this definitely deserves much more detailed analysis in the future—this technological-environmental complex could be understood in two senses, which are seemingly different yet remain intimately related. First, it is what the paleoanthropologist André Leroi-Gourhan terms a technical milieu.[16] The technical milieu is that which acts as a membrane between the internal milieu conceived as an unstable and dynamic 'mental tradition', and the external milieu consisting of the climate, natural resources and the influences of other tribal groups.[17] Leroi-Gourhan uses the cell as an organic metaphor to explain the relation between three milieus (technical, internal and external) and the permeability and resistance against technical tendencies. The technical milieu is that which is produced by the irreducible differences between the internal and external milieus, while at the same time it filters and diffuses what comes from the external milieu so that it can maintain the consistency of the internal milieu. In other words, the internal milieu and the external milieu form a reciprocal relation through the mediation of the technical milieu.

The second sense of the technological-environmental complex concerns a techno-geographical milieu, a term coined by Gilbert Simondon. It literally means that the geographical milieu, including natural resources, is no longer simply an object of exploitation but is rather integrated into the functioning of the technical object. In *On the Mode of Existence of Technical Objects*, Simondon gives us the famous example of the Guimbal turbine, which successfully integrates the river as both the driving force of an engine and its cooling agent.[18] The engine is immersed in oil at a high temperature. Oil effectively insulates and protects the engine from water, at the same time acting as a lubricant. In the case of the Guimbal turbine, the functionality of the river is multiplied; it becomes an organ belonging to the technical objects. The river is also what Simondon calls an associated milieu which provides a feedback mechanism for stabilizing and regulating the dynamic system: the stronger the current, the faster the

16 André Leroi-Gourhan, *Milieu et technique* (Paris: Albin Michel, 1973), 340–50.
17 Ibid., 334–35.
18 Simondon, *Technical Objects*, 57–58.

turbine moves. Theoretically, more heat is produced which may burn the engine, while since the current is also fast, the heat can be more effectively carried away. The river and the turbine thus form a techno-environmental complex.

Both Leroi-Gourhan and Simondon were influenced by the metaphor of the organism in their conceptualization of the technical milieu and the associated milieu. This aspiration to an organismic or holistic model was a significant intellectual movement of their time. The role of the technical milieu for Leroi-Gourhan as a membrane between the internal and external milieus, is similar to what Simondon calls the associated milieu, with the difference that Leroi-Gourhan still wants to single out the technical from the cultural (internal) and natural (external), while in the scheme of Simondon such distinctions have already disappeared. Simondon calls it a techno-geographical milieu (this is also the reason why Simondon was able to conceive of a conceptual plan for overcoming the antagonism between culture and nature, nature and technology, culture and technology). Simondon's interpretation of the significance of the Guimbal engine and the notion of the associated milieu was very much influenced by Wiener's cybernetics; and the reflective logic in cybernetics seems to Simondon to have displaced philosophy. It is from this point that we can understand Heidegger's claim that cybernetics marks the end of philosophy. Simondon's river stands in a peculiar relation to what Heidegger says in *The Question Concerning Technology* about the hydroelectric plant in the Rhine river, where the river becomes a mere standing reserve, to be constantly challenged and exploited by modern technology.[19] Peculiar because, at first glance, Simondon's formulation of the river as a techno-geographical milieu expresses an optimism, while Heidegger's description of the Rhine river as standing reserve is, though not necessarily pessimistic, a criticism of the 'technization' of *phusis*; they both refer to the same end of philosophy, but with two different attitudes.

Simondon's emphasis on what concerns the Guimbal engine is not simply about the exploitation of the river, but also demonstrates a reciprocity between the technological and the natural, or what Simondon himself calls 'co-naturality'. The reciprocal and communal structure demonstrated by the Guimbal engine is only one case of

19   Martin Heidegger, *The Question Concerning Technology and Other Essays*, trans. William Lovitt (New York: Garland, 1977), 16.

the cybernetic thinking to which Simondon aspires, in order to overcome dualism—or its more aggressive form, antagonism—between
culture and technology, nature and technology. After cybernetics,
especially with biologists Huberto Maturana and Francisco Varela's
notion of 'structural coupling', the technical functionality of the river
described by Simondon seems to be present as a generic model of
the techno-geographical complex. Environment is not only that which
is modified by technology, but rather it is also increasingly constituted by technology. Ecological thinking is not simply about protecting
nature, but fundamentally a political thought based on environments
and territories. Technology's increasing capacity to participate in the
modulation of the environment forces us to develop a geophilosophy.
This is by no means a new discovery, however, it is essential to analyse this historical trajectory in order to understand what is at stake in
technological development today:

1   The relation between the human and the environment is com-
           plexified in the course of time and the semiotics that defines
           perception and interpretation has to be constantly updated
           according to the evolution of technical objects in Simondon's
           sense. The continuity and discontinuity from biological sen-
           sory detection, to the display of signs and symbols, and to
           the invention of electronic sensors that gradually cover the
           urban and rural area, today entails a technological trajecto-
           ry that constantly defines and redefines human and nature,
           which Peter Sloterdijk might term the domestication of hu-
           man beings.[20]

2   The technology that is used for the domestication of livestock
           is fundamentally a modulation of the relation between live-
           stock and its environment; or in other words, human beings
           intervene in the environment by controlling its fertility and
           sterility in order to modulate the behaviour of the livestock on
           a large scale. Human communities maintain an apparent au-
           tonomy through the invention of laws, customs and symbolic

20   Peter Sloterdijk, *Nicht gerettet: Versuche nach Heidegger* (Frankfurt am
Main: Suhr-kamp, 2001), especially the chapter 'Domestikation des Seins: Die
Verdeutlichung der Lichtung.'

systems that define taboos and transgressions. These constitute social norms and therefore also their opposite, social inadaptability, which is central to Michel Foucault's analysis.

3   The technology of livestock domestication has gradually merged with the self-domestication of the human being, which may be understood in terms of what Foucault calls governmentality. Human beings' intervention in the environment constitutes a specific kind of governmentality, which Foucault calls environmentality. At the beginning of this environmental thinking, we see that, and here I quote Foucault, 'the population is the object that government must take into account in all its observations and knowledge [*savoir*], in order to be able to govern effectively in a rational and conscious manner'.[21]

4   The control of the population represents a *molar* type of governmentality, which treats human beings in large quantities, therefore its technique can only be implemented through the mediation of laws and regulations that treat each subject as an equal and particular being. Technological inventions since the twentieth century supplement this molar mode of control with a *molecular* mode, meaning that each human being is treated as an individual who differs from other individuals. Such individuals are defined by the relation between the individual and their environment constantly captured and capitalized in the form of data. This form of governmentality became dominant during the coronavirus pandemic.

The generalization of recursive algorithms and its implementation in digital computers concretize cybernetic thinking and its applications in almost all social, economical and political domains. Capital moves from a mechanistic model, accurately observed by Marx, towards an organismic model realized by informational machines equipped with complex recursive algorithms. Data is the source of information; it is

---

21   Michel Foucault, *Power: Essential Works of Foucault, 1954–1984*, ed. James D. Faubion, trans. Robert Hurley et al. (London: Penguin Classics, 2020), 217.

that which allows the recursive models to be ubiquitous and effective. The digital urbanism that is in the process of developing, and which will be the central theme of the digital economy, is driven by the recursive operation of data. Data, in Latin, means something that is already given, like sense data that determines the falling of the tick, or the red colour of the apple in front of me. Since the mid-twentieth century, data has acquired a new meaning, namely, computational information, which is no longer merely 'given' as such, but is rather produced and modulated by human beings.[22] In this sense, we can see that the notion of 'societies of control' described by Gilles Deleuze is far beyond the common discourse of a society of surveillance; it rather means societies whose governmentality is based on the auto-position and auto-regulation of automatic systems. These systems vary in scale; it can be a global corporation like Google, a city like London, a nation state like China and also the whole planet.

Towards an ecology of machines

Here I would like to return to the question raised earlier: Is cybernetics and its continuation in the twenty-first century, via the systems theory of Niklas Luhmann et al., already a response to the critique of industrialism, which inherited the dualistic tendency of early modern thought, as outlined by Ludwig von Bertalanffy in his 1936 *General System Theory*?

> The mechanical world view, taking the play of physical particles as ultimate reality, found its expression in a civilization which glorifies physical technology that has led eventually to the catastrophes of our time. Possibly the model of the world as a great organization can help to reinforce the sense of reverence for the living which we have almost lost in the last sanguinary decades of human history.[23]

22   Hui, *Digital Objects*, 48.
23   Ludwig von Bertalanffy, *General System Theory* (New York: George Braziller, 2015 [1968]), 49.

With the becoming reflective of cybernetic machines, is it possible to surpass modernity, and hence the epistemologies that accompany it? Or is the generic model suggested by cybernetics for overcoming dualism still within the paradigm of modernity, as Heidegger suggested in the 1930s? What does it mean to still be within the paradigm of modernity? It means, I suggest, that such a concept of modernity undermines the necessity of locality and diversity, because it insists upon a universal episteme and upon the concept of progress.

Although it is true that machines are becoming organismic, it is, as Simondon has observed, in the permanent process of 'becoming', no matter how concrete a technical object is, that it still retains reminiscences of abstract schemes, while a living being is always already completely concrete. It is within the parallax between the 'not being completely concrete' and the illusion of being able to replace nature with digital informational technology that we find the question of politics today. The former remains a humanist critique, while the latter is transhumanist. Heidegger's response is neither humanist nor transhumanist, but rather, according to our interpretation, local. Being, for Heidegger, is a notion specific to a locality, called the land of the evening (*Abendland*). The concept of being does not have a corresponding term in Chinese language and thought, at least, not from a linguistic point of view.[24] We find it, for example, in Heidegger's reading of Hölderlin's hymn 'Der Ister', in which the river is conceived as both locality (*Ortschaft*) and wandering (or journeying) (*Wanderschaft*) at its origin.[25]

> The river is the locality of the locale of the home. The river at the same time determines the becoming of human beings as historical in their being at home. The river is the wandering of that journey in which the becoming of being at home has its essence.[26]

24   A.C. Graham, *Studies in Chinese Philosophy and Philosophical Literature* (New York: SUNY, 1990), 322–59.
25   Martin Heidegger, *Hölderlin's Hymn 'The Ister'*, trans. William McNeill and Julia Davis (Indianapolis: Indiana University Press, 1996), 30.
26   Ibid., 42.

The river, which is the external milieu for Leroi-Gourhan and the associated milieu for Simondon, is the locality that is, by default, keeping stationary, and it is the wandering that moves forward. This seemingly contradictory movement, forward and backward, constitutes the historicity of 'being there' (*Da-sein*). However, the destiny of locality is not yet clear in the technological epoch, and this ambiguity is the source of reactionary politics. It is because the reactionaries search for a *Heimat* without differentiating it from locality. However, the truth of Being can only take place in the danger brought about by humanity's frenzy for the gigantic, in the form of an event of appropriation initiated by a 'shock of deep awe' (*Schrecken der Scheu*).[27] Ought we to wait for this eschatology to happen, or should we instead take other paths that do not follow the history of Western thought, as long as the universal has to be contested? The question of Being, which Heidegger explores, brings us back to the question of locality and historicity; one that is in tension with Heidegger's own longing for the *Heimat*.[28] One may claim, as many sociologists do, that with the invention of network technology, time and space are both increasingly compressed. Such a claim prevents us from seeing what has always already been there and beyond. Indeed, one of the major failures of the twentieth century is the inability to articulate the relation between locality and technology, and the reliance on an almost standardized ecological thinking endowed with a strong European humanism. Technology became a provocation of either reactionary politics based on a dualism between tradition and modernity, or a fanatical accelerationism, which believes that the problems that we have and have inherited will finally be resolved by technological advancement, be it geoengineering for repairing the earth or the subversion of capitalism by accelerating towards full automation. From the economic and technocratic perspective, there is very little value in taking locality into consideration, other than accounting for the availability of natural resources. The advancement of network technology will speed up the spatial compression, and therefore it is of no use to discuss what could be called 'geographicality', since all exchanges are done at the speed of light. This ignorance of the milieu is also an

27   Martin Heidegger, *Beiträge zur Philosophie (vom Ereignis)* (Frankfurt am Main: Vittorio Klostermann, 1989), 8.
28   I will treat this question more fully in Yuk Hui, *Post-Europe* (New York: Sequence/Urbanomic, forthcoming 2024).

ignorance of locality; it fails to establish an intimate and complicit relation between the earth seen from the perspective of the territory and globalizing technology.

We still have to add why cybernetics is not yet sufficient as a non-dualistic solution before we arrive at understanding locality. The logic of cybernetics remains formal; therefore, it underestimates the milieu by reducing it to mere functionality based on feedback, so that the milieu can be integrated into the operation of the technical object. In this respect, the milieu is exposed as a scientific and technological object, while its position within the genesis of technicity is ignored. This is also why in the introduction to Part III, 'Genesis of Technicity', of *On the Mode of Existence of Technical Objects*, Simondon claims that the analysis of the evolution of technical objects (Part I) and the analysis of the relation between the human and technics (Part II) are not sufficient to understand technicity. Instead, he says, it is necessary to situate technical concretization within the genesis of technicity, which means to relate technological thought to other thoughts. Simondon's unfinished project (judged from the standpoint of cosmotechnics) suggests that we think of a genesis with a first magic phase which constantly bifurcates, first into technics and religion and then, in the second stage, each of them bifurcates into the theoretical and practical parts. Simondon understands technological development as a constant entanglement with religious thinking, aesthetic thinking and philosophical thinking, oscillating between technology's need to diverge and thinking's desire to converge. Technicity means here the cosmo-geographical specificity of technology and how such cosmogeographical particularity has participated in shaping the technological mentality, which includes an understanding of technology, a sensibility towards matter, form and other forms of existence, the relation between art and spirit, and so on. It is also for this reason that Simondon's project has to be pursued further by looking into the cosmological specificity of cultures. For example, Tetsurō Watsuji pointed out almost a century ago how the milieu affects the way of seeing and painting. The Japanese word *fûdo* (literally wind and soil, often rendered in English as climate) comes from the two Chinese characters for wind (fû 風) and soil (do 土). Watsuji classifies three types of *fûdo*, namely, monsoon, desert and meadow. To give brief examples of Watsuji's observations, he thinks that, since Asia is heavily affected by monsoons, the resulting relative lack of seasonal change creates an easy-going personality. In

Southeast Asia especially, since the weather is always very warm, nature provides a plenitude of foodstuffs, and therefore there is no need to labour too much in order to survive, or to worry about the demands of day-to-day living. Similarly, he argues that the lack of natural resources in the deserts of the Middle East creates solidarity between peoples, so that the Jewish people, although they live in diaspora, remain united; while in the meadowlands of Europe, clear and regular seasonal changes demonstrate the constancy of the laws of nature, thus suggesting the possibility of mastering nature with science.

This cosmological specificity gives rise to different technics, for example, in Greece the plenitude of sun and clear sky gives priority to the form, while the obscure *fûdo* in Asia gave rise to the style of haziness in painting.[29] Cosmo-geography constitutes an important dimension of locality.

Cybernetic thinking remains a thinking of totalization, since it aims to absorb the other into itself, like Hegelian logic, which sees polarity not as oppositional but rather as a motivation towards synthesized identity. The Hegelian and cybernetician Gotthard Günther considers cybernetics fundamentally the operational (technical) realization of Hegelian reflexive—that is, dialectical—logic.[30] The complexification of cybernetic logic finally leads to an absolute totality. Bearing this in mind, without being able to reiterate Günther's interpretation of the place of Hegelian reflexive logic in cybernetics here,[31] my claim could be formulated as follows: To think beyond cybernetics is to think beyond the totalizing effect of a nondualist thinking. In other words, how can we reintroduce the question of locality into the discourse of machine and ecology today? And how does this reintroduction of locality contribute to the discourse on machines?

We are not opposing machine and ecology as if machines are those things that only rape Mother Nature and violate the harmony between the human and nature, an image attributed to technology since the end of the eighteenth century. Neither are we following the Gaia theory that the earth is a single super-organism or a collectivity

29   Tetsurō Watsuji, *Climate and Culture: A Philosophical Study*, trans. Geoffrey Bownas (Westport, CT: Greenwood, 1961), 90.
30   Gotthard Günther, *Das Bewußtsein der Maschinen: Eine Metaphysik der Kybernetik* (Baden-Baden: Agis, 1963), 95.
31   For a more detailed analysis see Yuk Hui, *Recursivity and Contingency* (London: Rowman and Littlefield International, 2019), Chapter 2.

of organisms in line with the thought of James Lovelock and Lynn Margulis. Instead, I would like to propose that we reflect on an ecology of machines. To open this ecology of machines, we will need first to go back to the concept of ecology. The foundation of ecology is diversities, since it is only with biodiversities (or the co-existence of multiple species, including all forms of organisms, even bacterial) that the ecological system can be conceptualized. To discuss the ecology of machines, we will need a different notion in parallel to biodiversity, which I call technodiversity. Biodiversity is the correlate of technodiversity, since without technodiversity, we will only witness the disappearing of species by a homogeneous rationality. Take the example of pesticide, which is made to kill a certain species of insect regardless of its geographical location, precisely because the pesticide is based on chemical and biological analysis. However, we know that the use of the same pesticide may lead to different disastrous consequences in different environments. Before the invention of pesticides, different techniques were employed to combat insects threatening the harvest, for example, natural resources found in the region. Which is to say, there was a technodiversity prior to the employment of pesticides as a universal solution. Pesticides are apparently more effective in the short term, but it is well established today that we have only been looking as far as our noses in thinking about the distant future. We can say that technodiversity is fundamentally a question of locality. Locality does not necessarily mean ethnocentrism, nationalism or fascism, but rather, it is that which forces us to rethink the process of modernization and globalization and allows us to reflect on the possibility to *resituate* modern technologies. Locality is also key to conceive of a multiplicity of cosmotechnics. Locality does not mean identity politics here, but rather the capacity to reflect on the technological becoming of the local, not to retreat to traditionalism of one form or another, but rather for multiple localities to invent their own technological thought and future—an immunology, or rather immunologies, yet to be written.

What are the localities of non-European countries such as Japan, China and Brazil today? Heidegger's long exposition on the relation between technology and Western philosophy is occidentally oriented. We should take the term orientation in a literal sense here, namely, as *Erörterung* (orientation), that is, an identification of where one is and what one will become. It is in this sense that Heidegger is also a thinker of geopolitics. To take up Heidegger's project today, but also to go beyond him, is to carry his reflection beyond Europe. I want to put this challenge into a speculative question: For non-European cultures, can we identify their own technological thought in the same way that they also have different *fûdo*? Can these technological thoughts contribute to the imagination of technological futures, which are now unfortunately dominated by the transhumanist ideology? I tend to believe that it is possible and necessary to rediscover different technologies, which I call cosmotechnics. Cosmotechnics is not simply about different ways of making things, for example, different techniques of knitting or dyeing. I gave it a preliminary definition in *The Question Concerning Technology in China* as the unification of the moral and the cosmic order through technical activities.[32] The term unification will have to be further elaborated,[33] but for our purpose here, cosmotechnics should be understood as an *Urtechnik*; it challenges our current understanding of technology and therefore also its future. This cosmological specificity must be rethought beyond astral physics, beyond the conceptualization of the universe as a thermodynamic system; it also reopens the question of morality beyond ethical rules that are added after the fact as constraints to new technologies. Technical activities unify the moral order and the cosmic order—by unification I mean reciprocal processes which constantly enforce each other to acquire new meanings. This is why I wanted to reinterpret what Leroi-Gourhan calls the *technical tendency* and *technical facts*.[34] The technical tendency is what seems to be universal, like laws of nature. For example, the use of flint to produce fire and the invention of the wheel for transportation can be found in almost every civilization. Technical facts are the particular features that vary from one civilization to another; in the process of diffusion, technology was filtered and modified according to constraints intrinsic to the internal milieu. For Leroi-Gourhan, technical facts are determined by numerous factors, but largely by material constraints, while I tend to think that the differences in technical facts entail different cosmologies and their moral constraints, which encompass far more than functional aesthetics.

32   Yuk Hui, *The Question Concerning Technology in China: An Essay in Cosmotechnics* (Falmouth: Urbanomic, 2016).
33   I elaborate on this notion of unification in *Art and Cosmotechnics* (Minneapolis: University of Minnesota Press, 2021).
34   André Leroi-Gourhan, *L'homme et la matière* (Paris: Albin Michel, 1973), 27–35.

I would like to conclude by picking up the biochemist-turned-sinologist Joseph Needham's question here, namely: Why did modern science and technology not develop in China and India, but only in Europe?[35] Historians who attempt to answer this question tend to carry out comparative studies on the advancement of technology in Europe and China as if the essence of technology concerns merely efficiency and mechanical causalities; for example, papermaking in the second century in China was more advanced than in Europe. However, this line of inquiry, it seems to me, has betrayed Needham's own stance. This is so because Needham was actually suggesting that there were two different trajectories of technology in China and in Europe, which were less constrained by material causes than by their different ways of thinking and forms of life. To put it in other words, answering Needham's question is not to show who is more advanced, but rather to elaborate on the different systems of technological thought. In *The Question Concerning Technology in China* I aim to respond to Needham by taking his implicit thesis further.

The technological upheaval since the nineteenth century has presented us with a convergence which at times seems inevitable, while at the same time it is clearly problematic and has to be fragmented in favour of other social and political visions. The inquiry into the relation between machine and ecology is not so much about how to design more intelligent machines, but rather requires a discovery of cosmotechnical diversity; while such diversity has to be thought through by going back to the question of locality, therefore re-articulating the concept of technics by resituating it within the geographical milieu, culture and thinking. The task that is left to all of us is to rediscover these cosmotechnics in order to reframe modern technologies, namely, by reframing the enframing (*Gestell*). Only through such a reframing can we imagine a 'new earth and people that do not yet exist'.[36]

---

35 Joseph Needham, *The Grand Titration: Science and Society in East and West* (London: Routledge, 2013).

36 Gilles Deleuze and Félix Guattari, *What is Philosophy?* trans. Hugh Tomlinson and Graham Burchell (New York: Columbia University Press, 1994), 108: 'We lack creation. *We lack resistance to the present.* The creation of concepts in itself calls for a future form, for a new earth and people that do not yet exist. Europeanization does not constitute a becoming but merely the history of capitalism, which prevents the becoming of subjected peoples'.

Note

This chapter was originally published, in a slightly different version, in *Angelaki* 25, no. 4 (2020): 54–66. I want to thank the editors of *Angelaki* for their permission to reprint it in this volume.

Reference

Arendt, Hannah. *The Human Condition*. Chicago: Chicago University
    Press, 1998 [1958].
Bergson, Henri. *Time and Free Will: An Essay on the Immediate Data of
    Consciousness*. London: Allen Lane, 1913.
Berque, Augustin. *Thinking Through Landscape*. Trans. Anne-Marie
    Feenberg-Dibon. London: Routledge, 2014.
Bertalanffy, Ludwig von. *General System Theory*. New York: George
    Braziller, 2015 [1968].
Deleuze, Gilles, and Félix Guattari. *What is Philosophy?* Trans. Hugh
    Tomlinson and Graham Burchell. New York: Columbia University
    Press, 1994.
Foucault, Michel. *Power: Essential Works of Foucault, 1954–1984*. Ed.
    James D. Faubion. Trans. Robert Hurley et al. New York: Penguin,
    2001.
Graham, A.C. *Studies in Chinese Philosophy and Philosophical Literature*.
    New York: SUNY, 1990.
Günther, Gotthard. *Das Bewußtsein der Maschinen: Eine Metaphysik der
    Kybernetik*. Baden-Baden: Agis, 1963.
Haeckel, Ernst. *Generelle Morphologie der Organismen*. Berlin: Georg
    Reimer, 1866.
Heidegger, Martin. *Beiträge zur Philosophie (vom Ereignis)*. Frankfurt am
    Main: Vittorio Klostermann, 1989.
Heidegger, Martin. *Hölderlin's Hymn 'The Ister'*. Trans. William McNeill
    and Julia Davis. Indianapolis: Indiana University Press, 1996.
Heidegger, Martin. *Ponderings XII–XV: Black Notebooks 1939–1941*. Trans.
    Richard Rojcewicz. Indianapolis: Indiana University Press, 2017.
Heidegger, Martin. *The Question Concerning Technology and Other
    Essays*. Trans. William Lovitt. New York: Garland, 1977.
Hui, Yuk. *On the Existence of Digital Objects*. Minneapolis: University of
    Minnesota Press, 2016.

Hui, Yuk. *The Question Concerning Technology in China: An Essay in Cosmotechnics*. Falmouth: Urbanomic, 2016.

Hui, Yuk. *Recursivity and Contingency*. London: Rowman and Littlefield International, 2019.

Hui, Yuk. *Art and Cosmotechnics*. Minneapolis: University of Minnesota Press, 2021.

Hui, Yuk. *Post-Europe*. New York: Sequence/Urbanomic, 2024.

Jonas, Hans. *The Phenomenon of Life: Toward a Philosophical Biology*. Evanston: Northwestern University Press, 2001.

Leroi-Gourhan, André. *L'homme et la matière*. Paris: Albin Michel, 1973.

Leroi-Gourhan, André. *Milieu et technique*. Paris: Albin Michel, 1973.

Lovelock, James. *Gaia: A New Look at Life on Earth*. Oxford: Oxford University Press, 2000 [1979].

McLuhan, Marshall. 'At the Moment of Sputnik the Planet Became a Global Theatre in which There Are No Spectators but Only Actors'. *Journal of Communication* 24, no. 1 (1974): 48–58.

Needham, Joseph. *The Grand Titration: Science and Society in East and West*. London: Routledge, 2013.

Richards, Robert J. *The Tragic Sense of Life: Ernst Haeckel and the Struggle over Evolutionary Thought*. Chicago: University of Chicago Press, 2009.

Simondon, Gilbert. *On the Mode of Existence of Technical Objects*. Trans. Cecile Malaspina and John Rogove. Minneapolis: Univocal, 2017.

Sloterdijk, Peter. *Not Saved: Essays after Heidegger*. Trans. Ian Alexander Moore and Christopher Turner. Cambridge: Polity, 2017.

Uexküll, Jakob von. *A Foray into the Worlds of Animals and Humans: With a Theory of Meaning*. Minneapolis: University of Minnesota Press, 2010.

Watsuji, Tetsurō. *Climate and Culture: A Philosophical Study*. Trans. Geoffrey Bownas. Westport, CT: Greenwood, 1961.

Wiener, Norbert. *Cybernetics: Or Control and Communication in the Animal and the Machine*. Cambridge, MA: MIT Press, 1985.

Ontology and the Politics of Information in the First Cybernetics

Mathieu Triclot

Does cybernetics still have anything to teach us in our present time? Not only does the term 'cybernetics' refer to the now distant post-World War II era of the twentieth century, but it also appears largely out of fashion. We would be hard pressed to find the word 'cybernetics' in our universities' curricula. Both the prefix 'cyber' and the word 'cybernetics' seem outdated, belonging to a realm of obsolete futures.

Why should we consider a cybernetics for the twenty-first century? I can identify four reasons. First, maybe 'twenty-first-century cybernetics' is, in a way, already there. It is clear that the concepts and technologies promoted by cybernetics have become more pervasive than ever. The dissemination of the terms 'feedback' and 'information' is monumental and disconnected from the declining usage of the signifier 'cybernetics'. In other words, we are witnessing what could be called 'a cybernetics without cybernetics', that is, a diffusion of its concepts and artefacts, but without the outdated label. There was a 'first cybernetics', associated with figures like Norbert Wiener, Warren McCulloch, and John von Neumann, and a 'second cybernetics' centred on self-organization, and associated with Heinz von Foerster and Francisco Varela, among others. Now, we may be at the beginning of a 'third cybernetics', no longer associated with the names of personalities, but names of firms like Google, Amazon, Facebook, or OpenAI. Could this be the elusive 'twenty-first-century cybernetics'?

Beyond the progressive diffusion of the terminology of information and feedback, the most striking development lies in the new social roles assumed by the artefacts, anticipated by cybernetics. These artefacts are now entering society on a grand scale. The first noteworthy instance is what has been called the machine learning tsunami, based on the resurgence of the neuroconnectionist models pioneered by cyberneticians.[1] But there is also the prospect of an industrial revolution

1   Dominique Cardon, Jean-Philippe Cointet and Antoine Mazières, 'Neurons Spike Back: The invention of inductive machines and the artificial intelligence controversy', *Réseaux* 211, no. 5 (2018): 173–220.

resulting form the convergence of digital technologies and traditional industries. This new industrial revolution was indeed one of the grand predictions of the original cybernetics. We can think here of Wiener's depiction of the automated factory: 'The all-over system will correspond to the complete animal with sense organs, effectors and proprioceptors, and not, as in the ultra-rapid computing machine, to an isolated brain, dependent for its experiences and for its effectiveness on our intervention.'[2] This description of the shift from the computer as a simple 'isolated brain' to 'the complete animal' evokes concrete figures today, such as Amazon's robotic warehouses or autonomous vehicles. It is only now, with a time lag of seventy years, that cybernetic artefacts are really imposing themselves, with the kind of autonomy and agency envisioned by the first cyberneticians.

This brings us to the second reason for considering a cybernetics for the twenty-first century, not merely as an odd descriptive term for the contemporary era, but prescriptive. We may need a 'cybernetics for our times'. One significant aspect of reclaiming the term lies in the fact that the original cybernetics produced a real-time critical discourse on these technologies. Cybernetics presents itself as a multidisciplinary endeavour open to philosophical and critical inquiry. Heidegger expressed the fear that cybernetics would 'replace philosophy'.[3] However, this overlooks the fact that within cybernetics itself there is a philosophical production, claimed as such. The impetus for revisiting and inheriting cybernetics lies in the significance of this inherent philosophical production endogenous to the technical milieu.

The third reason that justifies this return to cybernetics is that we find, within this philosophical production, a unique stance regarding the nature of information. Cyberneticians advocated for a non-symbolic, physicalist conception of information, which I refer to as information-signal, as opposed to an information-code.[4] This distinction is important, given the inextricably conceptual and technical significance of the term. Information has emerged as a new universal equivalent, applicable to everything and ensuring the reduction of everything to computational devices. What can we learn from this alternative view

2   Norbert Wiener, *Cybernetics, or Control and Communication in the Animal and the Machine* (Cambridge, MA: MIT Press, 2000), 157.
3   Martin Heidegger, *Écrits politiques 1933–1966*, trans. and ed. François Fédier (Paris: Éditions Gallimard, 1995), 262.
4   Mathieu Triclot, *Le moment cybernétique* (Seyssel: Champ Vallon, 2008), 405–11.

of information to critically assess the current digital technologies? But the discourse on information extends beyond ontology and the philosophy of science: we encounter, particularly in Wiener's writings, a discourse that links this ontology of information with politics. This nexus of ontology and the politics of information seems particularly interesting to re-examine today.

This brings me to the fourth and final reason supporting a return to cybernetics: we cannot pretend that the arguments of the first cyberneticians are applicable as they are to the present state of affairs. The time gap between the first cybernetics and our twenty-first-century cybernetics is intriguing in its own right, primarily because the mode of science and technology production has undergone profound changes. Hence, we cannot merely transplant the old cybernetic arguments to the contemporary landscape; instead, we must exploit this temporal gap to shed light on the characteristics of the current regime of science and technology.

The first cyberneticians were working at a turning point in the history of science and technology, during the Cold War, with sciences nationalized by the state and enlisted in the war effort. Cyberneticians, beginning with Wiener, took a stand against this transformation and advocated for an alternative way of doing science. Today, we inhabit a totally different mode of production of science and technology, in which the market has taken on an increasingly important role since the 1980s. Consequently, cybernetics becomes relevant not because it fills the gap between the post-war and contemporary worlds, but because it exposes that gap. By revisiting Wiener's arguments, we can assess these changes and their implications.

In this essay I revisit the debates surrounding the nature of information, particularly the intersection of ontology and politics in Wiener's work. I aim to confront these positions with the contemporary moment, as a step toward a cybernetics for the twenty-first century. I will proceed in three stages. First, I will provide a brief historical overview of cybernetics to contextualize the movement. Next, I will delve into the debate that took place during the seventh Macy Conference, in 1950, on the meaning of the terms 'digital' and 'analogue'. This debate is a key document to understanding the cybernetic conception of information. Finally, I will present a small sample of precepts for an information politics, as they can be extracted from Wiener's writings, and discuss their relevance in light of the contemporary situation.

The paradox of cybernetics

In the first part of this essay, I aim to highlight three messages. First, it is important to recognize that cybernetics is an object that can be difficult to pin down. Indeed, there have been many 'cybernetics', sometimes incompatible with each other. The term cybernetics functions as a floating signifier, which can be reappropriated in very diverse contexts. There have been several cybernetics in the United States,[5] but also in the United Kingdom.[6] It existed as a distinct discipline in the Soviet Union, studied notably by Slava Gerovich.[7] The experiments conducted by Stafford Beer in Chile are also noteworthy.[8] Additionally, cybernetics found its way into the structuralist social sciences in France, through figures like Levi-Strauss and Lacan, among others.[9] There was also a Chinese cybernetics, as I recently discovered thanks to Dylan Levi King's research.[10]

This uncontrolled diffusion of cybernetics can be attributed, in my view, to a key phenomenon: the failure of cybernetics to establish itself as a formal science or discipline; had that been the case, it would still be taught in our universities. This was the original intention of the first cyberneticians, particularly Wiener, but instead of having dedicated cybernetics departments in universities, the field relied on events such as the Macy conferences. This inherent fragility led to the fragmentation of cybernetics, driven by interpersonal difficulties and a questioning of its scientific agenda, with the emergence of the symbolic artificial intelligence research programme.[11] The word 'cybernetics' resembles the word 'psychoanalysis' in the first half of the twentieth century, in

5   Steve Heims, *John Von Neumann and Norbert Wiener: From Mathematics to the Technologies of Life and Death* (Cambridge, MA: MIT Press, 1980); Steve Heims, *Constructing a Social Science for Postwar America: The Cybernetics Group 1946–1953* (Cambridge, MA: MIT Press, 1991).
6   Andrew Pickering, *The Cybernetic Brain: Sketches of Another Future* (Chicago: University of Chicago Press, 2010).
7   Slava Gerovich, *From Newspeak to Cyberspeak: A History of Soviet Cybernetics* (Cambridge, MA: MIT Press, 2002).
8   Eden Medina, *Cybernetic Revolutionaries: Technology and Politics in Allende's Chile* (Cambridge, MA: MIT Press, 2014).
9   Ronan Le Roux, *Une histoire de la cybernétique en France (1948–1975)* (Paris: Garnier, 2018).
10   Dylan Levi King, 'The Genealogy of Chinese Cybernetics', *Palladium* (2023), https://www.palladiummag.com/2022/10/17/the-genealogy-of-chinese-cybernetics.
11   On the interpersonal problems, see Flo Conway and Jim Siegelman, *Dark Hero of the Information Age: In Search of Norbert Wiener the Father of Cybernetics* (New York: Basic Books, 2005).

that the first cyberneticians struggled to regulate its use.[12] As a result, it circulated widely, and was reappropriated in various contexts, often with conflicting interpretations. For instance, I recall a letter from the artist Nicolas Schöffer, who created 'cybernetic light towers' and organized 'cybernetic ballets' featuring robots dancing alongside human performers. In 1957, Schöffer reached out to Wiener, who responded dryly, acknowledging the interest but asserting that these endeavours had no direct connection to cybernetics.[13]

The second element to keep in mind when approaching the first cybernetics is the originality of its way of doing science. Cybernetics is a scientific movement that is marked by multidisciplinarity. It is a well-known fact that cybernetics brings together mathematicians, engineers, members of the life sciences, psychology and the social sciences. This original style of science is also open to philosophy. Wiener, Rosenblueth and Bigelow's 1943 paper on feedback as a model for understanding living organisms—which laid the foundation for the cybernetics research programme—was published in *Philosophy of Science*.[14] We have an article co-authored by a physiologist, an engineer and a mathematician, published in a philosophy journal.

Thus, cybernetics represents a style of science that is open to various disciplines and to philosophical reflection. In this regard, cybernetics can be seen as carrying forward the spirit of 1930s physics, which embraced philosophical inquiry. However, cybernetics found itself at odds with the emerging structures of 'big science', shaped by the war. There is, in the very way Wiener put together the cybernetics group, a rejection of the enlistment of science in the Cold War. This refusal is expressed in the influential 1947 open letter 'A Scientist Rebels'.[15] One cannot understand the form of the cybernetics group without these commitments.

If I had to delimit the first cybernetics in time, I would propose the year 1943 as the start and 1956 as the end. The year 1943 marks a significant milestone with the publication of two foundational articles:

12   Elisabeth Roudinesco, *L'histoire de la psychanalyse en France: Jacques Lacan* (Paris: Livre de Poche, 2009).
13   Maude Ligier and Mathieu Triclot, 'L'art cybernétique de Nicolas Schöffer' (paper presented to the third Congrès de la Société Française d'Histoire des Sciences et des Techniques, 6 September 2008).
14   Norbert Wiener, Arturo Rosenblueth and Julian Bigelow, 'Behavior, Purpose and Teleology', *Philosophy of Science* 10, no. 1 (1943): 18–24.
15   Norbert Wiener, 'A Scientist Rebels', The Atlantic Monthly 179, January 1947, 46.

the aforementioned work by Wiener, Rosenblueth, and Bigelow on feedback; and McCulloch and Pitts's paper on formal neurons.[16] The 1956 date is less obvious. It corresponds to the Dartmouth summer school that launched the symbolic AI program, which was to supplant the cybernetic paradigms in the field of computer science. One could also consider the death of von Neumann in 1957 to symbolize the end of the movement, which declines as a research programme in the United States after this date. This is the paradox of cybernetics: while the movement achieved remarkable success both technically and conceptually, it failed to establish itself as an independent discipline within the academic realm.

What is information?

After this brief overview of the key elements for framing the history of cybernetics, I now come to what seems to me one of the most interesting aspects to be re-interrogated today: the debate on the nature of information. Cybernetics played a pivotal role in establishing the concept of information, which emerged at the intersection of two technical fields. The first is the theory of telecommunications, or 'information theory', established in the work of Claude Shannon.[17] Shannon introduced a mathematical measure of the quantity of information. The second field is mechanical computation, where Shannon's measure, based on bits, was promptly adopted, as the new machines were seen as operating on information. However, cybernetics went beyond merely promoting and consolidating a technical vocabulary at the intersection of these fields. It delved deeper by questioning the very nature of this new term, 'information'. One might have expected this question to be dismissed as a philosophical inquiry secondary to technical advancements. Yet, within cybernetics, the question arises due to the multidisciplinary nature of the field and its ambition to transfer the technical vocabulary of information and feedback to other domains such as the life sciences, psychology and the social sciences.

16 Warren McCulloch and Walter Pitts, 'A Logical Calculus of the Ideas Immanent in Nervous Activity', *Bulletin of Mathematical Biophysics* 5 (1943): 115–33.
17 Claude Shannon, 'A Mathematical Theory of Communication', *Bell System Technical Journal* 27 (1948): 379–423, 623–56.

So, what is information? The discussions following Ralph Gerard's presentation at the seventh Macy Conference on 23 March 1950 provide a remarkable glimpse into the debates that permeated cybernetics at the time.[18] The conversation was initiated by Gregory Bateson and J.C.R. Licklider, who expressed concern about a confusion in the terminology, between digital and analogue. Here is what Bateson says:

> It should be a good thing to tidy up our vocabulary. We have the word 'analogical', which is opposed to the word 'digital'. We also have the word 'continuous', which is opposed to the word 'discontinuous'. And there is the word 'coding', which is obscure to me. First of all, as I understand the sense in which 'analogical' was introduced to this group by Dr von Neumann, a model plane in a wind tunnel would be an 'analogical' device for making calculations about a real plane in the wind. Is that correct?"[19]

Von Neumann acknowledges the need for a clarification, while admitting its difficulty. Indeed, the discussion goes on for about twenty pages: 'Von Neumann: It is very difficult to give precise definitions of this, it has been tried repeatedly. Present use of the words "analogical" and "digital" in science is not completely uniform'.[20]

The ensuing discussion offers two valuable insights. First, it highlights what I call the physicalist orientation of the cyberneticians. Von Neumann and Wiener's answers have in common that they prioritize the signal or analogue dimension over the symbolic dimension of information:

> Von Neumann: Thus, both for the man-made artefact as well as for the natural organ, which are supposed to exercise discrete switching actions, the 'discrete actions' are in reality simulated on the background of continuous processes. ... To restate: the organs that we call digital are, in reality, continuous, but the main aspects of their

18   Heinz Von Foerster, *Cybernetics, Circular Causal and Feedback Mechanisms in Biological and Social Systems: Transactions of the Seventh Conference, March 23–24, 1950* (New York: Caldwell, 1951): 11–57.
19   Ibid., 26.
20   Ibid., 27.

> behaviour are rather indifferent to limited variations of
> the input stimuli…
>
> Wiener: May I speak of the real distinction between the
> digital and the analogical situation? This is a comment
> on what Professor von Neumann has said. … The digital
> element lies in the fact that the things to which we are
> referring are not precise positions but fields of attraction
> which impinge upon one another so that the field where
> there is any substantial indetermination as to whether the
> thing goes to one or the other is as small as possible.[21]

This is a key point: in the last resort, symbols are always signal, material configurations. As Pitts explains, 'we should speak of physical systems in general, not computers'.[22] What is the difference between a symbol and a signal? The symbol is always two-sided: it is a form that is inscribed in matter, but in a conventional way. It is by convention that such and such a material configuration—for example, the presence of an electric current—refers to such and such symbolic content; for example, the value 1 rather than 0. The symbol is inscribed in matter, but the matter is indifferent. The matter could be anything and everything, as long as it can function as a medium of inscription. By contrast, the notion of a signal carries another type of relation between matter and signification, since in the case of the signal, the information is not separable from the material configuration (which by convention is susceptible to finding a new inscription): the information is the material configuration and vice versa.

Cyberneticians do not deny that information can function in a symbolic way. On the contrary, it is how digital mechanical calculators function, as do the lines of communication modelled by Shannon. However, as in the declarations of the seventh Macy Conference, cyberneticians regularly insist on the fact that this symbolic functioning is only a simplification or an abstraction compared to the 'real' functioning which, on the physical level, operates in an analogical way.

But the seventh Macy Conference also reveals variations in this materialist or physicalist stance. Three distinct viewpoints can be

---

21   Ibid., 20–21.
22   Ibid., 32.

identified. The most radical physicalist reductionism is found in von Neumann, who repeats several times that 'in reality' we are dealing primarily with the continuous: 'To conclude, one must say that in almost all parts of physics the underlying reality is analogical, that is, the true physical variables are in almost all cases continuous, or equivalent to continuous descriptions. The digital procedure is usually a human artefact for the sake of description'.[23]

Wiener expresses a more pragmatic position, which consists of explaining that we can choose the 'code' according to the situation: 'I say that the whole habit of our thinking is to use the continuous where that is the easiest and to use the discrete where the discrete is the easiest. Both of them represent abstractions that do not completely fit the situation as we see it. One thing that we cannot do is to take the full complexity of the world without simplification of methods.'[24]

Pitts introduces a third variation, emphasizing that the opposition between digital and analogue is not strictly binary, and that there can exist intermediate systems—in particular forms of continuous calculation at the biological level—which do not however correspond to the model of analogical calculators: 'There is a third between the two, because they are not opposite. The digital and analogical sorts of devices have been defined quite independently and are not logical opposites. ... There can be devices which are computing machines which are continuous without being analogous in the sense that the engineer assumes.'[25]

If we agree that cybernetics defends an original conception of information, we are left with a question: What is the point? What difference does it make? Three theoretical sectors are directly concerned by this discussion on the nature of information, which can be briefly outlined. The first sector is related to the theory of telecommunications. We find traces of it in the dispute over priority between Shannon and Wiener. Wiener reproached Shannon for having pre-empted the theory of communications from a digital conception of the signal, whereas Wiener had developed a model of information based on the physics of the continuous signal.[26]

23   Ibid., 27.
24   Ibid., 50.
25   Ibid., 48.
26   David Mindell, *Between Human and Machine: Feedback, Control, and Computing before Cybernetics* (Baltimore: Johns Hopkins University Press, 2002), 286.

The second area concerns the analogy between information and entropy. Wiener and von Neumann, in particular, advocated for a physicalist interpretation of the formal analogy between entropy and the quantity of information, interpreting information as the inverse of entropy. Information would then be a measure of the amount of order in a physical system, while entropy represents the measure of system disorganization. Wiener revisits the Maxwell's demon thought experiment to provide a framework for interpreting information as a physical quantity.[27]

The most significant impact of the conception of information lies in the development of computer science around the question of the brain-computer relationship, particularly as it appears in von Neumann's work.[28] The discussion at the seventh Macy Conference directly concerns the computer-brain analogy. The history of these debates can be summarized as a return to the 'original sin' of the first draft of a report on the EDVAC, the technical document where von Neumann formalized the operations of digital computers. To carry out this formalization of logical-mathematical operations, von Neumann relies on what he calls 'E-Elements': binary automata with a threshold, directly inspired by the formal neurons of McCulloch and Pitts's 1943 article, to which he directly refers.[29] Von Neumann never ceased to return to this shortcut of the 'E-Elements'—by considering the processes in a digital way, the complexity of the real processes is masked. This complexity reappears in the failure or the error of calculation. This 'physics of information' gives rise to two scientific programmes: alternative models of basic components at the technological level, motivated by the desire to obtain stable behaviour with unstable elements;[30] and a focus on cellular-level processes in the modelling of living beings, pushing a research agenda for artificial life.[31]

27   Wiener, *Cybernetics*, 58.
28   John von Neumann, *The Computer and the Brain* (Yale: Yale University Press, 2000 [1958]).
29   John von Neumann, 'First draft of a report on the EDVAC', *IEEE Annals of the History of Computing* 15, no. 4 (1993), 5.
30   John von Neumann, 'Probabilistic Logics and the Syntheses of Reliable Organisms from Unreliable Components', in *Automata Studies*, ed. Claude Shannon and John McCarthy (Princeton: Princeton University Press, 1952), 43–98.
31   John von Neumann, 'Letter to Norbert Wiener, November 29th 1946', in *John von Neumann: Selected Papers*, ed. Miklos Rédei (American Mathematical Society, 2005), 280.

As Andrew Pickering has shown, the machines envisioned by the first cybernetics are not so much intended to manipulate representations, but to act on the world; to orient themselves in a changing environment by adapting their ways of doing things according to a goal.[32] In this sense, the model remains that of the living being rather than that of the mind manipulating symbols. Cybernetics had in view other kinds of computer science and calculation machines, which we can hardly imagine today. In essence, cybernetics presents an original conception of information, rejecting its reduction to a mere set of symbols. This division leads to specific research orientations such as artificial life, neuro-connectionism, and Wiener's interest in prostheses, which subsequently influenced Licklider's paradigm of 'man-machine symbiosis'.[33]

But what significance can the symbol-signal partition still have today, when the tsunami of machine learning has brought neuroconnectionist models back to the fore? Apparently, cybernetics has won: the parallels between the cyberneticians' arguments and the approaches of machine learning are obvious. Yann LeCun's team's demonstration of character recognition in 1993 follows the same problem of recognition of incomplete forms as in von Neumann's 'General and Logical Theory of Automata' in 1948. But, despite the continuity of the research programmes, contemporary machine learning relies on two technical conditions that were foreign to cyberneticians. First, the explosion of computing power, particularly with the use of GPUs (Graphics Processing Units), plays a crucial role. Second, the availability of massive amounts of data (referred to as big data) is essential for the effectiveness of machine learning, without which it loses its supremacy over other techniques such as classical AI or statistical processing.

We may wonder if we are not dealing with a 'revenge of symbols' within the neuroconnectionist paradigms themselves: the models only work on the condition of a prior reduction of the world into data, into symbolic information. These observations about the technical, economic, legal, and political conditions underlying the resurgence of cybernetic approaches point to a fundamental difference in machine design. Contemporary machine learning is a technique for processing massive amounts of data, whereas cyberneticians envisioned

32   Pickering, *The Cybernetic Brain*, 5–7.
33   J.C.R. Licklider, 'Man-Computer Symbiosis', *Transactions on Human Factors in Electronics* 1 (1960): 4–11.

machines where manipulating representations was secondary to their performative abilities. Hence the resurgence of neuroconnectionism relies on a considerable shift from the physicalist orientation of cyberneticians. This shift remains unexplored and extends beyond the binary choice between machine learning and symbolic artificial intelligence.

Politics of information

So far, I have been interested in the impact of the cybernetic conception of information on technoscientific programmes. However, the influence of this conception extends beyond the scientific domain. The style of science original to cybernetics offers us a last remarkable component, in the form of a transposition of arguments about the nature of information to the field of politics, particularly developed in Wiener's work.

Here, I must call attention to Wiener's singular position within the cybernetic group, as demonstrated by Steve Heims.[34] Multiple competing political orientations emerged from the early days of cybernetics, only to proliferate even more among the subsequent variations that followed. For example, Wiener's programme is diametrically opposed to von Neumann's game-theoretic perspective of calculating optimal decisions. It also differs from Bateson and Mead's intention of employing cybernetic modelling in the social sciences.

Wiener's unique stance lies in his refusal to simply 'apply' engineering sciences to the social world. He argues that such an application is impossible and would amount to a form of fraud. The social, historical world is marked by the singularity of its trajectories and does not present the regularity necessary to be subjected to calculation. There is something very surprising in this refusal to make cybernetics work as a 'science of government', departing from the explicit meaning of the term 'cybernétique' in Ampère. Wiener states that

> in the social sciences we have to deal with short statistical runs, nor can we be sure that a considerable part of what we observe is not a an artefact of our own creation. … We cannot afford to neglect [the natural sciences]; nei-

34 Heims, *John Von Neumann and Norbert Wiener.*

ther should we build exaggerated expectations of their possibilities. There is much which we must leave, whether we like it or not, to the un-'scientific' narrative method of the professional historian.[35]

Yet, we do find a cybernetic politics in Wiener. What does it entail? It involves a strategic use of cybernetic concepts to understand political and social issues, rather than a straightforward application. Cybernetics, with its conception of information, provides strategic argumentative resources, without indulging in a scientistic reduction of the social world to engineering sciences.

I present three samples of Wiener's political use of the notion of information. The first and most obvious is his refusal to consider information as an immaterial term. Considering information as a physical quantity—the opposite of entropy—nurtures in Wiener a form of tragic humanism. The world is inevitably going to waste, as the second law of thermodynamics indicates that entropy necessarily increases in any isolated system. The role of political action, in Wiener's view, is to create and maintain local enclaves of organization and knowledge to resist chaos. He says: 'We are shipwrecked passengers on a doomed planet. … We shall go down, but let it be in a manner to which we may look forward as worthy of our dignity.'[36]

Beyond that, the axiom of the physicality of information leads Wiener to an ecological style of thinking. In his article 'Too Big for Private Enterprise', he defends the role of public power in managing long-term interests that cannot be left in the hands of the 'first businessman who comes along'.[37] *The Human Use of Human Beings* extends this argument in the form of a critique of the 'American philosophy of progress'. Wiener argues:

> We have a good deal of experience as to how the industrialists regard a new industrial potential. … They have very few inhibitions when it comes to taking all the profit

35   Wiener, *Cybernetics*, 164.
36   Wiener, *The Human Use of Human Beings: Cybernetics and Society* (London: Eyre and Spottiswoode, 1950), 26.
37   Norbert Wiener, 'Too Big for Private Enterprise', in *Collected Works with Commentaries, Volume IV*, ed. Pesi Masani (Basel: Birkhäuser Verlag, 1990), 702–3.

out of an industry that there is to be taken, and then letting the public pick up the pieces. This is the history of the lumber and mining industries, and is part of what we have called in another chapter the traditional American philosophy of progress.[38]

This first epistemological-political maxim regarding the materiality of information resonates strongly today. It challenges the discourse of dematerialization and digital dualism, urging us to scrutinize the material, technical, and extractive mediations that underpin information systems. If we return to the autonomous car, let us start with rare metals, and let us not forget assembly lines and the global division of labour.

The second of Wiener's political maxims is encapsulated in the statement: 'Information is not meant to be a commodity'. This can be deduced, once again, from the physics of information, as the inverse of entropy: information cannot retain its value, it is always a function of time and inevitably gains noise. Wiener explains:

> What makes a thing a good commodity? Essentially, that it can pass from hand to hand with substantial retention of its value... Communication is based on a notion allied to entropy, known as the amount of information. ... Just as entropy tends to increase spontaneously in a closed system, so information tends to decrease... . Information and entropy are not conserved, and are equally unsuited to being commodities.[39]

Here Wiener mobilizes a line of reasoning that may seem singularly out of step with contemporary thinking that would lead to the same conclusion. Indeed, contemporary arguments against the commodification of information insist on the possibility of information being shared without loss of value. But this argument rests precisely on a distinction between material and immaterial goods, which is problematic in the spirit of the first cybernetics. This being so, this second maxim leads to a political perspective critical of intellectual property rights, which

38   Wiener, *The Human Use of Human Beings*, 188.
39   Ibid., 128–29.

would not be out of place in contemporary movements in favour of free software or the digital commons, for example.

A third maxim, which follows directly from the cybernetic conception of information, can be expressed as a rejection of the 'myth of the robot'. One of Wiener's major political concerns revolved around automation, particularly the idea of automated factories, mentioned at the beginning of this article. Wiener engaged with union leaders, professional organizations, and political figures. Notably, his conversation with Indian Prime Minister Jawaharlal Nehru emphasized the importance of intermediate professional training and technical culture.[40]

Wiener feared that computers would facilitate the automation of production, leading to a 'new industrial revolution' and significant job losses. However, his argument goes beyond mere fear of replacement. He posits that the prospect of replacing humans with machines ignores the difference between human and mechanical capabilities. Humans excel at reasoning in undefined contexts, while machines are superior in logical calculation. Thus, the ideal relationship with machines is one of coupling, or what Licklider termed a symbiosis between two different beings.

The cybernetic reflection on the computer-brain relationship leads to this political position: the objective of replacing humans with machines supposes, in reality, a considerable reduction of human capabilities. Such replacement is only possible due to of the existence of 'inhumane uses of human beings'.[41] The robot is not dangerous in itself, because pure replacement is a myth. It is dangerous because it is put at the service of social forces that have an interest in extending the inhumane use of human beings. The robot embodies a political and economic domination that drastically reduces human potential. Wiener says:

> Our view of society differs from the ideal of society
> which is held by many Fascists, Strong Men in Business,
> and Government. ... Such people prefer an organization
> in which all orders come from above, and none return.
> The human beings under them have been reduced to the
> level of effectors for a supposedly higher nervous organ-

40   Norbert Wiener, *I am a Mathematician: The Latter Life of a Prodigy* (New York: Doubleday, 1956), 335–56.
41   Wiener, *The Human Use of Human Beings*, 16.

> ism. I wish to devote this book to a protest against this
> inhumane use of human beings.[42]

What to do with this argument today? This is perhaps one of the places where Wiener's position is most endangered—insofar as the cybernetic programme reaches a new stage, with the emergence of artificial entities that possess learning capabilities, exhibit a form of intuition, and take a new step forward in the kind of purposeful behaviour that machines are capable of producing. In other words, Wiener's old argument that robot replacement is a myth because there is a complexity in humans that resists the machine seems to be threatened by a novel combination of machine learning and big data, that cybernetics could not see coming. However, Wiener's plea prompts us to resist this vertigo, and draws our attention to the human part of AI and the way it can only work by enlisting human labour in the loop. Behind the robot, there is digital labour: proletarized forms of work, which serve to train and monitor AI.

Cybernetics as a 'counter-discipline'

Returning to cybernetics—the original scene of information technologies—allows us to exhume a set of theoretical resources that are challenged by contemporary configurations. One of the lessons of cybernetics may nevertheless lie in the constitution of a 'counter-discipline', bringing the life sciences and engineering together in a unique manner.

Wiener used the authority of cybernetics to critically analyse the new modes of production of American science. Cybernetics promoted small democratic collectives, marked by both a high level of individual and collective information. These collectives ensure, in Bernard Stiegler's vocabulary, the formation of 'circuits of transindividuation'; a requirement for the crisis of the technical milieu to end on other perspectives than 'arch-proletarianization'.

42   Ibid.

Reference

Cardon, Dominique, Cointet Jean-Philippe and Mazières Antoine. 'Neurons Spike Back: The invention of inductive machines and the artificial intelligence controversy'. *Réseaux* 211, no. 5 (2018): 173–220.

Conway, Flo and Jim Siegelman. *Dark Hero of the Information Age: In Search of Norbert Wiener, the Father of Cybernetics*. New York: Basic Books, 2005.

Gerovich, Slava. *From Newspeak to Cyberspeak: A History of Soviet Cybernetics*. Cambridge, MA: MIT Press, 2002.

Heidegger, Martin. *Écrits politiques 1933–1966*. Translated and edited by François Fédier. Paris: Gallimard, 1995.

Heims, Steve. *John von Neumann and Norbert Wiener: From Mathematics to the Technologies of Life and Death*. Cambridge: MIT Press, 1980.

Heims, Steve. *Constructing a Social Science for Postwar America, The Cybernetics Group, 1946–1953*. Cambridge: MIT Press, 1991.

Le Roux, Ronan. *Une histoire de la cybernétique en France* (1948–1975). Paris: Garnier, 2018.

Levi King, Dylan. 'The Genealogy of Chinese Cybernetics.' *Palladium*, 17 October 1922, https://www.palladiummag.com/2022/10/17/the-genealogy-of-chinese-cybernetics.

Licklider, J.C.R. 'Man-Computer Symbiosis.' *Transactions on Human Factors in Electronics* 1 (1960): 4–11.

Ligier, Maude and Mathieu Triclot. 'L'art cybernétique de Nicolas Schöffer.' Paper presented to the third Congrès de la Société Française d'Histoire des Sciences et des Techniques, 6 September 2008.

McCulloch, Warren and Walter Pitts. 'A logical calculus of the ideas immanent in nervous activity'. *Bulletin of Mathematical Biophysics* 5 (1943): 115–133.

Medina, Eden. *Cybernetic Revolutionaries: Technology and Politics in Allende's Chile*. Cambridge, MA: MIT Press, 2014.

Mindell, David. *Between Human and Machine: Feedback, Control, and Computing before Cybernetics*. Baltimore: Johns Hopkins University Press, 2002.

Pickering, Andrew. *The Cybernetic Brain: Sketches of Another Future*. Chicago: University of Chicago Press, 2010.

Roudinesco, Elisabeth. *L'histoire de la psychanalyse en France: Jacques Lacan*. Paris: Livre de Poche, 2009.

Shannon, Claude. 'A mathematical theory of communication.' *Bell System Technical Journal* 27 (1948): 379–423, 623–656.

Triclot, Mathieu. *Le moment cybernétique*. Seyssel: Champ Vallon, 2008.

Von Foerster, Heinz. *Cybernetics, Circular Causal and Feedback Mechanisms in Biological and Social Systems: Transactions of the Seventh Conference, March 23–24, 1950*. New York: Caldwell, 1951.

Von Neumann, John. *The Computer and the Brain*. Yale: Yale University Press, 2000 [1958].

———. 'First draft of a report on the EDVAC.' *IEEE Annals of the History of Computing* 15, no. 4 (1993).

———. 'Letter to Norbert Wiener, November 29th 1946.' In John Von Neumann, *Selected Papers*, edited by Miklos Rédei. American Mathematical Society, 2005.

———. 'Probabilistic Logics and the Syntheses of Reliable Organisms from Unreliable Components.' In *Automata Studies*, edited by Claude Shannon and John McCarthy. Princeton: Princeton University Press, 1952.

Wiener, Norbert. *Cybernetics, or Control and Communication in the Animal and the Machine*. Cambridge: MIT Press, 2000[1948].

———. *The Human Use of Human Beings: Cybernetics and Society*. London: Eyre and Spottiswoode, 1950.

———. *I am a Mathematician: The Latter Life of a Prodigy*. New York: Doubleday, 1956.

———. 'A Scientist Rebels.' *The Atlantic Monthly* 179, , January 1947, 46.

———. 'Too Big for Private Enterprise.' In Norbert Wiener, *Collected works with Commentaries, Volume IV*. Edited by Pesi Masani. Basel: Birkhäuser Verlag, 1990.

Wiener, Norbert, Arturo Rosenblueth and Julian Bigelow. 'Behavior, Purpose and Teleology.' *Philosophy of Science* 10, no. 1 (1943): 18–24.

Detoxifying Cybernetics: From Homeostasis to Autopoiesis and Beyond

N. Katherine Hayles

To start, a mystery. By 1970, most academic departments of cybernetics had disappeared, even though many of the ideas from cybernetics were still circulating both in both cultural and scientific disciplines. Why did they suddenly become defunct? There are various explanations; one is the multidisciplinary nature of cybernetics. Because it encompassed many fields, integrating it with academic structures based on separate disciplines was difficult. Another factor was the militarism and the black box psychology of first wave cybernetics. To explore these ideas, I will focus on the figure of Norbert Wiener, who loomed large in the period from 1945 to 1960. I will engage specifically with his World War II work on an anti-aircraft predictor; he subsequently built on this scientific research to expand his view of human behaviour.

As Peter Galison explains in 'The Ontology of the Enemy: Norbert Wiener and the Cybernetic Vision', Wiener postulated that there were two sorts of adversaries to scientific inquiry.[1] One he called the Augustinian Devil, which he equated with nature. Nature might resist your inquiries, but it does not try to deliberately trick or mislead you. In contrast is the Manichean Devil, which he associated with US adversaries during World War II, who would use any kind of tactics, including lies and deceptions, to prevail in a conflict. As he focused on this Manichean Enemy, he pictured it in servomechanical terms, translating deception into mechanical actuators that incorporate feedback loops.

Thus Wiener envisioned the defensive situation against this Manichean adversary as a human (an anti-aircraft gunner), a calculator and a weapon, forged into a single integrated system in which feedback mechanisms were crucial. Under stress, humans tend to act repetitively and therefore predictably. Building on this premise, he built a mechanism that would try to predict the evasive manoeuvres of an enemy

---

1   Peter Galison, 'The Ontology of the Enemy: Norbert Wiener and the Cybernetic Vision,' *Critical Inquiry* 21: 1 (Autumn 1994): 228–66.

aircraft under fire. To test it, he created two simulated lights on a wall; one for a dodging aircraft, and the other for the gunner trying to shoot the aircraft down. When he tested this against actual data in which gunners were looking for enemy aircraft, the data showed that the predictor worked well for a single pilot under different circumstances, (that is a single pilot making more than one run) but not for different pilots. This was an important realization which he could not capitalize on at the time, because the computer power he had available was not sufficient for the task. Knowing what we know now about neural nets, if one knew that any given enemy pilot tended to act predictably, one could use a neural net to build a mechanism that would reliably predict the actions of that pilot and any number of others, based on their characteristic manoeuvre patterns. But with the technology Wiener had, he was not able to build a predictor that would work in all circumstances. In that sense, his research was a failure.

In another sense, however, it allowed him to forge an important bridge between humans and feedback mechanisms. In an article he published with Arthuro Rosenblueth, a physiologist, and Julian Bigelow, an electrical engineer, Wiener proposed that human behaviour could be treated like a black box.[2] Black boxes are units designed to perform a function without an observer knowing what exactly is happening inside the box, in contrast to white boxes, which specify the inner mechanism. So, he proposed that human behaviour is a black box. Along with colleagues such as John von Neumann, Wiener formed a research group they called the Teleological Society, which treated human behaviour in a purely behaviouristic fashion. In this research group, mechanical engineering and neurology were seen as essentially the same field. In the above article that he co-published, he drew the conclusion that 'the term purposeful is meant to denote that the act or behavior may be interpreted as directed to the attainment of a goal'.[3] Hence, he was connecting purpose with teleology.

A theology professor, Richard Taylor, objected, stating that this definition of purpose was much too broad. Taylor proposed a counter example of a weighted roulette wheel. Was that purposeful?, Taylor asked. In response, Wiener and his colleagues made a distinction between passive devices and active devices. The antiaircraft predictor

2   Arturo Rosenblueth, Norbert Wiener and Julian Bigelow, 'Behavior, Purpose, and Telelogy,' *Philosophy of Science* 10.1 (January 1943): 18–24.
3   Ibid., 18.

used feedback, so it was an active device. The weighted roulette wheel was a passive device and did not use feedback. Moreover, here they reiterated their claim that as objects of scientific inquiry, 'humans do not differ from machines'. Therefore, in their view, human intentionality does not differ from machine self-regulation. This article marks the limits of first-order cybernetics.

In retrospect, we can see what was achieved by this vision, and also what was obscured. Obviously, such a mechanistic interpretation of human behaviour has many limitations and drawbacks. In the 1980s, as World War II faded into history, new visions began to emerge that tried to remedy some of these limitations. The period between 1979 and 1981 was particularly important. Heinz von Foerster's *Observing Systems*, published in 1981, initiated what is now called second-order cybernetics. There is a pun in the title: the observer is observing a system, but the observer himself is also a system that can be observed in turn. This kind of cycling between what the observer sees and the observer himself was typical of second-order cybernetics, which emphasized recursivity, the inclusion of the observer into the systemic dynamics, and system-environment couplings. This perspective provided a basis for a bridge between first-order cybernetics and new ideas that were surfacing in the environmental realm, which came to be associated with second-order cybernetics.

In 1979, James Lovelock published his book *Gaia: A New Look at Life on Earth*, which marks the turn toward an environmental emphasis.[4] In Lovelock's Gaia hypothesis, the earth is seen as a self-regulating entity in which life forms and environments are tightly coupled into a single feedback system. In his book, Lovelock included a chapter on cybernetics in which he focused on homeostasis, that is, maintaining a stable state, which was crucially important in first-order cybernetics. Lovelock argues that the earth, and all the biological life forms on it, constitute a cybernetic system. He has three principal examples to illustrate this idea. He points out that the earth's atmosphere is roughly 20 per cent oxygen. Oxygen is a reactive gas, therefore earth's atmosphere is a system far from equilibrium. What keeps it from going toward equilibrium? His argument: the action of biological organisms is what maintains the stability of the atmosphere.

---

4   James Lovelock, *Gaia: A New Look at Life on Earth* (Oxford: Oxford University Press, 1979).

A second example is the acidity or alkalinity of the oceans. He demonstrates by a series of calculations that the salt content of the oceans should be constantly increasing, because as water evaporates, the salt has nowhere to go. What actually happens, by contrast, is that the salt content remains approximately constant. This could only be the case, he argues, because of the action of organisms within the ocean.

In his third example, he notes that, in the four billion years since earth was formed, the sun has been constantly growing larger. The sun's heat is therefore increasing, but nevertheless earth systems show a maintenance of a steady temperature, even though the sun is much hotter that it was four billion years ago. Again, he attributes this tendency toward a more or less steady temperature to biological organisms.

Finally, to illustrate how organisms could stabilize a system, he creates a simulation called Daisyworld. Daisyworld has black daisies, and white daisies. When the temperature is cool, the black daisies that absorb sunlight, proliferate and are predominant, thus warming the planet. When the temperature gets hotter, white daisies, that reflect sunlight, begin to take over. In this simple simulation, he illustrates his ideas of how biological organisms react with the environment to create a homeostatic or steady situation.

We are now ready to trace the transition from the military-industrial emphasis of first-wave cybernetics in the 1940s, '50s and '60s to environmental concerns that began to appear in the 1980s and '90s. The emphasis here turns from human-machine fusion to biota-environmental coupling. This now makes cybernetics about the characteristics of the living in the context of their environments rather than predominantly about mechanical fusions. Now we introduce a new thread into this tapestry that we are weaving. Huberto Maturana and Francisco Varela's important book *Autopoiesis and Cognition: The Realization of the Living* was published in 1980, right in that crucial period between the 1970s and '80s.[5] One of their central concepts is autopoiesis. Poiesis comes from a Greek root meaning 'to make'; 'poetry' comes from the same root. Auto, of course, means emerging from the self. Thus autopoiesis means self-making or self-organizing. Maturana and Varela sketch a feedback system in which the organization of an organism

5   Humerto R. Maturana and Francisco J. Varela, *Autopoiesis and Cognition: The Realization of the Living* (Dordrecht: D. Reidel: 1980).

produces the components, and the components simultaneously also produce the organization. This kind of recursivity, they argue, is intrinsic to the process of living. Moreover, they weave cognition into this idea as well: 'A cognitive system is a system whose organization defines a domain of interactions in which it can act with relevance to the maintenance of itself, and the process of cognition is the actual acting or behaving of this domain. Living systems are cognitive systems, and living as a process is a process of cognition. This statement is valid for all organisms with and without a nervous system'.[6] Essentially, they argue that cognition is co-extensive with life.

Now we will begin to build out this environmental theme as it merges with cybernetics. The next important event is the work of Lynn Margulis, a microbiologist, and her 1970 book *The Origin of Eukaryotic Cells*.[7] Eukaryotic cells are cells that have a membrane and nucleus. Margulis upended conventional ideas about evolution by arguing that the origin of eukaryotic cells came about because of a fusion of two independent prokaryotic bacteria. Prokaryotic cells are cells that do not have a nucleus. Those were the original living cells, but at the end of the Archaean period, eukaryotic cells (cells with a nucleus) began to appear, which initiated a whole new trajectory in evolution. Margulis argues that the origin of eukaryotic cells came about when one microbe ingested the other; but it was incompletely digested and continued to live within its predator. The ingested organism becomes the mitochondria within the nucleated cell, which powers the cell by providing energy. The two previously independent organisms fused into what today we know as the eukaryotic cell. Later, her theory was verified when it was determined that mitochondrial DNA is different from the DNA of the nucleus, and that the mitochondria reproduce on a schedule different from the nucleus of a cell. This established that the mitochondria, in fact, have their own separate DNA and hence must have previously been independent organisms.

Expanding on this idea, Margulis argues that bacteria are the only true individuals. Every organism larger than a single bacteria, in fact is a community of organisms. Of course, we know that as humans we have a whole microbiome inside us (the gut bacteria) as well as all kinds

6   Ibid., 13.
7   Lynn Margulis, *Origin of Eukaryotic Cells: Evidence and Research Implications of a Theory of the Origin And Evolution of Microbial, Plants, and Animal Cells on the Precambrian Earth* (New Haven: Yale University Press, 1970).

of other bacteria and viruses that live within our bodies. Margulis argued that humans, mammals, and every other macro-organism should be seen as a community, not as an individual. Moreover, she rejected the idea that new species come about primarily through random mutations, as orthodox evolutionary theory maintained. On the contrary, she believed that evolution is driven primarily by symbiosis—the joining of two or more microbial species. Hence she argued for symbiogenesis as the primary driver of evolutionary novelty.

Things really start to get interesting when Margulis discovers Lovelock's work and begins to collaborate with him. Each of these major figures contributed something to the other's ideas. Margulis expanded Lovelock's archive of biotic-environmental coupling by contributing all the ways in which micro-organisms coupled with the environment to produce either new organisms or new kinds of situations. She argued, for example, that photosynthesis, the basis for all life on earth, occurred through such an environmental coupling. Photosynthesis in plants have its origin in sulphur-eating bacteria, which used the sun's energy to fuel their metabolism. These bacteria fused with plants, giving plants the ability to use sunlight as energy. Lovelock, for his part, provided the basis for an expanded view of evolution. Margulis always had a problem extending her arguments beyond micro-organisms to macro-organisms. Even today, most biologists do not accept the idea that mammals, for example, evolve primarily through symbiosis. Rather they fall back on the received ideas of natural selection and fitness criteria. Margulis, I think, has won the day for micro-organisms, but not for macro-organisms.

You can see how Lovelock now becomes important for Margulis's leap into macro-organisms, and we see this in her book *Microcosmos: Four Billion Years of Microbial Evolution*, published in 1989.[8] Notice the time span: we have gone from 1980 to almost 1990, and in those nine years, all the interpretations of environment-organism coupling were expanded. Here is what Margulis wrote about Lovelock in 1989: 'According to Lovelock's ideas, which he calls the Gaia hypothesis, the biota itself, which includes Homo Sapiens [and you see there the leap to macro-organisms] is autopoietic'. Here she is picking up on Maturana

8   Lynn Margulis and Dorion Sagan, *Microcosm: Four Billion Years of Microbial Evolution* (Berkeley: University of California Press, 1997).

and Varela's idea of autopoiesis:[9] 'It recognizes, regulates and creates conditions necessary for its own continuing survival'. In the second edition of the *Origin of Eukaryotic Cells* in 1993, we find multiple references to Lovelock and to autopoiesis, and after that, Margulis typically refers to the earth or Gaia as an autopoietic system.

However, there was a problem with the way Maturana and Varela defined cognition. You recall that for them, cognition was co-extensive with living systems: to live is to cognize. But by making it co-extensive with living systems, the concept does not extend to non-living entities, such as computational media. For this reason, machines tend to fade from the picture in autopoietic discourses, which typically focus on the relation between biota and the environment (as with Lovelock and Margulis). At about the same time, evolutionary explanations, among those aware of and persuaded by Margulis, tend toward symbiosis for micro-organisms, versus establishment biologists, especially neo-Darwinists, who focus on natural selection and fitness for macro-organisms.

There is one exception to this general tendency, in a brief essay that Dorion Sagan and Margulis published in 1985. It is only seven pages long and appeared in the successor to the *Whole Earth Catalog* called the *Whole Earth Review*, which is not a scientific journal.[10] Dorion Sagan, son of Margulis and Carl Sagan, became an important co-author of many of Margulis's later publications. In her scientific publications, she is listed as the first author and Dorion Sagan as the second. However, in this essay, Sagan is the first author. I think this may be significant, indicating that these ideas are really more his than Margulis's. Sagan (and Margulis) recognize in this essay that machines are not self-making or self-producing, hence not autopoietic. Machines must have people to produce them, maintain them, and so forth. In the terminology of Maturana and Varela, they are not autopoietic, they are allopoietic. But Sagan argues that they do not need to be autopoietic because they evolved by using humans, who are operating as self-maintaining and self-reproducing autopoietic organisms.

9   Ibid., 266.
10   Dorion Sagan and Lynn Margulis, 'Gaia and the Evolution of Machines,'
Whole Earth Review (Summer 1987): 15–21.

Bruce Clarke has emphasized the importance of this essay in what he sees as Margulis's turn toward what he calls neo-cybernetics.[11] In neo-cybernetic systems theory, we get a combination of the thread we have been tracing through Maturana, Varela, Margulis, and Lovelock with cybernetic systems, as they appeared in Niklas Luhmann's social systems.[12] This constellation emphasizes the hallmarks of second-order cybernetics: recursivity, re-entry, the observer in the system, and system-environmental coupling. As an advocate for neo-cybernetic systems theory, Clarke asks a question latent in the idea of cognition as co-extensive with the process of living. If the earth is considered a single entity in which living organisms are tightly coupled with the environment, that is, Lovelock's Gaia hypothesis, could there be a planetary cognition? If you argue that the earth is a single organism and all living organisms are cognitive, then you could hypothesize that there is something we might refer to as planetary cognition. This represents the conclusion that emerges from neo-cybernetic systems theory and the culmination of the tapestry woven with threads coming from Lovelock, Margulis, and Maturana and Varela in second-order cybernetics.

Now I will turn to some of the fractures in these constellations, where the threads become frail or fail to connect. To trace one of these fractures, I will go back to Maturana and Varela. Part of their theory is that no information from the environment reaches the organism. This is highly counter-intuitive. You are reading what I have written, and hopefully you are thinking about it, so it seems obvious that information is flowing from me to you. But Maturana and Varela argue that an environmental stimulus can only 'trigger' an organism's responses, not cause it. This can be traced to the fact that Maturana was a junior co-author of a very important biological paper: 'What the Frog's Eye Tells the Frog's Brain.'[13] The argument of that paper is this much information processing occurs in the frog's eye itself before it communicates anything to the brain. Hence the information coming from the environment is so hyper-processed by the organism's nervous system and way of processing information, that it is not accurate to say that the frog reacts to

11   Bruce Clarke, *Gaian Systems: Lynn Margulis, Neocybernetics, and the End of the Anthropocene* (Minneapolis: University of Minnesota Press, 2020).
12   Niklas Luhmann, *Social Systems*, trans. John Bednarz, jr. with Dirk Baecker (Redwood City: Stanford University Press, 1995).
13   Jerome Y. Lettvin, Humberto R. Maturana, Warren S. McColluch and Water H. Pitts, 'What the Frog's Eye Tells the Frog's Brain', *Proceedings of the Institute for Radio Engineers* 47, no. 11 (November 1959): 1940–51.

information; rather, information *impinges* on the frog's sensory system and is then processed in a way specific to the frog. Maturana argues that we cannot use causality when we talk about organisms and environments; instead we have to assume this triggering rather than direct causality. This results in a very strained vocabulary, because causality is built into our way of talking from the ground up. If you jettison everyday vocabulary, if you jettison causality, you really have to go around the barn to get in the door. For example, when Maturana and Varela talk about language, the primary mode in which humans communicate information, they do not call it language, they call it 'languaging'; that is, a process that triggers responses rather than directly causes them.[14] We are 'languaging' at present; a vocabulary they devised to remove the causal implication that I am directly imparting information to you. Instead, in their view, I am creating triggers that impinge on your nervous system, and so you think in ways specific to your experience, your sensory systems, and so forth. I am not causing you to do anything. Your response—in fact, in their view it would be a mistake to even call it a response—is completely determined by your own systems, not by anything that I am communicating to you. You can see how convoluted this way of thinking and talking quickly becomes.

I regard this part of Maturana and Varela's work as mistaken. I think I understand where it comes from: the 'Frog's Eye' research. In my view, it would be more accurate and sensible to say that information is *transduced* as it moves from the environment to the organism. I grant their point that any environmental stimulus is completely transformed by the organism's own sensory system, but nevertheless this transduction only reconfigures the information; it does not block it altogether. This view removes the idea of some kind of absolute barrier existing between what is happening in the environment and what is happening in the organism. From my point of view, the idea that an organism is informationally closed to the environment is a fracture because it results in some very convoluted and unnecessary complications.

Moreover, if you are going to say that there are feedback loops between the organism and the environment, and at the same time you are saying that no information can move from the environment to the organism, you have a problem. Maturana and Varela have tried to say that

---

14   Humerto R. Maturana and Francisco J. Varela, *The Tree of Knowledge: The Biological Roots of Human Understanding*, revised ed. (Boulder: Shambhala, 1992), 210.

the organism is open to material and energy exchanges but not to information. But then, flows of information and their transformations are crucial both in first and second-order cybernetics, so the result is a kind of incoherence in the way different parts of the constellation interact with one another.

If we go back to first-wave cybernetics, we may ask: What made first-wave cybernetics possible? Otto Mayr has looked into this extensively in his book *The Origins of Feedback Control*.[15] He goes back to the Greeks, who knew about self-regulating mechanisms. They used self-regulating mechanisms on water flow, for example. Moving into the nineteenth century, engineers created thermostats and governors on steam engines—all feedback devices. Consequently, as Mayr shows, feedback mechanisms have been known since antiquity. What happened with cybernetics? In the twentieth century, a crucial new element was added: the concept of information developed simultaneously by Claude Shannon and Norbert Wiener. As Mayr points out, it was only in the twentieth century that electrical self-regulation began to appear, and that became possible in part because of Shannon's work on quantifying information. What is added to this ancient knowledge that makes first-wave cybernetics possible is a concept of quantifiable information.

Now we have seen how cybernetics turns from mechanisms to organisms, and we have seen an early attempt by Sagan and Margulis to reintroduce machines. Really to reintroduce machines, however, we need to heal some of those fractures that appeared. A clue for this endeavour is offered by the emergence of the concept of information. Instead of making cognition co-extensive with life, which leaves machines out of the picture, we can begin with a definition of cognition that includes machines, because it highlights information flows. In my book *Unthought* I devised this definition for cognition: 'Cognition is the process of interpreting information in contexts that connect it with meaning'.[16] This has something in common with Maturana and Varela's ideas. Like them, I see cognition as a process; and like them, I maintain that all biological organisms have cognitive capacities. But the difference is that this definition also allows computational media to have cognitive

---

15   Otto Mayr, *The Origins of Feedback Control* (Cambridge, MA: MIT Press, 1975).
16   N. Katherine Hayles, *Unthought: The Power of the Cognitive Nonconscious* (Chicago: University of Chicago Press, 2017).

capacities. Like biological organisms, computational media interpret information in contexts that connect them with meaning.

Now we have an integrated framework incorporating humans, living nonhuman organisms, and computational media. I call these cognitive assemblages. Cognitive assemblages are collectivities, not exclusively human, not exclusively organic, through which information, interpretations, and meanings circulate. Another way that my view departs from the constellation we have been tracing is the idea that Gaia could be a single organism. Of course, by adopting the name of a Greek goddess, Lovelock implies personhood for the planet. Personhood in turn implies intentionality. Hence if the planet has intentionality, the idea of something like planetary cognition naturally arises. Margulis, with her background in biology, was initially sceptical of the Gaia terminology, and even though she eventually began using Lovelock's terminology, she remained somewhat uneasy with it. She is not alone in her skepticism. The Gaia terminology has led to all kinds of problems, including the reactions of many scientists who do not like this implication of intentionality and personhood (notwithstanding that Lovelock occasionally tried to deal with the scepticism by conceding that the earth is not a person, and does not directly manifest intentionality).

My own solution to this difficulty is to focus on cognition. Defining it as I do allows a clear distinction between agents and actors, because it focuses on a capacity to interpret information. Material processes like erosion, breakdown of rocks, and so forth, have agency, but they do not perform interpretations or make selections and decisions. Actors, by contrast, *do* make decisions. Actors in this sense include all biological organisms as well as computational media. Returning to Lovelock's vision of organisms and the environment as one highly interactive system, I agree about the coupling part, but I would also argue that it is always the living organisms, not the environment as such, that catalyse and direct the changes. Material processes by themselves do not have stakes in outcomes; a mountain does not care—indeed, cannot care—that it erodes. But organisms *do* care if they survive, and their drive to survive adds direction and intentionality to the changes that occur as evolution proceeds. Consequently, I regard the material processes as agents, while living organisms are actors. For different reasons, computational media are also actors because they are programmed and designed to have specific outcomes and goals—that is, they too have intentionality, albeit not in the same way that organisms do.

Now, instead of symbiosis or symbiogenesis, we have *techno-symbiosis*. It incorporates and extends biosymbiosis into the technical realm. Like the early essay by Sagan and Margulis on the evolution of machines, I argue that machines do evolve, and they evolve through incorporating humans into their collectivities. Because this is mutually beneficial both to machines and humans, it counts as symbiosis. Humans have their cognitive capacities extended through cognitive machines. I can talk to you in China from Los Angeles precisely because I have a cognitive machine that I am hooked up to, and you have the cognitive machine that you are hooked up to, so a coupling can occur between us.

We can observe biota and environmental couplings of the kind that Lovelock emphasized. We also now have human and machine couplings, and environments are increasingly co-constructed between humans, machines, and the natural world. These environments include not only couplings between biota and the world, but also couplings between humans, computational media and the environment. Moreover, we, as humans, benefit from the computational media we create—increasingly so as computational media interpenetrate virtually all of our technical infrastructures. And computational media obviously benefit from our constructions, because we humans are what bring them into existence, maintain them, supply energy to them, and so forth. This mutual benefit is what I mean by technosymbiosis.

Part of this argument depends on the idea that machines have interpretive possibilities; machines interpret information from their environment. Using the terminology of Jakob von Uexküll, I would say machines have *Umwelten*, or world-horizons.[17] Uexküll, of course, argued that living organisms all have specific world views. The frog, for example, thinks and perceives like a frog, which is dramatically different from how a human perceives. Today, computational media also have inputs and outputs. Even stand-alone computers have a vision of the world they construct through their relatively narrow and deterministic inputs. Once we begin to move into computational networks that have sensors and actuators, it becomes even clearer that they perceive the world through their sensors, and they act on the world through their

17   Jakob von Uexküll, *A Foray into the Worlds of Animals and Humans with a Theory of Meaning*, trans. Joseph D. O'Neil (Minneapolis: University Of Minnesota Press, 2010).

actuators, so they have their own *Umwelten*, which are distinctive to them and different from us—although overlapping with humans in ways that allow us to communicate with them and form cognitive assemblages that include them.

Now we can speculate about a third-wave of cybernetics that includes insights from first-order cybernetics, for example, mechanistic couplings of the kind that Wiener talked about. It also includes second-order cybernetics (specifically Maturana and Varela, as well as Margulis and Lovelock) so it focuses on couplings between the observer and the environmental system dynamics. In addition, the new constellation, tentatively called third-order cybernetics, incorporates the co-evolution of humans and machines into an integrated cognitive framework.

Third-order cybernetics opens new possibilities for research and development both in cybernetics and in environmental programmes. For example, the Australian National University wanted to establish a multidisciplinary school—not just a department, an entire school. They chose to name the new entity the School of Cybernetics. It is radically multidisciplinary, including environmentalists, computer specialists, biologists, activists, etcetera. Thus, we begin to see how the events that we have been tracing allow a fusion between the idea of human-machine feedback, and human-environmental feedback, extended to the entire biosphere, which now also includes technosymbiosis between humans and computational media, all coming together in an integrated framework. I think these possibilities opened by technosymbiosis and cognitive assemblages are going to reinvigorate interest in cybernetics. The fusion of cybernetics with environmental concerns offers potent new possibilities for research, analysis, and perhaps most importantly, interventions. I would not be surprised if this idea, appealing on many levels in our age of environmental crises, spread very quickly. This is what I call 'detoxifying cybernetics' through redefining its collectivities and refocusing its mission through its environmental and computational concerns.

In conclusion, we went from antiaircraft designs, of the kind Wiener was working on, to environmental problems and solutions. We went from symbiosis between organisms, which Margulis emphasized in symbiogenesis, to technosymbiosis between humans, nonhumans and computational media. As computational media become increasingly integrated with human and natural environments, their inclusion in a cybernetic approach oriented to analysing and solving environmental problems is more urgent now than ever. This reorientation can reinvigorate cybernetic thinking and make significant contributions to our global environmental crises. Realizing the full potential of a detoxified cybernetics requires a theory robust enough to overcome the historical fractures and provide a basis for new challenges that will inevitably arise as we humans grapple with the implications of computational media, including increasingly powerful and pervasive artificial intelligences.

Reference

Clarke, Bruce. *Gaian Systems: Lynn Margulis, Neocybernetics, and the End Of the Anthropocene*. Minneapolis: University of Minnesota Press, 2020.

Galison Peter. 'The Ontology of the Enemy: Norbert Wiener and the Cybernetic Vision'. Critical Inquiry 21: 1 (Autumn 1994): 228–66.

Hayles, N. Katherine. *Unthought: The Power of the Cognitive Nonconscious*. Chicago: University of Chicago Press, 2017.

Lettvin, Jerome Y., Humberto R. Maturana, Warren S. McColluch and Water H. Pitts. 'What the Frog's Eye Tells the Frog's Brain'. *Proceedings of the Institute for Radio Engineers* 47, no. 11 (November 1959): 1940–51.

Lovelock, James. *Gaia: A New Look at Life on Earth*. Oxford: Oxford University Press, 1979.

Luhmann, Niklas. *Social Systems*. Translated by John Bednarz, jr. with Dirk Baecker. Redwood City: Stanford University Press, 1995.

Margulis, Lynn. *Origin of Eukaryotic Cells: Evidence and Research Implications of a Theory of the Origin And Evolution of Microbial, Plants, and Animal Cells on the Precambrian Earth*. New Haven: Yale University Press, 1970.

Margulis, Lynn and Dorion Sagan. *Microcosm: Four Billion Years of Microbial Evolution*. Berkeley: University of California Press, 1997.

Maturana, Humerto R. and Francisco J. Varela. *Autopoiesis and Cognition: The Realization of the Living* (Dordrecht: D. Reidel: 1980).

———. *The Tree of Knowledge: The Biological Roots of Human Understanding*. Revised edition. Boulder: Shambhala, 1992.

Mayr, Otto. *The Origins of Feedback Control*. Cambridge, MA: MIT Press, 1975.

Rosenblueth, Arturo, Norbert Wiener and Julian Bigelow. 'Behavior, Purpose, and Telelogy', *Philosophy of Science*, Vol. 10, No. 1 (Jan., 1943): 18–24.

Sagan, Dorion and Lynn Margulis, 'Gaia and the Evolution of Machines,' *Whole Earth Review* (Summer 1987): 15–21.

Uexküll, Jakob von. *A Foray into the Worlds of Animals and Humans with a Theory of Meaning*. Translated by Joseph D. O'Neil. Minneapolis: University Of Minnesota Press, 2010.

James Lovelock, Gaia, and the Remembering of Biological Being

Dorion Sagan

The occasion of the passing of James Lovelock (1919–2022) provides us the luxury of attempting to look back on the life, not only of a great scientist, but of the major object of his intellectual attention, the life of the biosphere, whose status as (to quote David Bowie) a space oddity, he discovered. The Gaia hypothesis was a response to the search for extraterrestrial life, specifically NASA's Viking mission of robotic landers to see if there were life on Mars. Self-described as an engineer and inventor more than a scientist, Lovelock invented the electron capture device, an extremely sensitive chemical detector that found human-made industrial products (such as DDT and PCB toxins) in remote regions of Earth, helping to spur Rachel Carson's *cri de cœur*, the 1961 book *Silent Spring*, itself a spur for the environmental movement. Introduced by my father, Carl Sagan, with whom he shared an office at the NASA's Jet Propulsion Laboratory in Pasadena, to my mother, Lynn Margulis, who was interested in the composition of Earth's early atmosphere, the two, Lovelock and Margulis, went on to develop the Gaia theory, which explored how Earth's biosphere, far from being a planet with some life on it, was a giant thermodynamic system away from chemical equilibrium. Lovelock's idea for detecting the presence of life in space—which, inverted, revealed that Earth had a living body, a kind of planetary physiology—depended on his studies which showed and continued to show multiple chemicals in Earth's atmosphere that existed in concentrations orders of magnitude out of chemical and thermodynamic equilibrium. But they were there. Methane, butyl mercaptan and many organic compounds should disappear in our atmosphere steeped in reactive oxygen (O_2), they should react and disappear. But they do not. Because life put them there, and continues to put them there, replenishing its reactive compounds.

But how? Who? Microbial ecologist Margulis pointed to the gene-trading bacteria, with their many forms of metabolism, or metabolic virtuosi, as she put it. They completed chemical cycles and produced the atmosphere; the oxygen-rich atmosphere with its redox gradient. The cyanobacteria, evolving to use the hydrogen in water (H_2O) as a source of electrons for photosynthesis, released O_2, loosing free radicals in to the world. Anaerobic life, primarily archaea, suffered and died, while some survived by taking refuge in the anoxic muds. Oxidized iron, Margulis pointed out, such as that from which the iron for cars in Ontario and Michigan is mined, shows evidence for global oxidation some two billion years ago. Ozone (O_3) also arose from the surfeit of water-using green life. The very planet's blue colour, Lovelock pointed out, was the result of the light-scattering properties of oxygen atoms loosed by energetically lustful life. The collaboration between the atmospheric chemist and the microbial ecologist was especially fruitful. An example of this is Margulis's identification of the source of the persistence of methane, which immediately reacts with oxygen to become carbon dioxide and water in Earth's atmosphere. It is produced by methanogens, considered methanogenic bacteria at the time, and now usually classified as archaea. In termites and cows, helping to digest the refractory cellulose of wood and grass in anaerobic environments, symbiotic microbial communities produced methane, as did prokaryotes in seaside expanses called microbial mats. The metastable atmosphere of Earth was like part of the body, in this case inside-out relative to mammals, with the circulatory system on the outside rather than the inside. Whereas Lovelock characterized Gaia as an organism, Margulis differed, pointing to the datum that no organism completely recycles its own material waste. Gaia is better characterized as planetary life form; a body, yes, but subtler than an organism, it produces waste mostly as heat, the end product of metabolism that cannot be used by any living organisms. Like all lifelike and living cycling systems it produces entropy, in thermodynamics, a measure of the spread of energy.

That Carl Sagan, who was suspicious of the grand claims that Earth itself was alive, knew of Gaia, is apparent from his first sole-authored book, *Planetary Exploration* (1970). In the book, based on his Condon lecture at Portland University on his ex-wife's birthday, Sagan takes the reader on a thought experiment on how to detect life on other planets. If one approaches a planet relatively closely, one might notice life by the shadows of structures that would seem quite unlikely geologically (for example, the stilt-like feet of animals). Even from further out, the perspicacious observer could detect, say, the lights of cities at night, while from astronomic distances one might still be able to receive electromagnetic messages. But, Sagan says, without mentioning Gaia by name, the best evidence might be the unexpected presence of methane in an oxygen-rich atmosphere; the clearest message of life on Earth might be, he drily jokes, an unintended consequence of 'bovine flatulence'.

Leaving aside that cows belch almost all their methane from the other end, the point is well taken. Gaia's inside is our outside. 'She' could be detected spectroscopically by extraterrestrials, say martians, with our level of scientific chemical voyeurism. Alas, Mars's atmosphere was found, prior to the landing of Viking's robotic landers, to have an atmosphere almost completely of carbon dioxide, showing no obvious chemical signs of life, let alone a planetary surface steeped in it. Like many of science's great discoveries, Gaia was not directly sought, or supported by funding agencies, but discovered serendipitously. In retrospect one might argue that Gaia, the notion that Earth is no more a rock with some life on it than you are a skeleton infested with cells, may be considered the most striking result of NASA space exploration, as well as SETI, the search for extraterrestrial intelligence. Life is an open thermodynamic system in space, transforming the solar gradient between the sun and space, primarily through the advanced, sensitive natural nanotechnics of water-using photosynthesis, into the redox potential of Earth's highly energized, because continuously oxygen-supplied, biosphere. Lovelock, with Marguilis, probably deserved a Nobel Prize in Physiology or Medicine for their work. More important, however, is the intellectual and affective sequelae of the scientific idea that our planet is a living body, of which we are in no way a key part. Lovelock's thought experiment, that Mars did not harbour life because its atmosphere was in chemical and thermodynamic equilibrium, turns out to be right.

However, and although my Gaian matchmaker was not thinking directly of Lovelock when he said this, that aging British scientists tend to go a bit dotty in their later years, an argument can be made that Lovelock did not fully appreciate the consequences of the Gaia theory he helped spawn. Carl Sagan said this to me in a conversation about a review of a book by Fred Hoyle, the astronomer who precisely predicted the means by which helium turns to carbon atoms inside stars, and who termed the term big bang, but believed life and the universe might both be eternal. Hoyle argued that bacteria and viruses existed throughout space, further suggesting that Mars's rusty regolith might be the product of *Pedobacterium*, an iron-oxidizing bacterium, and that the odds of life evolving on the Earth, or at all, were incalculably small.

With his deep insight that the atmosphere is as highly organized and unexpected as a beehive or a sandcastle on the beach, Lovelock's notion of planetary chemical disequilibrium as a way of detecting life on a planet, matured from a hypothesis of life regulating the planet's atmospheric chemistry, to, with Margulis, a theory recognizing microbes as the main actors. The 'bovine flatulence' that might alert aliens to life's terrestrial presence is in fact from methanogens, archaea that have survived from the Archean Eon prior to the build-up of oxygen on the planet and iron and uranium oxides in the fossil record. As mentioned, Margulis differed from Lovelock in describing Earth life as an organism. But although the metaphorical matrix spurred on by looking at life as an organism—later Lovelock would say that deforestation and industry are destroying Gaia's 'skin'—could be fruitful, it also overreached, for example, when Lovelock compared Earth to being an old lady on dialysis who needed human help, that is, geoengineering. Margulis told me that Lovelock excused such overreach by saying that if people thought of Earth as an organism, they would be less likely to destroy it. There was something of Mother Mary in it. But given the treatment of women in a patriarchal society—or even of female-associated symbols, such as in the secret Cold War Air Force Project A119 to detonate a nuclear device on the moon, of which my father was apprised—the Soviets had a similar plan—the notion seems doubtful. 'Love your mother', said my mother's T-shirt, over an image of Earth from space, in a smiling photo of her from the 1970s. But Gaia is not a mother or an organism, but something stranger, an alien body, based on the metabolism, gene-trading, and symbioses of prokaryotes, that we are just beginning to understand. His later works, playing with notions of planetary medicine and technological salvation, culminate in *Novacene* (2019), where Lovelock suggests he knows that only Earth in the cosmos is alive. The comment is suggestive, even exemplary of, the general anthropocentrism that renders the aliens of *Star Trek* as humans; a self-centredness which shows up too in the bloating of our individual fears of death into worries over the death of the planet.

The theory of Gaia is, in a sense, an autobiography of a planet; an autobiography told by very small part of the vast nexus of life, with its estimated thirty million species, not including the prokaryotes, which trade genes so often, and do not reproduce sexually so do not conform to the traditional biological species concept, which like the rest of human knowledge must take into account the provinciality, the particularity of human observers. The genesis of Gaia was thermodynamic but its description by Lovelock was cybernetic. Certainly there are loops, feedbacks, responses by sensing living matter, which are not just reactive. The growth of algae and trees in the sun produces volatiles that not only signal in nonhuman chemical languages but also serve as nuclei for raindrops, making a loop between the growth of organisms under the sun and the production of clouds and rain blocking the sun's light and adjusting the shutters, as it were, of life's more-than-human home. Cybernetics was attractive at the time of the early development of Gaia because it linked the mind-like loops of sensing machines to the real minds, or awarenesses, of organisms. In retrospect Lovelock and Andrew Watson's Daisy World model, which showed in principle how coloured daisies could cool a planet showered with increasing energy from its star (by, for example, white daisies growing and reflecting more light as the sun's luminosity increased), can be said to have mimicked mind, fooling mechanist scientists—men that denied that planetary thermoregulation was possible without human-like intelligence or communication between organisms, or aeons of evolution by natural selection. Simple cybernetic feedback, modelling growth within a temperature range, which even some non-living thermodynamic systems can do, suffices in principle, without natural selection, to thermoregulate a planet. But cybernetic descriptions, linked with computers, ultimately became a sterile path. In *Novacene*, Lovelock, who once in *Nature*, in an article titled 'Life Span of the Biosphere', calculated that Gaia would end in secular biological hellfire when it ran out of carbon dioxide to counter the increasing luminosity of the sun, argues that AIs may be needed to calm Earth's anthropic fever. But philosopher Yuk Hui seems right to me when he says, in an interview with Anders Dunker, that 'when we think of humans and the Earth as a cybernetic system, we have already lost the world', and then goes on to talk about Heidegger and the forgetting of being. The most cited scientist by Heidegger is Jakob von Uexküll, who, as a scientist, shamanized himself into what it must feel like to be other organisms, including, famously, (as Deleuze and Guattari reprise) a tick. Heidegger argued that nonhuman animals are 'poor in world'. But maybe not, maybe not at all. I would argue that every organism may have a world, a full world, an *idios kosmos*, as well as a *koinos kosmos* insofar as it interacts with members of its own and other kinds. The terms are those of Greek philosopher Heraclitus, the first referring to our private worlds, as when we dream, the second, to the world we share. The thermodynamic dissipative spaces where living beings find their homes—necessarily using energy, taking in substrate, and producing waste—encompass a feeling of being alive, if not freedom to move, act, and be. Other beings may have worlds as rich, and in some cases richer, than our own. In the nineteenth century, Samuel Butler argued that microbes (our ancestors), far from being unfeeling automatons, have their own sensations and little purposes, and their own technics, or 'tool-kits' as he put it. Their activities, their technics, over hundreds of millions of years, created bodies. 'We don't remember', Butler (whom Gregory Bateson described as 'Darwin's most able critic') says, 'when first we grew an eye'. Living being is rich, on Earth and perhaps elsewhere throughout the cosmos. Our present infatuation with technology may be terminal, but the present technological malaise may also be growing pains, as were, for example, the situations encountered with the calcium ions that toxified Archaean marine protists, eukaryotic cells on the line to the ancestors of animals, including us. The calcium ions, in some cases, were stockpiled extracellularly, jump starting the evolution of microscopic marine exoskeletons, which it is theorized may sometimes, after falling to the ocean floor, become subducted, greasing the skids of continental plates.

Unlike in human society, where particulate pollution, which blocks light by day, incrementally cooling, but more than makes up for it by increasing temperatures at night (when particles reradiate solar and Earth-absorbed energy), profligately damaging waste is not a feature of the smoothly entropy-producing Gaian living nexus, about one-third the age of the universe dated from the Big Bang. Indeed, our own bodies, insofar as we age, seem to show a kind of unconscious physiological wisdom, one that evolved in clades of organisms that tend to overgrow their environments, thus exposing them to mass die-offs via predation, starvation, and infection. Gaia is more than cybernetic; it is autopoietic, self-producing, as are its constituent cellular members. We would do well to remember this biological being, which far transcends our computer models (although, as mentioned, even some of these may effectively pass a version of the Turing Test). Cybernetic thinking (even though IPCC models do not incorporate Gaian living feedbacks into their supercomputer models) as an adequate description of the real biosphere is failing. We need to have more respect for the unknown, for the metabolically diverse microbial life from which Earth life comes, and from a small subsection of which we and our brains evolved, and in whose ecosystems we are embedded.

When I asked Margulis how scientists can claim to predict the climate when I do not even know how I will feel after eating lunch at a restaurant, she said 'no one knows'. She also surmised that the major evidence for humankind remaining in the fossil record will be a very thin layer of iron, 'from the cars'. A little humility is a good thing, whether on the question of life existing throughout the cosmos on untold planets, or its being confined to our pale blue dot, quickly becoming a pinpoint as we move away from our privileged realm. As the example of those toxic calcium ions that must be exported across cell membranes by marine eukaryotic cells suggests, we humans are not the first to make a mess of things. Elements necessary for life include cosmically common carbon, hydrogen, nitrogen, oxygen, phosphorus, and sulphur. Elements partly under Gaia's planetary control include calcium, originally a toxin to marine eukaryotic cells, but eventually stockpiled outside multiple forms of algae as exoskeletons, such as those produced by *Emiliania huxleyii* in the English Channel, sometimes growing in blooms so large that they are visible by satellite as white submarine clouds. Their intricate skeletons look like Venetian blinds, and may be used accordingly, adjusting incoming levels of light. Gaian theorizers have suggested that the gas dimethyl sulphide, released by the microbes, may serve as nuclei for the formation of raindrops, thus establishing a link between growth of massive blooms of plankton in the hot sun and subsequent cooling by clouds. Gaian control does not appear to have arisen from processes that are top-down, let alone ones involving non-living computer chips. The multibillion-year complexity and ecological recycling of Gaia, the transition of calcium waste into bones and shells and skulls, of toxic O_2 into a vibrant atmosphere, and so on, came about not through ape overseers but by countless individual actions; a billions-year reign of sensuous anarchies, a more-than-human ecological being maintained by countless autopoietic actions, intentional and not. Let us not forget our biological being.

Note

This article was commissioned by the Research Network for Philosophy and Technology and first appeared on the website of *Technophany—A journal for philosophy and technology* in April 2023.

Part II: Territories

Cybernetics in Britain

Andrew Pickering

Cybernetics was invented in the 1940s, around the time of World War II. In 1948 Norbert Wiener defined it as the science of communication and control, describing it as a synthesis of ideas about information, digital computing and feedback.[1] These fields have since developed in very different ways in different times and places. In this essay I explore an important but relatively little known version of cybernetics that grew up in Britain, and which was organized especially around ideas of feedback.[2]

I will start with the distinctive worldview or ontology that has characterized British cybernetics, and with related issues of power and control that interest many people. Then I will talk about the early days of cybernetics in Britain which focused on the brain as well as robotics and psychiatry, and I will try to clarify the contrast between cybernetics and mainstream AI. After that, I can look at the extension of cybernetics into fields like management and the arts. Most of my examples are historical, but in the last section I will talk about some neo-cybernetic work on our relations with the environment that relates to the problems of the Anthropocene. Finally I will connect the story of British cybernetics to what Yuk Hui suggestively calls cosmotechnics.

Ontology

The easiest way to get at what is special about British cybernetics is to talk about its ontology, by which I mean its overall vision of what the world is like. This hinges on questions of knowability and unknowability. Conventional sciences, like physics, take it for granted that the world is knowable and that we will sooner or later find out what it is made of—quarks, black holes, the double helix of DNA, and so on.

1   Norbert Wiener, *Cybernetics, or Control and Communication in the Animal and the Machine* (Cambridge, MA: MIT Press, 1948).
2   For extensive discussion and full documentation of what follows, see Andrew Pickering, *The Cybernetic Brain: Sketches of Another Future* (Chicago: University of Chicago Press, 2010).

That is the ontology or worldview of modern science and of Western common sense; an ontology, we could say, of knowability. That is what we teach our children. Cybernetics went in the opposite direction. In 1959, Stafford Beer, the founder of management cybernetics, defined cybernetics as the science of exceedingly complex systems, meaning systems that are either so complex we will never fully understand them, or systems that are lively and always changing so that we can never pin them down. The key point then is, that unlike the conventional sciences, cybernetics did not aim at producing positive knowledge about the world. Instead it was about getting along, we could say, with an unknowable and unmasterable universe. More prosaically, it was about adaptive systems—systems that can somehow come to terms with the unexpected.

Seen from this angle, cybernetics can seem almost magical—how can we operate in an unknowable world?—but the examples that follow explore some ways in which the cyberneticians brought this vision down to earth with a surprising and diverse array of practices, projects and artefacts. The sheer variety of these projects is one thing I want to emphasize. Before we get to the examples, I will make two important points.

First, in its emphasis on exceedingly complex systems, cybernetics foregrounded performance—action in the world, doing things—rather than knowing, so that a key feature of cybernetic projects and artefacts was, what I call, performative experimentation—trying things out to find out how the world will respond, and then responding to that—a kind of looping and spiralling back and forth that I call a dance of agency.[3] We will see this looping movement played out in many different ways in what follows.

Second, I want to think about the political critique of cybernetics. Ever since Wiener called cybernetics a science of control, critics have fixated on this word 'control'. Do we need a science of control? Aren't we controlled more than enough already? These questions are fair enough in respect of Wiener's vision of cybernetics, which grew out of engineering control mechanisms like the domestic thermostat, which tries to keep the temperature fixed and under control, come what may. But we should note that this sort of control is just impossible in the

---

3   Andrew Pickering, *The Mangle of Practice: Time, Agency, and Science* (Chicago: University of Chicago Press, 1995).

case of exceedingly complex systems—we can never, so to speak, dictate terms to them. As I said, the best we can do with such systems is get along with them, hopefully drawing them into our activities in a non-hierarchic process, which another cybernetician, Gordon Pask, suggestively called 'conversation'. Control in British cybernetics meant conversation. The moral is thus that critics of cybernetics should be positively interested in this distinctive branch of British cybernetics, as a way to elaborate the field's most valuable features without propping up an authoritarian state and its institutions.

The brain

In his 1956 book, *Thinking by Machine: A Study of Cybernetics*, Pierre de Latil identified a group he called 'the four pioneers of cybernetics'.[4] One of them was Norbert Wiener, a mathematician. The other three were brain scientists. One of them was American; Warren McCulloch, the chair of the famous Macy meetings. The other two were Englishmen who worked in mental hospitals; Grey Walter and Ross Ashby. Cybernetics was, then, originally a science of the brain, and that is what I want to think about now.

The key point is that although cybernetics was about the brain, it had an unusual understanding of what the brain is and what it does. We usually think of brains as organs of cognition and representation—of *knowing*—and that is the idea that has dominated mainstream AI from the computer programs of the mid-1950s to the neural nets of today. So it is important to stress that cybernetics went in a very different direction from conventional AI in terms of its understanding of the brain. As Ashby put it in 1948, 'the brain is not a thinking machine, it is an *acting* machine; it gets information and then it does something about it'.[5] The initial goal of British cybernetics was precisely to understand the brain as an acting machine, and it did this by building electromechanical models of the brain. This was the cybernetic counterpart to writing programmes in conventional AI. In line with the unconventional ontology of unknowability, the primary function of the cybernetic brain

4   Pierre de Latil, *Thinking by Machine: A Study of Cybernetics* (London: Sidgwick and Jackson, 1956).
5   W. Ross Ashby, 'Design for a Brain,' *Electronic Engineering* 20 (December 1948): 379–83.

was understood as that of exploring and adapting to the unknown, and Walter and Ashby both built devices that did that.

First Walter. He is famous for the machines he built in 1948, generally referred to as 'tortoises' or 'turtles' because of their physical appearance. They were small mobile robots, which used a photocell to locate and home in on lights, while going into a back-and-forth motion to get around any obstacles they encountered. The key point about them is that they exemplified the cybernetic focus on performance rather than knowledge. They did not try to map and understand their environment, which is how conventional AI-robots work. Instead, they explored their worlds of lights and obstacles in real time and reacted to whatever turned up. The 'intelligence' of the tortoises thus depended on feedback from the world and a sort of embodied looping through the world rather than inner computation. Before we move on, it is worth mentioning that they inspired the very successful tradition of situated robotics re-invented by Rodney Brooks at MIT in the 1980s.

More important to the development of British cybernetics in the long run is Ashby's model brain, which he called the 'homeostat', and featured in his 1952 book, *Design for a Brain*.[6] Like the tortoise, the homeostat also explored its world, though it did it electrically rather than physically, and it went one step further in reconfiguring its own inner workings in response to what it found there. I should now explain how that worked.

The homeostat was an electro-mechanical device that turned electrical inputs into outputs. In isolation, a single homeostat was inert—it did not do anything. But Ashby experimented on combinations of homeostats, in which one homeostat could be thought of as a brain and the others as its environment. When several homeostats were connected together, feedback loops were set up, and the combination of homeostats might turn out to be stable—meaning that the currents within them tended to zero—or unstable—with the currents tending to grow. If the set-up was unstable, a stepping switch within each homeostat would move to the next position, randomly changing the parameters of the circuit, and this process would continue until a condition of stable equilibrium was found. The homeostat was thus what Ashby called an 'ultrastable machine'—a machine that, whatever the initial conditions, would come into a situation of balance with its surroundings.

6   W. Ross Ashby, *Design for a Brain* (London: Chapman and Hall, 1960 [1952]).

What can we say about this? I think of a multi-homeostat set-up as an ontological theatre, a material model of the overall cybernetic worldview, as I described it at the beginning. The homeostat-brain *knew* nothing of its world in a cognitive sense; instead it explored the world performatively via its electrical outputs and reacted adaptively to the inputs that came back to it. So, if you want to grasp the ontology of cybernetics, just think of a bunch of interacting homeostats and you've got the picture. The subsequent history of cybernetics in Britain can be seen as one of variations and elaborations of this homeostat-ontology, as I will try to show in the rest of this essay. The centrality of the homeostat and homeostat-like couplings is what distinguishes most clearly between British cybernetics and other branches of cybernetics as they developed elsewhere.

To continue our exploration of cybernetics, we can stay with the brain for a while. Ashby built an adaptive system, the homeostat, and called it a brain. Ten years later, two other cyberneticians, Stafford Beer and Gordon Pask, reversed the logic and argued that any adaptive system found in nature was, in some sense, already a brain. Beer's favourite example was a pond, a body of water. His point was that the ecosystem of a pond is adaptive, in that the balance of species within it reacts constructively to changes in its environment, just like the homeostat. This idea is at the root of Beer and Pask's incredibly imaginative biological computing project, which aimed to entrain living systems as controllers of human organisations—as, for example, managers of a factory. Get rid of the human managers and plug in a pond instead, that was the idea! This project fizzled out, alas, in the early 1960s, not due to any problem of principle, but because of the practical difficulty of getting ecosystems to care about the key variables of factories.

From a different angle, Ashby's image of the homeostatic brain fed into a radical approach to psychiatry. In contrast to biological and psychoanalytic approaches to madness, in the 1950s Gregory Bateson associated schizophrenia with his famous double-binds. These were situations in which children and parents could find no satisfactory way to go on, which Bateson analogized to homeostats becoming locked in pathological oscillations, leading to madness. In the 1960s, R. D. Laing and his colleagues put this vision to work at Kingsley Hall in London, where psychiatrists and the patients lived communally together. The idea of the anti-psychiatry movement, as it was called, was to do away with orthodox treatments like shock therapy and drugs. Instead the psychiatrists would latch onto otherwise uncommunicative patients in any way they could find—in animal games of fighting and biting, for example—in the hope of breaking up double binds and finding new equilibria. Like homeostats, the expectation was that the psychiatrists as well as the mad would be themselves transformed in this process of open-ended exploration, becoming new kinds of selves—the mad teaching the sane to go mad, as Laing put it. Again, an enormously imaginative project.

So: brain science, an alternative approach to AI, robotics, psychiatry, biological computing—this starts to convey some of the range and diversity of British cybernetics that I am trying to get at. Now we can go beyond the brain, starting with social science.

Beyond the brain: organisations and management

From the 1960s onwards, Stafford Beer pioneered the extension of cybernetics to understanding and designing social organisations. Biological computing had been a first step in that direction, but Beer's later work focused on what he called the Viable System Model (VSM), which is still an important approach to management today. Modelled on the human nervous system, the VSM divided organisations in to five levels, running from production through planning to higher management, all linked via feedback loops. The most dramatic implementation of the VSM was to the entire Chilean economy in the early 1970s under the Allende regime, brought to a premature end by the Pinochet coup in 1973.[7] The point I want to emphasize here is that the links between the levels of the VSM (as well as the links to the organisation's environment) were supposed to be homeostat-like, centred on repeated give and take between levels until some sort of agreed equilibrium was reached—a process of 'reciprocal vetoing' as Beer called it, just like that modelled by Ashby's homeostats. Management, for example, could propose changes in production to the planning level, but the planners could then evaluate those changes and propose different ones back to management, and so on, repeatedly around all of the feedback loops.

7   See also Eden Medina, *Cybernetic Revolutionaries: Technology and Politics in Allende's Chile* (Cambridge, MA: MIT Press, 2014).

I stress this because it bears on the questions of power and control I mentioned at the start. Project Cybersyn (the Chilean application of the VSM) was criticized as technocratic, but these homeostatic couplings were intended to diffuse power and decision-making symmetrically throughout the organisation. The contrast here is with the top-down structure of conventional management, in which orders flow downwards without any return feedback from below—as, for instance, in British universities today. As Beer put it, the VSM aimed to maximize organisational freedom.

Beers's later work, up to his death in 2002, focused on ways of organising these homeostatic interactions between levels. He began by inviting managers and union leaders to his office to drink whisky after work on Friday afternoons, hoping the alcohol might lead to an openness to change. Subsequently he devised a process that he called 'syntegration', in which decision-makers were assigned to the edges of a notional geometrical figure—an icosahedron—and discussions alternated over several days between the vertices of the diagram, just like a constellation of homeostats bouncing off one another. There are two points worth noting here. First, the figure is symmetrical and has no privileged centre. Beer thus regarded syntegration as a perfect form of democracy (unlike, say, conventional committees with chairmen and fixed agendas).

Second, syntegration also points to a key cybernetic variable known as 'variety'. Variety is a measure of the number of different states a system can be in. Thus Ashby's standard configuration of four homeostats had relatively low variety and could reach equilibrium in a short time. But Ashby showed in the 1950s that as variety increases, the time to reach equilibrium increases exponentially, quickly becoming greater than the age of the universe. This has always been a problem in experiments in radical democracy. By all accounts, attempts in the 1960s in the USA and Europe to organize fully democratic institutions foundered on the impossibility of reaching collective decisions except by the exhaustion of the participants—the same problem turned up in the Occupy movement more recently. Letting everyone argue with everyone else all the time just does not work.[8] Syntegration's great

---

8   Andrew Pickering, 'Islands of Stability: From Cellular Automata to the Occupy Movement,' *Zeitschrift für Medien- and Kulturforschung* 14, no. 1 (2014): 121–34.

achievement was to reduce variety and solve this problem by its geo-metrical arrangement, without imposing any sort of hierarchy (unlike conventional political arrangements—elections, for example).

The arts

Another important line of cybernetic development up to the present has been in the arts.[9] Another cybernetician, Gordon Pask, was a key figure here, beginning with his *Musicolour* machine in the early 1950s. The input to *Musicolour* was an improvised musical performance which the machine then used to modulate a light show in real time as a multimedia light and sound experience. *Musicolour*'s key feature was that it was an exceedingly complex system within Beer's definition. Its internal parameters varied in use so that it was impossible to master it cognitively. Instead of a linear relation between sound input and light output, the machine would adapt to each performance as it took place and eventually it would 'get bored', as Pask put it. It would cease, for example, to respond to repetitive inputs, thus encouraging the human performer to adapt in turn to the machine and try something new. Then the machine would get bored again, and so on and so on, back and forth between the human and the machine.

Again, we have here a version of the multi-homeostat set-up in which the human performer explores and adapts open-endedly to the unknowable machine and vice versa—now as a work of art. And again we can think of *Musicolour* as ontological theatre, showing us the fundamental ontology of cybernetics in action. I often think of cybernetic artworks as ontological pedagogy, teaching us in a nonverbal way about the ontology of unknowability.

Whole traditions of cybernetic art have grown up, especially since the 1960s. Just to stay with Pask, he devised an interactive theatre in which the audience could collaborate with the performers in structuring the development of a play, and in 1968 he exhibited a dynamic sculpture called the *Colloquy of Mobiles* at the famous Cybernetic Serendipity exhibition in London. The *Colloquy* featured five interacting

9   See also Andrew Pickering, 'Cybernetic Art,' to appear in *The Bloomsbury Encyclopaedia of New Media Art*, ed. Charlie Gere (London: Bloomsbury, forthcoming).

robots that communicated like multiple homeostats via light and sounds. Pask also made an important contribution to the development of interactive architecture in the design of Cedric Price's Fun Palace in London in the early 1960s. Though it was never actually built, the Fun Palace was designed as a public building that would be reconfigurable in use, responding to different patterns of use but also getting bored, like *Musicolour*, and thus encouraging people to find new uses and activities; new ways to be.

The environment

My examples so far have been historical. We can finish with something closer to the present, and important for the future. I have been writing recently about neo-cybernetic approaches to the environment—floods, farming and wildfires—and I will say a bit about this.[10]

In the late 1960s, Gregory Bateson—who I mentioned earlier in connection with schizophrenia—became very concerned with the environmental crisis.[11] His basic idea was simple; the environment is itself an exceedingly complex system that we can never fully understand or master. That means, according to Bateson, that targeted environmental interventions might work on some level, but might also have bad unexpected consequences. In the 1960s, one would think, for example, of Rachel Carson's famous book, *Silent Spring*, on how agricultural pesticides killed pests but turned out to poison songbirds too.[12] Today we might think about the Anthropocene more generally, for example, the way in which burning fossil fuels serves to generate power, but also leads to climate change and global warming as an unwanted spin-off.

10   Andrew Pickering, 'Poiesis in Action: Doing without Knowledge' in *Weak Knowledge: Forms, Functions, and Dynamics*, ed. Moritz Epple et al. (Frankfurt: Campus Verlag, 2019), 61–84; Andrew Pickering, 'Acting With the World: Doing Without Science,' to appear in *Beyond the Anthropocene: Climate Crisis, New Ontologies and Alternatives to the Anthropocentric Modernity*, special issue of *e-cadernos CES*, ed. António Carvalho and Mariana Riquito, forthcoming 2023; Andrew Pickering, *Acting with the World: Floods, Farming, Fires and Spirits* (in prep.).
11   Gregory Bateson, 'Conscious Purpose Versus Nature,' in *To Free a Generation: The Dialectics of Liberation*, ed. David Cooper (New York: Collier, 1968), 34;49; Gregory Bateson, *Mind and Nature: A Necessary Unity* (Cresskill, NJ: Hampton Press, (2002 [1979]).
12   Rachel Carson, *Silent Spring* (New York: Houghton Mifflin, 1962).

Having identified the basic problem, Bateson's solution was simply that we should learn to *think* differently and just abandon our dreams of mastering nature. But I think cybernetics enables us to go further and imagine different patterns of *action* as well as thought. As our previous examples suggest, this would involve the same sort of back-and-forth experimentation with the environment that we have already been looking at, regarding the model of Ashby's homeostats searching for collective equilibrium, and I can run through just one example to see how this can go.[13]

The giant Glen Canyon Dam was completed on the Colorado River in the USA in 1963 to control the flow of water and generate electricity. But its unintended consequence was to degrade the river's downstream ecosystem (which includes the famous Grand Canyon). Sandbanks started to disappear and local species were threatened with extinction. The question was, what could be done about that? The outline of a solution first appeared in 1983, when Lake Powell, above the dam, was in danger of overflowing. In desperation, engineers released large amounts of water through the dam, in effect staging an artificial flood on the river. This flood turned out to have a surprisingly beneficial effect, rebuilding sandbanks and their associated ecosystems.

This effect was only temporary—the sandbanks began to erode again soon afterwards—but led to the establishment of the Glen Canyon Dam Adaptive Management Program (AMP) which continues to the present. The AMP consists of periodically staging more artificial floods on the river, finding out how the downstream ecosystem reacts, and modifying later floods in the light of that—another dance of agency. And I want to make two points about this programme. First, it is distinctively cybernetic. In place of the command-and-control stance that Bateson criticized, we find the multi-homeostat model again, with the dam operators and the river searching together, open-endedly and

13   Lisa Asplen, 'Going with the Flow: Living the Mangle in Environmental Management Practice,' in *The Mangle in Practice: Science, Society and Becoming*, ed. Andrew Pickering and Keith Guzik (Durham, NC: Duke University Press, 2008), 163–84; James Rice, 'Further Beyond the Durkheimian Problematic: Environmental Sociology and the Co-Construction of the Social and the Natural', *Sociological Forum* 28, no. 2 (2013): 236–60; Andrew Pickering, 'Wicked Problems and the Cybernetic Method,' to appear in *Critical Studies of Complexity: Theories, Notions, Translations and Normativity*, ed. Pablo Jensen and Fabrizio Li Vigni (Editions Matériologiques, 2023); Andrew Pickering, *Acting with the World: Floods, Farming, Fires and Spirits* (in prep.).

performatively, for collective equilibrium. And second, the AMP works, in an interesting sense.

The AMP is not a permanent solution to environmental degradation. Sandbanks still erode between floods. But it turns out that they can be more or less maintained if the artificial floods on the Colorado are timed to coincide with natural floods on two other rivers that join the Colorado below the dam. The trick is that the artificial floods carry along the sediment brought down by the natural floods, and this is what rebuilds the sandbanks. I am struck by the fact that this synchronisation couples the actions of the human dam operators tightly with the actions of the rivers, in a kind of choreography of agency, a regularisation of the dance of human and non-human agency I talked about before.

This choreography interests me a lot as a different way to interact with the environment; a way of acting *with* nature, accommodating ourselves ourselves to it and going along with it, in sharp contrast to the linear acting *on* the world which has got us into so much trouble in the Anthropocene. I believe this homeostatic tuning into nature and the environment points to an important way forward in the evolution of cybernetics.

Cosmotechnics

I have been reviewing the very wide-ranging history of British cybernetics—from robots and schizophrenia, to adaptive architecture and the Colorado River—with the homeostat and the ontology of unknowability as the defining thread. To close, I want to summarize what we have seen from a different angle, by thinking about Yuk Hui's conception of what he calls cosmotechnics.[14] The point of this word, I think, is to suggest that technology is not a universal category. That is not to say that one cannot find things that can be called 'technology' at all times and places, but that different forms of technology (techniques, technics) hang together with different cosmologies or ontologies, as I have been calling them. Different ontologies feed into different technological

14   Yuk Hui, *The Question Concerning Technology in China: An Essay in Cosmotechnics* (Falmouth: Urbanomic Media: 2016).

paradigms and vice versa. Joseph Needham, for example, the great historian of science and civilisation in China, distinguished between Confucian and Daoist styles of engineering.[15] The latter sought somehow to go with the flow in line with the fluidity of the Dao itself, and is exemplified in the ancient Dujiangyan Dam on the Min River in China, which acts differently depending on the volumes of water flowing past it. Confucian engineering, according to Needham, sought instead to act on rivers by the familiar tactic of building dykes and levees to control them.

I want to say that cybernetics illustrates very nicely the cosmotechnical inner connection of technology and ontology, in fact coming down on the Daoist side of Needham's contrast. We could say that cybernetics and its ontology of unknowability is part of a very different cosmotechnical paradigm from the command-and-control paradigm in modern science and engineering and its ontology of knowability and controllability.

The clearest example of this is the cybernetic biological computing project, which, as I said, aimed to draw the open-ended liveliness of biological systems into the human world of management. The stark contrast here is with conventional computing, which depends not on the liveliness of matter, but the opposite: taming and domesticating silicon chips right down to the atomic level and then writing computer programmes to instruct them in precisely what to do.[16] These two paradigms thus diverge profoundly at the level of hardware: ponds vs chips. And one could say much the same about the contrast between antipsychiatry, which entailed no hardware at all, and mainstream psychiatry, with its scalpels, electroshock machines, and psychoactive drugs.

But to make the contrast hinge on hardware alone is to create a problem, since my other cybernetic examples in fact used much the same hardware as their enframing counterparts. Cybernetic robots, say, used many of the same components as AI robotics. The adaptive management of the Colorado likewise depended on waterflows through the same Glen Canyon Dam which created the ecological problem in the first place. What can we say about that?

15   Joseph Needham, *Science and Civilisation in China, Vol 4, Physics and Physical Technology, Part III, Civil Engineering and Nautics* (Cambridge: Cambridge University Press, 1971), 234–50.
16   Andrew Pickering, 'Beyond Design: Cybernetics, Biological Computers and Hylozoism', *Synthese*, 168 (2009): 469–91.

The point, I believe, is that in thinking about cosmotechnics we should not focus exclusively on hardware but also on how the hardware is arranged. Different arrangements of the same hardware conjure up, we could say, different worlds and ontologies. The sensors and actuators of AI-robots are configured to map and respond to a knowable world, while the same components in cybernetic robots serve to explore and respond to the unknown. We thus need to think here of a foreground/background gestalt switch in which one ontology or the other is brought to the fore through the artful design of technological assemblages. This is how to think about cosmotechnics, even when material technologies are themselves the same.

So much for technology. One final thought about cosmology. I have been talking about the cybernetic ontology of unknowability and contrasting it with the scientific ontology of knowability. But it is worth saying that beyond this contrast, the cybernetic ontology has many positive affinities with nonmodern, non-Western and mystical cosmologies. I just mentioned cybernetics' affinity with Daoism, and the British cyberneticians themselves made many similar connections. In his work on schizophrenia, for example, Gregory Bateson collaborated with Alan Watts, the great popularizer of Buddhism in the West, and Watts in turn drew on cybernetics in his explanations of Buddhist concepts. The very notion of unknowability connects directly to mystical experience of the infinite, and Stafford Beer drew on this in arguing for the existence of God. Beer was likewise fascinated by the mystical figure called the enneagram, which he found repeated many times in the syntegration diagram. He was fascinated by Indian philosophy, too, and besides working as a management consultant, he studied and taught tantric yoga.

In the end, then, thinking about cosmotechnics can take us a very long way, from the down-to-earth projects and artefacts of British cybernetics, into distinctly non-British cosmologies, worldviews and religions. This emphasizes, for me, just what a strange and wonderful field British cybernetics has been.

Reference

Ashby, W. Ross. 'Design for a Brain'. *Electronic Engineering* 20 (December 1948): 379–83.

———. *Design for a Brain*. London: Chapman & Hall, 1960 [1952].

Asplen, Lisa. 'Going with the Flow: Living the Mangle in Environmental Management Practice'. In *The Mangle in Practice: Science, Society and Becoming*. Edited by Andrew Pickering and Keith Guzik, 163–84. Durham, NC: Duke University Press, 2008.

Bateson, Gregory. 'Conscious Purpose Versus Nature'. In *To Free a Generation: The Dialectics of Liberation*. Edited by David Cooper, 34–49. New York: Collier, 1968.

———. *Mind and Nature: A Necessary Unity*. Cresskill, NJ: Hampton Press, 2002 [1979].

Carson, Rachel. *Silent Spring*. New York: Houghton Mifflin, 1962.

de Latil, Pierre. *Thinking by Machine: A Study of Cybernetics*. London: Sidgwick and Jackson, 1956.

Hui, Yuk. *The Question Concerning Technology in China: An Essay in Cosmotechnics*. Falmouth, Urbanomic Media, 2016.

Medina, Eden. *Cybernetic Revolutionaries: Technology and Politics in Allende's Chile*. Cambridge, MA: MIT Press, 2014.

Needham, Joseph. *Science and Civilisation in China, Vol. 4, Physics and Physical Technology, Part III, Civil Engineering and Nautics*. Cambridge: Cambridge University Press, 1971.

Pickering, Andrew. 'Acting With the World: Doing Without Science'. To appear in *Beyond the Anthropocene: Climate Crisis, New Ontologies and Alternatives to the Anthropocentric Modernity*, special issue of *e-cadernos CES*, edited by António Carvalho and Mariana Riquito (forthcoming 2023).

———. *Acting with the World: Floods, Farming, Fires and Spirits*. In preparation.

———. 'Beyond Design: Cybernetics, Biological Computers and Hylozoism'. *Synthese* 168 (2009): 469–91.

———. 'Cybernetic Art'. To appear in *The Bloomsbury Encyclopaedia of New Media Art*. Edited by Charlie Gere. London: Bloomsbury, forthcoming.

———. *The Cybernetic Brain: Sketches of Another Future*. Chicago: University of Chicago Press, 2010.

———. 'Islands of Stability: From Cellular Automata to the Occupy Movement'. *Zeitschrift für Medien- and Kulturforschung* 14, no. 1 (2014): 121–34.

———. *The Mangle of Practice: Time, Agency, and Science*. Chicago: University of Chicago Press, 1995.

———. 'Poiesis in Action: Doing without Knowledge'. In *Weak Knowledge: Forms, Functions, and Dynamics*. Edited by Moritz Epple et al., 61–84. Frankfurt: Campus Verlag, 2019.

———. 'Wicked Problems and the Cybernetic Method'. To appear in *Critical Studies of Complexity: Theories, Notions, Translations and Normativity*. Edited by Pablo Jensen and Fabrizio Li Vigni. Editions Matériologiques, forthcoming 2023.

Rice, James. 'Further Beyond the Durkheimian Problematic: Environmental Sociology and the Co-Construction of the Social and the Natural'. *Sociological Forum* 28, no. 2 (2013): 236–60.

Wiener, Norbert. *Cybernetics, or Control and Communication in the Animal and the Machine*. Cambridge, MA: MIT Press, 1948.

Cybernetics Across Cultures: The Localization of the Universal

Slava Gerovitch

The history of cybernetics is a story of crossing cultural, political, and disciplinary boundaries. Cybernetics, or the science of control and communication in the animal and the machine, was articulated in the 1948 book of the same title by Professor of Mathematics at the Massachusetts Institute of Technology, Norbert Wiener. A display of Wiener's historical photographs and documents is placed in the hall of the MIT Mathematics Department, not far from my office.

Wiener's work on cybernetics draws on his wartime research on anti-aircraft gun control. He designed and built an anti-aircraft predictor, a feedback-operated servomechanical device for predicting the trajectory of an enemy airplane. This function was usually performed by human gun-pointers and gun-trainers, and Wiener's device would therefore 'usurp a specifically human function'.[1] This work led Wiener to the far-reaching analogy between the operation of servomechanisms, feedback-based control devices, and human purposeful behaviour. In 1943 Wiener, physiologist Arturo Rosenblueth, and engineer Julian Bigelow, jointly published an article in which they suggested that purposeful human behaviour was governed by the same feedback mechanism that was employed in servomechanisms.[2] Combining terms from control engineering (feedback), psychology (purpose), philosophy (teleology), and mathematics (extrapolation), they constructed a classificatory scheme of behaviour equally applicable to human action and machine operation.

1   Norbert Wiener, *Cybernetics, or Control and Communication in the Animal and the Machine* (Cambridge, MA: MIT Press, 1961 [1948]), 6.
2   Arturo Rosenblueth, Norbert Wiener, and Julian Bigelow, 'Behavior, Purpose and Teleology', *Philosophy of Science* 10 (1943): 18–24.

Cyberspeak between human and machine

In his book *Cybernetics*, Norbert Wiener further generalized these ideas and introduced a new, 'universal' language, which I call cyberspeak. It tied together a diverse set of human-machine metaphors. Cutting across various disciplines—computing, information theory, control theory, neurophysiology, and sociology—cybernetics described living organisms, control and communication devices, and human society in the same cybernetic terms: information, feedback, and control.

Travelling across the Atlantic Ocean to Europe and then to the Soviet Union, cybernetics changed its guise multiple times: it appeared at different times and places as an instrument for devising sophisticated weapons, a theoretical underpinning for the freedom of speech, a method for designing intelligent machines, a model for describing the functioning of the human brain, a vehicle of interdisciplinarity, and a tool for reforming the theoretical apparatus of a wide range of life and social sciences with formal models from mathematics and computing. At times it was filled with strong ideological messages, at other times it was presented as allegedly politically neutral. Every time cybernetics crossed a new cultural, political or disciplinary boundary, its connotations were questioned, and new ones attached.

The universalist aspirations of cybernetics and artificial intelligence

One particularly salient example of cyberneticians' universalist aspirations is the design of computer programmes capable of carrying out some human cognitive tasks, known as artificial intelligence (AI). The aspiration of AI is to grasp the universal principles of thought in order to implement them in a computer. In 1984, Patrick Winston articulated the goals of AI research as follows: 'Artificial Intelligence excites people who want to uncover principles that all intelligent information processors must exploit'.[3] At the same time in the Soviet Union, a budding AI community formulated its own goals, which sounded remarkably

3   Patrick Winston, *Artificial Intelligence* (Reading, MA: Addison-Wesley, 1984 [1976]), 2–3.

similar: 'to understand how the human being thinks, what are the mechanisms of thought'.[4] On both sides of the Iron Curtain, AI research was understood as a search for fundamental principles of human thinking.

Both American and Soviet scientists believed that there existed a general, universal, ahistorical mechanism of human thought. Yet as these scientists themselves belonged to different cultures, they had distinct, culturally specific intuitions about human thinking. The 'humans' whom they took as universal categories were, in fact, people who belonged to specific cultures. Their AI models thus reflected the specificity of their cultures.

Everyday practice in the USA and the USSR

Everyday practice in any society is based on commonly accepted patterns of behaviour—actions perceived as typical and normal—and also on various strategies of handling daily situations, known as common sense. John McCarthy famously called AI systems 'programmes with common sense', implying that a fundamentally universal common sense knowledge underlies human thinking.[5] As the anthropologist Clifford Geertz suggested, however, common sense is 'historically constructed and… subjected to historically defined standards of judgment. It can… vary dramatically from one people to the next. It is, in short, a cultural system'.[6] Geertz warned against 'sketching out some logical structure [that common sense] always takes, for there is none', thus unfortunately undermining McCarthy's basic premise.[7]

Everyday practice serves as a mediator for the constant exchange of cultural symbols, and shapes the cultural vocabulary for any given group. For Americans during this period, everyday experiences ranged from reading *The New York Times* to watching political debates on television to shopping at supermarkets that stocked a great variety of products. Soviet people's everyday experience looked quite different.

4   Mikhail S. Smirnov, ed., *Modelirovanie obucheniia i povedeniia* (The modelling of learning and behaviour) (Moscow: Nauka, 1975), 3.
5   John McCarthy, 'Programs with Common Sense', in *Semantic Information Processing*, ed. Marvin Minsky (Cambridge, MA: MIT Press, 1968), 403–9.
6   Clifford Geertz, 'Common Sense As a Cultural System', in *Local Knowledge: Further Essays in Interpretive Anthropology* (New York: Basic Books, 1983), 76.
7   Ibid., 92.

They never read *The New York Times*, never watched political debates, and never had a problem choosing which brand to buy. They read *Pravda* and underground literature, sat at Party meetings, and stood in lines at food stores. What seemed typical and normal to them looked peculiar and exotic to Americans, and vice versa. Yet even if common sense is not universal, AI models do tell us something—if not about the fundamentals of human thinking in general, then perhaps about specific cultural constructions of common knowledge.

Cultural influence manifests itself not only through typical patterns of behaviour and strategies of everyday life, but also through language, via the metaphors by which we live and think, including thinking about thought itself.[8] In this essay, I discuss the different cultural metaphors for thought prevalent among American and Soviet intellectuals and explore their connections with specific AI systems. I argue that deep cultural factors lie beneath the considerable differences in the approaches to AI developed by American and Soviet scholars. While looking for general principles of thinking and behaviour, AI specialists actually implemented their own cultural stereotypes in their models.

Different cultural metaphors for freedom: choice vs creativity

If we consider such an everyday situation as shopping, the main problem for American customers is how to make the right (one may say, 'healthy') choice among an appealing variety of foods and goods. The ability to make the right choice is also a very important part of academic training in the United States. College students choose most of their courses from a great variety of courses being offered; routine multiple-choice tests require selecting one right answer among several possibilities. Election ballots list multiple candidates for every office.

By contrast, most everyday situations in the Soviet Union left the citizen no choice at all. Higher education curricula prescribed a fixed, pre-determined sequence of courses for every major. The only choice students had was in selecting a preferred athletic activity. Multiple-choice tests were rare. Instead, the student was required to spell

8   George Lakoff and Mark Johnson, *Metaphors We Live By* (Chicago: University of Chicago Press, 1980).

out all the intermediate steps, and if the algorithm was inefficient (or simply different from the one in the textbook), the grade was lowered, even if the answer was correct. Election ballots always included only a single candidate, to simplify political choices. And finally, the Soviet way of shopping posed a different sort of problem for the customer. The problem was not what to choose, but how to find anything at all. With the shortage of many foods and household items, sought-after products could be obtained only via back channels. An ordinary Soviet citizen had to create a unique, long chain of informal social interactions through a network of friends, relatives, friends of relatives, and relatives of friends, so that a desired washing machine or a television set could be found at the other end.[9]

Cognitive psychological theories developed by American and Soviet scholars reflected the different cultural values of choice and creativity. The American cognitive psychologist Jerome Bruner, for example, described concept attainment as a process whose every step 'can be usually regarded as a choice or decision between alternative steps'.[10] Bruner's work showcased the 'cognitive revolution' in psychology, closely associated with the work of the American AI pioneers Herbert Simon and Allen Newell, who placed choice at the heart of their 'heuristic search' model of intellectual activity.

The Soviet psychologist Andrei Brushlinskii, by contrast, rejected the idea that thinking involved a choice among pre-existing alternatives. He argued that true thinking must produce a new alternative: 'Actual live thinking, for example, solving a task or a problem, always takes the form of prediction of an initially unknown, future solution. This prediction… makes the act of choosing among alternative solutions unnecessary'.[11]

AI specialists in the Soviet Union and in the United States sometimes drew on psychological theories, and sometimes psychologists drew on AI models. More habitually, however, AI specialists ignored psychologists' findings, believing that knowledge should flow from AI

9   See Alena Ledeneva, *Russia's Economy of Favours: Blat, Networking and Informal Exchange* (Cambridge: Cambridge University Press, 1998).
10   Jerome Bruner, *Beyond the Information Given: Studies in the Psychology of Knowing* (New York: Norton, 1973), 151.
11   Andrei Brushlinskii, 'Pochemu nevozmozhen "iskusstvennyi intellect "' (Why 'artificial intelligence' is impossible), *Voprosy filosofii* (Problems of philosophy) *no.* 2 (1979): 62.

to psychology, not the other way around.[12] When AI and psychology agreed, this often happened because they both relied on the same cultural stereotypes.

Bureaucratic man: striving for control of the social environment

One of the pioneers of American AI, Herbert Simon, explicitly referred to everyday experience when arguing that at the centre of intellectual activity was an act of choice:

> None of us is completely innocent of acquaintance with the gross characteristics of human choice, or of the broad features of the environment in which this choice takes place. I shall feel free to call on this common experience as a source of the hypotheses needed for the theory about the nature of man and his world.[13]

Simon drew on a wide array of mathematical theories that offered various formalizations of choice in well-structured environments—econometrics, game theory, operations research, utility theory, and the statistical decision theory—which his biographer Hunter Crowther-Heyck has termed 'the sciences of choice'.[14] All these theories assumed the act of choice to be free and rational: an individual acted upon the environment, but the environment did not affect the individual's goals or preferences.

---

12   Newell and Simon, for example, prophesied in 1958 that 'within ten years most theories in psychology will take the form of computer programs, or of qualitative statements about the characteristics of computer programs'; Allen Newell and Herbert Simon, 'Heuristic Problem Solving', *Operations Research* 6, no. 1 (1958): 7–8. In 1970, Allen Newell described AI as 'theoretical psychology', whose role was to generate problems for experimental psychologists to study; see Allen Newell, 'Remarks on the Relationship Between Artificial Intelligence and Cognitive Psychology', in *Theoretical Approaches to Non-numerical Problem Solving*, ed. Ranan B. Banerji and Mihajlo D. Mesarovic (Berlin: Springer-Verlag, 1970), 363–400.
13   Herbert A. Simon, 'A Behavioral Model of Rational Choice', *The Quarterly Journal of Economics* 69, no. 1 (February 1955): 100.
14   Hunter Crowther-Heyck, *Herbert A. Simon: The Bounds of Reason in America* (Baltimore: Johns Hopkins University Press, 2005), chap. 3.

Simon also borrowed from another set of disciplines: sociology, social psychology, anthropology, and political science. These 'sciences of control', by contrast, emphasized the malleability and docility of an individual, subjected to group and societal pressures and moulded by his social environment. The 'administrative man' of the sciences of control seemed utterly incompatible with the 'economic man' of the sciences of choice.

Drawing on both the sciences of choice and the sciences of control, Simon developed a theory of 'bounded rationality'. One could solve complex problems by reducing them to a limited set of alternatives and choosing rationally among them. Belonging to an organization limited an individual's choices and thus made rational decision-making possible.

In his 1956 paper, 'Rational Choice and the Structure of the Environment', Simon used the metaphor of a maze to introduce a mathematical model describing how an organism could meet a multiplicity of needs, making a sequence of rational choices at branch points, based on incomplete information.[15] This was not merely a convenient description. Extrapolating from his personal experience to the whole of humanity, Simon regarded a sequence of rational choices as a 'universal' model, a philosophy of life:

> A philosophy of life surely involves a set of principles.
> … Principles can provide a book of heuristics to guide
> choice at life's branch points, a thread to keep one on
> the right path in the maze. … In this chapter, I have been
> describing my life, and also my personal life philosophy,
> but I have also been describing the life of Everyperson.[16]

In the 1950s and 1960s, Simon and Allen Newell developed the heuristic search approach, which quickly became the dominant paradigm for American AI research. According to their model, problem solving activity consisted in finding a path from the initial to the goal state within the problem space. This space looked like a branching tree or a labyrinth; at every step of the process, the problem solver had to

15   Herbert A. Simon, 'Rational Choice and the Structure of the Environment', *Psychological Review* 63, no. 2 (1956): 129–38.
16   Herbert A. Simon, *Models of My Life* (New York: Basic Books, 1991), 360, 363.

choose one of the alternatives—one of the branches that diverged at the point of choice. In the absence of complete information about the labyrinth, or if the labyrinth was too large to make a feasible calculation, Newell and Simon suggested using heuristics—rules of thumb—to help make the right choice. They believed that labyrinth search was a universal model of intelligence and considered their computer programme, the 'General Problem Solver', to be a general 'theory of human problem-solving'.[17]

As Simon and Newell's conceptualization of human behaviour grew increasingly formal, the model situations they were drawing on became increasingly circumscribed and regulated; from semi-independent decisions by workers in big organizations, to semi-automatic actions of machine-bound operators in air defence control centres, to chess players' limited repertoire of permissible moves. In various computer implementations of the heuristic search model—the theorem-proving Logic Theorist, a chess-playing programme, and the 'universal' General Problem Solver—Newell and Simon tended to focus on situations with complete, unambiguous, computer-friendly descriptions.

Newell and Simon redefined the problem of choice: they no longer spoke of 'making decisions', but rather about 'solving problems'. If the decision-maker could consider different goals, the problem-solver had to focus on the assigned problem. Decisions turned into 'a less contentious, less political, process of allocating "processor time" to different tasks. Choices were now less decisions about which set of values to accept and more decisions about what set of data to process'.[18] Politics was reduced to technology: the liberal aspiration to control and purposefully transform the environment turned into a purely technical task of simplifying search in a labyrinth.

When elaborating her cultural 'grammar' of American storytelling, the anthropologist Livia Polanyi emphasized 'control' as one of the most important categories of American life. 'Proper people' as they are portrayed in everyday conversations, are those who 'can *control* the world sufficiently to be happy and have power'.[19] In the Soviet case,

17   Allen Newell and Herbert A. Simon, 'GPS, a Program that Simulates Human Thought', in *Computers and Thought*, ed. Edward A. Feigenbaum and Julian Feldman (New York: McGraw-Hill, 1963), 279.
18   Crowther-Heyck, *Herbert A. Simon*, 214.
19   Livia Polanyi, *Telling the American Story: A Structural and Cultural Analysis of Conversational Storytelling* (Norwood, NJ: Ablex, 1985), 140 (emphasis original).

by contrast, your social environment was something that could potentially control you, rather than something you could control. If one constructed a Soviet cultural grammar, this description could probably be rephrased as 'proper people are those who can sufficiently escape control by the world to be happy'. The independent-minded intelligentsia's everyday struggle for intellectual autonomy was translated, in a formalized and abstracted form, into Soviet AI models.

The Soviet controversy over 'thinking machines'

The idea that computers that could perform intellectual tasks stirred serious controversy in the Soviet Union in the early 1950s. In the paranoid Cold War context, scientific and technological innovations coming from the West were often viewed with great suspicion. In reaction to the popular discussions of 'thinking machines' in the West, the Soviet press condemned this idea as both a potential technological threat and an ideological subversion. Soviet journalists berated the capitalists for their hidden agenda to substitute a robot for a striking worker and to replace a human pilot who refused to bomb civilians with an 'indifferent metallic monster'. Soviet philosophers, for their part, attacked the idea of 'thinking machines' as both 'idealistic' (detaching thought from its material basis in the brain) and 'mechanistic' (reducing thought to computer operations). Soviet critics lumped all controversial uses of computers under the rubric of 'cybernetics' and labelled this field a 'reactionary, idealistic pseudo-science'. Despite its glaring logical contradictions—cybernetics was portrayed as both idealistic and mechanistic, utopian and dystopian, technocratic and pessimistic, a pseudo-science and a dangerous weapon of military aggression—the campaign had a serious impact on Soviet research. As a result of the media frenzy, work on 'thinking machines' became ideologically unacceptable, and early Soviet computer applications were limited to scientific calculations.[20]

20   On the Soviet anti-cybernetics campaign, see Slava Gerovitch, *From Newspeak to Cyberspeak: A History of Soviet Cybernetics* (Cambridge, MA: MIT Press, 2002), chap. 3.

Soviet cybernetics: a movement for reform

The anti-cybernetics campaign did not dampen the interest of Soviet scientists in computer systems that could perform intellectual tasks. All of the first large electronic digital computers in the Soviet Union were installed at defence research institutions, which were relatively protected from ideological pressure and also gave their employees access to most recent Western publications. Early Soviet champions of cybernetics and AI largely came from these institutions. The mathematician Aleksei Liapunov led the computer programming department at the Division of Applied Mathematics of the Mathematical Institute of the Soviet Academy of Sciences in Moscow. This division (after 1966, the Institute of Applied Mathematics) performed calculations for the Soviet nuclear weapons and rocketry programmes. These calculations were double-checked against the results obtained at Computer Centre No. 1 of the Ministry of Defence, where the computer specialist Anatolii Kitov was in charge of research and development. In 1955, taking advantage of the thawing political climate after Stalin's death, Kitov and Liapunov teamed up with the leading mathematician for the nuclear weapons programme, Sergei Sobolev, and published an article in the journal *Problems of Philosophy*, in which they publicly dismissed ideological charges against cybernetics and effectively legitimized research in this field.

As the cybernetics movement grew in strength, it brought under its umbrella all sorts of mathematical models and computer applications in 'cybernetic biology', 'cybernetic physiology', 'cybernetic linguistics', 'cybernetic economics', and many other fields. In 1960 Norbert Wiener attended a conference in Moscow and became an instant star. Party leaders became interested in computer technology and the prospects it opened for the socialist economy.

The pendulum of Soviet public attitudes toward 'thinking machines' swung in the other direction.[21] The Soviet press began extolling the intellectual abilities of the computer, portraying it as an all-powerful magical tool for solving any problem. Articles entitled '"Thinking" Machines' and 'Bordering on Science Fiction' mushroomed on the pages of newspapers and popular magazines. Journalists quickly dismissed

---

21   On the Soviet cybernetics movement, see Gerovitch, *From Newspeak to Cyberspeak*, chaps. 4–6.

the previous ideological critique by claiming that it applied only to capitalist society:

> If in the capitalist world the introduction of 'thinking' machines means the growth of unemployment, exploitation of workers, and fear of the future, in a socialist society, by freeing people from hard, uninteresting work, machines would provide an opportunity to focus on something lofty and joyful—to think, to create, and, in particular, to create new 'thinking' machines.[22]

The new 1961 Programme of the Communist Party of the Soviet Union proclaimed that 'cybernetics, electronic computers and control systems will be widely applied in production processes in industry, building and transport, in scientific research, planning, designing, accounting, statistics, and management'.[23] The Soviet media began calling computers 'machines of communism'.[24]

Despite the media hype, the Soviet government showed little interest in supporting AI research. The leaders of the cybernetics movement distanced themselves from AI aspirations, trying to cultivate an image of the computer as an efficient tool, rather than an autonomous agent. The chairman of the Cybernetics Council of the Soviet Academy of Sciences, engineer admiral Aksel Berg, publicly proclaimed that electronic computers 'will be increasingly providing help to man, but will never replace him and *will never think*'.[25] Computer time remained in short supply, and supervisors did not look favourably on computer programmers' attempts to divert valuable computational resources to investigate problems that aroused their own intellectual interest.

The tenuous position of Soviet AI was reflected in the language. The phrase 'thinking machines' was always put in quotation marks to stress its metaphorical meaning. The very term 'artificial intelligence'

22   Iu. Petrovskii, 'Na grani fantastiki' (Bordering on science fiction), *Znanie–sila* (Knowledge is power) no. 7 (1956): 23–24.

23   *Programme of the Communist Party of the Soviet Union. Adopted by the 22nd Congress of the C.P.S.U. October 31, 1961* (Moscow: Foreign Languages Publishing House, 1961), 66.

24   Viktor D. Pekelis, 'Chelovek, kibernetika i bog' (The human, cybernetics, and God], *Nauka i religiia* (Science and religion) no. 2 (1960): 27.

25   Aksel I. Berg, 'Problemy upravleniia i kibernetika' (Problems of management and cybernetics) (1961), in Berg, *Izbrannye trudy* (Selected works) vol. 2 (Moscow: Energiia, 1964), 87 (emphasis original).

remained controversial, and researchers avoided it. They preferred more neutral-sounding vocabulary, such as 'cybernetic psychology', 'the study of information processes', or 'heuristic programming'.[26]

The freedom not to choose

In 1964, when the mathematician Dmitrii Pospelov and the psychologist Veniamin Pushkin brought together computer specialists and psychologists interested in AI for a regular colloquium at the Moscow Power Engineering Institute, they named their field 'psychonics'. The psychonics group directly challenged the Simon-Newell model of thinking and put forward an alternative approach.

The term 'psychonics' was formed by analogy with bionics. While specialists in bionics hoped to imitate the 'design' of living organisms in engineering systems, Pospelov and Pushkin aspired to use psychological knowledge to construct intelligent computers. Pushkin conducted a number of eye-movement tracking studies of chess players and concluded that each player constructed a different mental model of the position on the board, rather than searching for the solution in a preset problem space. He asserted that the human problem space is not initially structured like a tree, and that the process of finding a solution involves creating a new problem space rather than 'pruning useless branches', as in the Newell-Simon labyrinth model.[27]

Soviet AI specialists disliked the labyrinth model not for its inefficiency, but for its departure from their cultural expectations. Even without knowing the conceptual origins of the General Problem Solver, they associated it with the 'bureaucratic apparatus' of labyrinth search. While some followed Newell and Simon's logic and asserted that 'the human being thinks by exhaustive search', many others suggested alternative models, for example, thinking as a chain of associations.[28]

Pushkin and Pospelov conceptualized thinking not as a search, but as a reflection of and on the problem. They argued that the descriptions

26   Evgenii I. Boiko et al., 'Kibernetika i p roblemy psikhologii' (Cybernetics and problems of psychology), in *Kibernetiku—na sluzhbu kommunizmu* (Cybernetics in service of communism), ed. Aksel I. Berg, vol. 5 (Moscow: Energiia, 1967), 314–50.
27   Veniamin Pushkin, *Psikhologiia i kibernetika* (Psychology and cybernetics) (Moscow: Pedagogika, 1971), 204.
28   Aleksandr Kronrod, *Besedy o programmirovanii* (Conversations about computer programming) (Moscow: URSS, 2001), 168, 139.

of the current situation and of the goal are often formulated in different terms. In the case of chess, for example, the initial position is described in terms of the location of specific pieces on the board, while the goal state—a checkmate—requires a higher-level description involving the inability to move the checked king. The human chess player must be able to go back and forth between low-level and high-level descriptions, that is, to build and manipulate various mediating models of the situation. Pushkin and Pospelov argued that situation modelling, rather than labyrinth search, was the basic intellectual procedure: 'Among all the existing words and notions used to describe productive thinking, the most adequate, the most suitable is the Russian word *soobrazhenie* (reflection/imagination). ... The solution *reflects* the situation, based on the *images* or models of its elements'.[29]

For Pospelov and Pushkin, human creativity manifests itself in abandoning the old labyrinth, re-conceptualizing the problem, and constructing a new problem space. For example, one cannot construct four equilateral triangles out of six matches if one seeks the solution on a plane. Constructing a new labyrinth of solutions—in the three-dimensional space—would produce the answer.[30]

While Newell and Simon started with a ready-made structure of the problem, Pushkin and Pospelov suggested that structuring the problem was an essential intellectual step in finding a solution. Building an adequate model of the situation was more important than powerful search algorithms. Pushkin and Pospelov proposed a semantic language for formal descriptions of the situation at various levels of generality and developed a system for building relational situation models. Pospelov and his team implemented this approach in computer systems for controlling loading operations in a sea port and other industrial operations, which combined technological and human elements.[31]

Pospelov and Pushkin's critique of the labyrinth theory echoed the Soviet cultural perception of choice as a restraint on creativity. For Eastern bloc intellectuals, the rigidly structured labyrinth of choices offered by the government seemed overly restrictive. Some chose to

29   Dmitrii Pospelov and Veniamin Pushkin, *Myshlenie i avtomaty* (Thinking and automata) (Moscow: Sovetskoe radio, 1972), 140–141 (emphasis added).
30   Ibid., 139.
31   For a historical overview, see Dmitrii Pospelov, *Situatsionnoe upravlenie: teoriia i praktika* (Situational control: theory and practice) (Moscow: Nauka, 1986), 254–58.

emigrate. Some, like Pospelov and Pushkin, chose to expose the limitations of choice-driven behaviour and to create new problem spaces.

An intellectual under an oppressive regime: striving for autonomy

Soviet intellectuals developed sophisticated strategies for living under surveillance. Recent studies of Soviet intelligentsia undermine the Cold War stereotypes of the Soviet scientist as either blindly supporting or passively resisting government policies.[32] A more typical figure would be a physicist working on nuclear weapons during the day, and reading underground literature at night.[33] Interested in results, the government allowed the scientists some intellectual license, as long as it was limited to their subject of study. The historian David Holloway called nuclear weapons laboratories 'islands of intellectual autonomy'.[34] One theoretical physicist later recalled:

> Physicists constituted a privileged caste, an aristocracy. There were fewer controls on our freedom than on those of any other member of Soviet civil[ian] society. The only laws we felt restricted by were those relating to the conventions of scientific work. Relatively speaking, we were free people.[35]

Mathematicians and computer specialists working on defence projects enjoyed a similar privileged status. As priests in a temple of the all-powerful goddess, the Computing Machine, they created their own dominions of intellectual autonomy in the climate-controlled, limited-access rooms housing mammoth-size computers of the first generation. The mathematicians Izrail Gelfand and Mikhail Tsetlin, of the defence-research-oriented Institute of Applied Mathematics, used

32   See *Osiris* vol. 23: *Intelligentsia Science: The Russian Century, 1860–1960*, ed. Michael D. Gordin, Karl Hall and Alexei Kojevnikov (2008).
33   Stanislav Rassadin, *Kniga proshchanii* (A book of farewells) (Moscow: Tekst, 2004), 217.
34   David Holloway, 'Physics, the State, and Civil Society in the Soviet Union', *Historical Studies in Physical and Biological Sciences* 30, no. 1 (1999): 175.
35   Mark Azbel, quoted in ibid., 187.

their portion of intellectual freedom to engage in a study of the central nervous system.

In 1958, Gelfand and Tsetlin organized an informal regular seminar on mathematical models in physiology.[36] Neurophysiologists traditionally assumed that various nodes within the central nervous system coordinated their activity via a complex system of interconnections. This assumption, however, baffled mathematicians: in a large system, the number of connections would grow so rapidly that any mathematical model would become too complex. Tsetlin and Gelfand, by contrast, proposed a model in which every node regarded the activity of all the other nodes as changes in its environment. They showed that individual nodes did not have to interact directly but could merely observe changes in their environment and follow a simple adaptive algorithm, minimizing their interactions with the environment. This resulted in purposeful behaviour of the system as a whole, if one defined purpose as minimization of the system's interaction with its environment. In this model, purposeful behaviour of the whole system did not require great complexity from its subsystems. All individual parts acted very simply: they tried to avoid interaction, rather than to build complex coordination networks. Gelfand and Tsetlin called this adaptive mechanism the 'principle of least interaction':

> At each moment, the subsystem solves its own 'particular', 'personal' problem—namely, it minimizes its interaction with the medium; therefore, the complexity of the subsystem does not depend on the complexity of the entire system. ... our mathematical models allow us (to a certain degree) to imagine the interaction of the nerve centers without considering the complex system of links and the coordination of their activity.[37]

36   Viacheslav Vs. Ivanov, 'Iz istorii kibernetiki v SSSR. Ocherk zhizni i deiatel'nosti M.L. Tsetlina' (From the history of cybernetics in the USSR: an outline of life and work of M. L. Tsetlin), in *Ocherki istorii informatiki v Rossii* (Essays on the history of informatics in Russia), ed. Dmitrii A. Pospelov and Iakov I. Fet (Novosibirsk: OIGGM SO RAN, 1998), 568.
37   Mikhail Tsetlin, *Automaton Theory and Modeling of Biological Systems*, trans. Scitran (New York: Academic Press, 1973), 150–52.

The peculiar definition of purposeful behaviour as the minimization of the system's interaction with its environment clearly resonated with the Soviet intelligentsia's drive to preserve maximum intellectual autonomy. Tsetlin argued that his model of the nervous system had the advantage of non-individualized control: there was no need to tell every node in the system what it was supposed to do; the system used its freedom of manoeuvre to self-organize under most general conditions. At a lecture before the Physiological Society in February 1965, Tsetlin explicitly brought up a comparison of free and forced labour to highlight the advantages of self-organization:

> The work of prisoners is more expensive than that of free men, even though the former are much worse fed and clad, and they work no less. The point is not only that the efficiency of prisoners is lower, but that a prisoner must be fed, clad, and watched by someone else. With a free person the matter is different: … my manager … doesn't have to think when to change my shoes or linen or what to do with my children.[38]

The MIT biophysicist Murray Eden once remarked: 'One wonders whether it is a reflection of cultural or social differences that Tsetlin chose to study cooperative phenomena in choosing "expedient" behaviour, while American game theory focuses on competition among the players'.[39] Tsetlin's model, strictly speaking, was not a mathematical implementation of socialist ideals. It reflected the intelligentsia's peculiar position within the Soviet system, in which 'cooperative phenomena' emerged out of individuals' efforts to escape control by the environment (the state) or by other individuals ('people's patrols'). Eden's suggestion of the social and cultural roots of different approaches to game theory, however, is worth exploring in greater detail.

38   Ibid., 125
39   Murray Eden, 'Foreword', ibid., xi.

Individualistic games of capitalism

In 1926, the Hungarian-born American mathematician John von Neumann developed an axiomatic formalization of two-person, zero-sum games with a finite number of 'strategies' (complete plans of the game). It was based on the Western concept of social interaction as a competition between self-interested, rationally calculating, yet cautious opponents.

Von Neumann proved the minimax theorem, asserting the existence of an optimal 'mixed', or randomized, strategy for each player, which would minimize the maximum loss, and would guarantee that each wins the 'value of the game'. He believed that the minimax strategy captured some fundamental aspect of human rationality: 'Any events—given the external conditions and the participants in the situation (provided that the latter are acting of their own free will)—may be regarded as a game of strategy if one looks at the effect it has on the participants'.[40]

Von Neumann's biographer Steve Heims has traced von Neumann's formalism to his perception of the world as filled with ruthless competitors who viewed all the other players as cunning enemies:

> His temperament was conditioned by the harsh political realities of his Hungarian experience. The recommended style of 'playing the economic game', the emphasis on caution, on calculation of expected consequences, the whole utilitarian emphasis aptly expresses the characteristic ideals of the middle class in capitalist societies.[41]

In 1944, von Neumann and his collaborator, the Austrian-born American economist Oskar Morgenstern, expanded the original conceptual framework of game theory to treat problems of economics in their book, *Theory of Games and Economic Behavior*. They explicitly challenged deterministic decision-making enshrined in neoclassical economics and presented the 'solution' of an economic game as a probabilistic

40   Von Neumann (1928), quoted in Robert J. Leonard, 'From Parlor Games to Social Science: Von Neumann, Morgenstern, and the Creation of Game Theory, 1928-1944', *Journal of Economic Literature* 33 (June 1995): 735.
41   Steve J. Heims, *John von Neumann and Norbert Wiener: From Mathematics to the Technologies of Life and Death* (Cambridge, MA: MIT Press, 1980), 296.

'stable set' of possible apportionments of payoff among the players. As the historian Philip Mirowski has argued, they treated mixed strategies as 'a representation of the stochastic nature of thought itself' and effectively turned minimax strategizing into 'the very epitome of the abstract rationality'.[42] Mirowski has further suggested that von Neumann and Morgenstern came to believe that game theory could 'simulate the behavior of any opponent and therefore serve as a general theory of rationality', and that in their writings 'game theory and artificial intelligence tended to blur together'.[43]

Among the indeterminism celebrated by von Neumann and Morgenstern, one thing remained stable throughout: the rules of the game. Fixing the rules of the game not only made it possible to derive powerful formal results in game theory. It also provided an anchor for the notion of rationality: the world was too complex for deterministic analysis, but it still followed rules, so a stochastically equipped mind could still calculate an optimal set of strategies.

American defence analysts asserted that 'the significance of game theory as a decision tool is that it eliminates guessing an opponent's intentions'.[44] While guessing seemed the opposite of rational problem-solving to American analysts, it was often the only option available to an intelligent decision-maker in the Soviet Union.

Collective games of socialism

Scholars studying Soviet science in the late Stalinist and Khrushchev periods have remarked on the ritualistic patterns of behaviour in the scientific community. Whether scientists were engaged in public discussions of the philosophical and ideological meaning of their discipline, or tried to jump on the bandwagon of a fashionable intellectual trend, they had to play a game according to the unspoken rules of the

42   Philip Mirowski, 'When Games Grow Deadly Serious: The Influence of the Military on the Evolution of Game Theory', in *Economics and National Security*, supplement to *History of Political Economy* 23, ed. Craufurd Goodwin, (Durham, NC: Duke University Press, 1991), 237.
43   Philip Mirowski, 'What Were von Neumann and Morgenstern Trying to Accomplish?' in *Towards a History of Game Theory*, supplement to *History of Political Economy* 24, ed. E. Roy Weintraub (Durham, NC: Duke University Press, 1992), 125, 127.
44   Quoted in Mirowski, 'When Games Grow', 251.

public behaviour of a Soviet scientist.[45] Ritual critique of ideological enemies, skilful manipulation with suitable quotes from Marx or Lenin, and ingenious translation of scientific terminology into an ideology-laden language, were among the indispensable strategies of Soviet science. The outcome of debates over the validity of scientific theories often depended on the discussants' abilities to play the game.

The play was complicated by the uncertainty over the rewards and punishment for specific strategies. Frequent swings in the direction of Stalinist ideological campaigns often left slow thinkers stuck with old, outdated slogans and made them vulnerable to attack. Those scientists who could not properly decipher 'signals' from above were often perplexed about the rules and direction of the most recent campaign.

The fundamental uncertainties of Soviet social games were reflected in Mikhail Tsetlin's theory of collective games of automata. An automaton is a mathematical model of a finite state machine that changes its state according to its transition diagram and the current input. Tsetlin interpreted an automaton as an agent acting in an environment that randomly penalized or rewarded specific behaviours. Unlike the classic von-Neumann-type games, Tsetlin studied games in which the automata faced a world filled with uncertainty. He wrote:

> It should be noted that the automaton games are discussed here from a viewpoint that differs from the one accepted in game theory. Indeed, it is normally assumed in the latter that the game is defined by a system of pay-off functions previously known to the players. … We thought it interesting to consider games played by finite automata having no a priori information about the game, and being forced to shape their strategies for each successive replay in the course of the game itself.[46]

In Tsetlin's games, 'the players have practically no information about the game. They are ignorant of the number of other players involved, of the situation at any particular moment and even of what kind of game

45   Alexei Kojevnikov, 'Rituals of Stalinist Culture at Work: Science and the Games of Intraparty Democracy circa 1948', *The Russian Review* 57 (January 1998): 25–52; Nikolai Krementsov, *Stalinist Science* (Princeton: Princeton University Press, 1997), esp. 239–48; and Gerovitch, *From Newspeak to Cyberspeak*.
46   Tsetlin, *Automaton Theory*, 6.

they are actually playing'.[47] Tsetlin informally compared his model of an agent operating in an environment with unknown and changing rules to a 'little animal in the big world'.[48] His friend, cybernetic neurophysiologist Nicholas Bernstein, used a similar metaphor to describe the fundamental uncertainties of intellectual activity: 'To use a metaphor, we might say that the organism is constantly playing a game with its environment, a game where the rules are not defined and the moves planned by the opponent are not known'.[49]

Tsetlin discovered that in a changing environment in which the probabilities of penalties and rewards varied over time, the most successful were the automata that did not have too many states. In other words, if the rules of the game constantly changed, it was not a good idea for the automaton to remember too much of its own history. The more dynamic the environment, the shorter was the optimal depth of the automaton's 'memory'.

In his study of collective 'distribution games', Tsetlin presented a thinly veiled commentary on the economic strategies of individuals under socialism. First, he considered a game in which a group of automata competed for resources (rewards or payoffs) by choosing different strategies. He designed automata that were completely unaware of the relative strengths of different strategies, but would eventually settle on the optimal strategy by reacting to rewards from their environment. Tsetlin showed, however, that their average gain could be increased if the automata played a game-theory version of socialism; a game with a 'common fund', in which all gains and losses of individual automata were summed up and then shared equally among them. The drawback was that the common fund camouflaged the link between individual contribution and reward and thus placed greater demands on the memory capacity of individual automata. One could 'reap the benefits of a common fund procedure starting from a certain level of complexity' of automata memory, he concluded, 'if the memory capacity is below this threshold, the introduction of a common fund reduces the average gain'.[50]

47   Viktor Varshavskii and Dmitrii Pospelov, *Puppets Without Strings*, trans. A. Kandaurov (Moscow: Mir, 1988), 97.
48   Tsetlin, *Automaton Theory*, 132.
49   Nicholas Bernstein, *The Co-ordination and Regulation of Movements* (Oxford: Pergamon Press, 1967), 173.
50   Varshavskii and Pospelov, *Puppets Without Strings*, 100.

In informal discussions, Tsetlin mockingly translated this rule into the clichéd parlance of the Soviet ideological discourse as 'the negative effect of [wage-]levelling and inadequate consciousness [of workers]'.[51] Indeed, the Soviet press often blamed the low quality of consumer products on workers' 'low level of consciousness'. Soviet propaganda routinely called on the workers to raise their consciousness and to work harder for a common fund. Tsetlin provided a mathematical formalization of this ideological dogma, calculating the precise memory capacity ('consciousness level') needed to find an optimal strategy in a game with a common fund.

Tsetlin's colleagues turned his result into a fundamental principle of human thinking and behaviour. Viktor Varshavskii and Dmitrii Pospelov interpreted memory capacity as a general measure of intellectual ability.[52] They correlated one's 'intellectual level' with the ability to find an optimal strategy in a game in which gains and losses were not explicitly tied to one's immediate actions but were produced at a higher level of organization. They concluded that 'capitalism is more profitable when the management system is simple and socialism is more profitable when the management system is elaborate'.[53] The writings of Soviet AI specialists paradoxically combined a thinly veiled critique of socialist redistribution and a peculiar definition of intellect as the ability to find an optimal strategy of living under socialism.

The notion of a game with unknown or changing rules was very familiar to the liberal intelligentsia. They played a cat-and-mouse game with the Soviet government, constantly challenging the fuzzy boundaries of permissible discourse. While Soviet laws ostensibly proclaimed many democratic freedoms, the actual practice was to suppress any significant dissent by placing it under the vague rubric of 'anti-Soviet activity'. Engaging in an open political protest would mean violating the most expedient strategy of behaviour under socialism: to minimize one's interactions with the political environment. Entering in a direct confrontation with the authorities was a flagrant violation of the 'principle of least interaction'.[54]

51   Ibid., 101.
52   Ibid., chap. 3.
53   Ibid., 102.
54   Evgenii L. Feinberg, 'Dlia budushchego istorika' (For a future historian), in *On mezhdu nami zhil: Vospominaniia o Sakharove* (He lived among us: memoirs about Sakharov), ed. Boris L. Altshuler et al. (Moscow: Praktika, 1996), 679.

Two central metaphors of AI: rats vs butterflies

Two metaphors capture crucial differences in the cultural stereotypes of thought and behaviour reflected in AI systems implemented in the Soviet Union and the United States. Life as a maze—a labyrinth in which we must find the right path—became the central metaphor for American AI. The metaphor of a labyrinth evoked the behaviourist pattern of B.F. Skinner's experiments on rats running T-shaped mazes and the popular American cultural image of the 'rat race'. In 1950 Claude Shannon designed a mechanical mouse that navigated a labyrinth in search of a metal 'cheese'. Herbert Simon's study of administrative behaviour, in turn, took rats running mazes as a paradigmatic case: 'A simplified model of human decision-making is provided by the behaviour of a white rat when he is confronted, in the psychological laboratory, with a maze, one path of which leads to food'.[55] Simon insisted that the limited knowledge and intellectual capacities of a rat better reflected the constraints on human rationality than the assumption of divine omniscience and perfect rationality: 'We need a less God-like and more rat-like chooser'.[56]

For Soviet AI specialists, the central metaphor for decision-making was not the search in a fixed labyrinth, but the flight of a butterfly, charting its flight trajectory through random streams of air. Viktor Varshavskii and Dmitrii Pospelov described a system that simulated the behaviour of a moth hunted by a bat. When the bat was too close and the moth could not fly away, the moth started dashing around in a chaotic flight:

> The chaotic flight is a series of passive falls with folded wings, sharp turns, loops and dives. In other words, the moth follows a trajectory which makes it more difficult for the bat to predict its location from one moment to the next. We should mention that in experiments the chaotic flight strategy saved the moth's life 70 percent of the time.[57]

55   Simon (1945), quoted in Crowther-Heyck, *Herbert A. Simon*, 112.
56   Simon (1954), quoted ibid., 6.
57   Varshavskii and Pospelov, *Puppets Without Strings*, 77.

A butterfly fluttering in a chaotic current of life and trying to escape a predator—this image was all too familiar to Soviet scientists, trying to preserve their intellectual autonomy.

American and Soviet AI specialists were seeking out general principles: universal, timeless mechanisms of thinking and behaviour. Their generalizations, however, were based on culturally conditioned cases. The examples that American and Soviet scientists had at their disposal, were, in fact, culturally specific patterns of social organization and decision-making. When trying to grasp universality, AI models manifested just the opposite: the specificity of cultural patterns.

Without knowing it, science often speaks with a national accent. Cultural symbolic systems can manifest themselves in scientific ideas as clearly as in literature or art. In their simulations of human thinking, AI systems truly reflect both mechanisms of reason and patterns of irrationality, individual creativity and social stereotyping, human nature and human culture.

Note

This article is a shortened and revised version of Slava Gerovitch, 'Artificial Intelligence with a National Face: American and Soviet Cultural Metaphors for Thought', in *The Search for a Theory of Cognition: Early Mechanisms and New Ideas*, ed. Stefano Franchi and Francesco Bianchini (Amsterdam: Rodopi, 2011), 173–194.

Reference

Berg, Aksel I. 'Problemy upravleniia i kibernetika' (Problems of manage-
    ment and cybernetics). In Berg, *Izbrannye trudy* (Selected works) vol.
    2. Moscow: Energiia, 1964.
Bernstein, Nicholas. The *Co-ordination and Regulation of Movements*.
    Oxford: Pergamon Press, 1967.
Boiko, Evgenii I. et al. 'Kibernetika i problemy psikhologii' (Cybernetics
    and problems of psychology). In *Kibernetiku—na sluzhbu kommu-
    nizmu* (Cybernetics in service of communism), edited by Aksel I.
    Berg, vol. 5, 314–50. Moscow: Energiia, 1967.
Bruner, Jerome. 'The Process of Concept Attainment'. In Bruner, *Beyond
    the Information Given: Studies in the Psychology of Knowing*. New
    York: Norton, 1973.
Brushlinskii, Andrei. 'Pochemu nevozmozhen "iskusstvennyi intel-
    lekt "' (Why 'artificial intelligence' is impossible). *Voprosy filosofii*
    (Problems of philosophy) no. 2 (1979): 50–64.
Crowther-Heyck, Hunter. *Herbert A. Simon: The Bounds of Reason in
    America*. Baltimore: Johns Hopkins University Press, 2005.
Feinberg, Evgenii L. 'Dlia budushchego istorika' (For a future historian).
    In *On mezhdu nami zhil: Vospominaniia o Sakharove* (He lived among
    us: memoirs about Sakharov), edited by Boris L. Altshuler et al.,
    652–711. Moscow: Praktika, 1996.
Geertz, Clifford. 'Common Sense As a Cultural System'. In Geertz, *Local
    Knowledge: Further Essays in Interpretive Anthropology*. New York:
    Basic Books, 1983.
Gerovitch, Slava. *From Newspeak to Cyberspeak: A History of Soviet
    Cybernetics*. Cambridge, MA: MIT Press, 2002.
Heims, Steve J. *John von Neumann and Norbert Wiener: From
    Mathematics to the Technologies of Life and Death*. Cambridge, MA:
    MIT Press, 1980.
Holloway, David. 'Physics, the State, and Civil Society in the Soviet
    Union'. *Historical Studies in Physical and Biological Sciences* 30, no.
    1 (1999): 173–92.
Ivanov, Viacheslav Vs. 'Iz istorii kibernetiki v SSSR. Ocherk zhizni i deia-
    tel'nosti M.L. Tsetlina' (From the history of cybernetics in the USSR:
    an outline of life and work of M. L. Tsetlin). In *Ocherki istorii informa-
    tiki v Rossii* (Essays on the history of informatics in Russia), edited by
    Dmitrii A. Pospelov and Iakov I. Fet, 556–80. Novosibirsk: Oiggm so
    ran, 1998.

Kojevnikov, Alexei. 'Rituals of Stalinist Culture at Work: Science and the
     Games of Intraparty Democracy circa 1948'. *The Russian Review* 57
     (January 1998): 25–52.
Krementsov, Nikolai. *Stalinist Science*. Princeton: Princeton University
     Press, 1997.
Kronrod, Aleksandr. *Besedy o programmirovanii* (Conversations about
     computer programming). Moscow: URSS, 2001.
Lakoff, George and Mark Johnson. *Metaphors We Live By*. Chicago:
     University of Chicago Press, 1980.
Leonard, Robert J. 'From Parlor Games to Social Science: Von Neumann,
     Morgenstern, and the Creation of Game Theory, 1928–1944'. *Journal
     of Economic Literature* 33 (June 1995): 730–61.
McCarthy, John. 'Programs with Common Sense'. In *Semantic
     Information Processing*, edited by Marvin Minsky, 403–9.
     Cambridge, MA: MIT Press, 1968.
Mirowski, Philip. 'What Were von Neumann and Morgenstern Trying to
     Accomplish?' In *Towards a History of Game Theory*, supplement to
     History of Political Economy 24, edited by E. Roy Weintraub, 113–47.
     Durham, NC: Duke University Press, 1992.
———. 'When Games Grow Deadly Serious: The Influence of the Military
     on the Evolution of Game Theory'. In *Economics and National
     Security*, supplement to *History of Political Economy* 23, edited by
     Craufurd Goodwin, 227–55. Durham, NC: Duke University Press,
     1991.
Newell, Allen. 'Remarks on the Relationship Between Artificial
     Intelligence and Cognitive Psychology'. In *Theoretical Approaches
     to Non-numerical Problem Solving*, edited by Ranan B. Banerji and
     Mihajlo D. Mesarovic, 363–400. Berlin: Springer-Verlag, 1970.
———. and Herbert A. Simon. 'GPS, a Program that Simulates Human
     Thought'. In *Computers and Thought*, edited by Edward A.
     Feigenbaum and Julian Feldman, 279–93. New York: McGraw-Hill,
     1963.
Newell, Allen, and Herbert Simon. 'Heuristic Problem Solving'.
     Operations Research 6, no. 1 (1958): 1–10.
Osiris vol. 23: *Intelligentsia Science: The Russian Century, 1860–1960*,
     edited by Michael D. Gordin, Karl Hall and Alexei Kojevnikov (2008).
Pekelis, Viktor D. 'Chelovek, kibernetika i bog' (The human, cybernetics,
     and God). *Nauka i religiia* (Science and religion) no. 2 (1960): 25–30.

Petrovskii, Iu. 'Na grani fantastiki' (Bordering on science fiction). *Znanie-sila* (Knowledge is power) no. 7 (1956): 17–24.

Polanyi, Livia. *Telling the American Story: A Structural and Cultural Analysis of Conversational Storytelling*. Norwood, NJ: Ablex, 1985.

Pospelov, Dmitrii. *Situatsionnoe upravlenie: teoriia i praktika* (Situational control: theory and practice). Moscow: Nauka, 1986.

Pospelov, Dmitrii, and Veniamin Pushkin. *Myshlenie i avtomaty* (Thinking and automata). Moscow: Sovetskoe radio, 1972.

Programme of the Communist Party of the Soviet Union. Adopted by the 22nd Congress of the C.P.S.U. October 31, 1961. Moscow: Foreign Languages Publishing House, 1961.

Pushkin, Veniamin. *Psikhologiia i kibernetika* (Psychology and cybernetics). Moscow: Pedagogika, 1971.

Rassadin, Stanislav. *Kniga proshchanii* (A book of farewells). Moscow: Tekst, 2004.

Rosenblueth, Arturo, Norbert Wiener and Julian Bigelow. 'Behavior, Purpose and Teleology'. *Philosophy of Science* 10 (1943): 18–24.

Simon, Herbert A. 'A Behavioral Model of Rational Choice'. *The Quarterly Journal of Economics* 69, no. 1 (February 1955): 99–118.

———. *Models of My Life*. New York: Basic Books, 1991.

———. 'Rational Choice and the Structure of the Environment'. *Psychological Review* 63, no. 2 (1956): 129–38.

Smirnov, Mikhail S., ed. *Modelirovanie obucheniia i povedeniia* (The modelling of learning and behaviour). Moscow: Nauka, 1975.

Tsetlin, Mikhail. *Automaton Theory and Modeling of Biological Systems*. Translated by Scitran. New York: Academic Press, 1973.

Varshavskii, Viktor, and Dmitrii Pospelov. *Puppets Without Strings*. Translated by A. Kandaurov. Moscow: Mir, 1988.

Winston, Patrick. *Artificial Intelligence*. Reading, MA: Addison-Wesley, 1984 [1976].

Cybernetics, Communism, and Romanticism: Cybernetic Thinking in the Polish People's Republic and in the Pre-Cybernetic Era

Michał Krzykawski

For the worldwide community of readers and scholars interested in science fiction literature, futurology, and technology, the juxtaposition of the words 'cybernetics' and 'Poland' brings to mind one name: Stanisław Lem. Those with a penchant for philosophy might point to *Summa Technologiae*, Lem's treatise on science and technology, originally published in 1962, where cybernetics provides the framework for his argument. As Joanna Zylinska, the translator of the book into English, has it, '*Summa* has lost none of its intellectual vigor or critical significance'.[1] The epistemological limits of Lem's empirical approach to biological, technological, and social phenomena notwithstanding, his futurologist observations are still worth discussing in light of today's advancements in artificial intelligence and, more broadly, in the so-called emergent technologies.

In this contribution, however, I offer a different take on the cybernetic moment in Poland, focusing on the political and scientific reception of cybernetics under communist rule. From this historical perspective, Lem's oeuvre is of lesser importance. In fact, for the state's apparatus, he was just a famous sci-fi writer.

My argument consists of two parts. In the first, I discuss the reception of cybernetics in the Polish People's Republic and the interdependence of science, economics, and ideology, with special emphasis on Oskar Lange's economic cybernetics and comments on the first issue of the journal *Postępy cybernetyki* (Cybernetic progress) published in 1978. In the second part, I go back to the pre-cybernetic era and discuss Bronisław Trentowski's *Stosunek filozofii do cybernetyki*

---

1   Stanislaw Lem, *Summa Technologiae*, trans. Joanna Zylinska (London, Minneapolis: University of Minnesota Press, 2013).

czyli sztuki rządzenia narodem (The relation of philosophy to cybernetics as the art of governing a nation). Trentowski was a romantic and liberal philosopher who introduced the term 'cybernetics' into the Polish language one hundred years before cybernetics gained its momentum with Norbert Wiener's seminal *Cybernetics: Or Control and Communication in the Animal and the Machine*, originally published in 1948. I suggest that the meaning of cybernetics as discussed by Trentowski at the very beginning of industrial revolution in this part of Europe can open a new perspective on the question of governance in the context of the relationship between artificial intelligence and political power.

Cybernetics and dialectical materialism

The Polish People's Republic, just to recall some basic historical facts, was a socialist one-party state with a unitary Marxist-Leninist government headed by the Polish United Workers' Party. The country existed from 1947 to 1989 and was a satellite country in the Soviet sphere of interest. When reconsidering the adventures of (Western) cybernetics in this context, we notice two kinds of tension: on the one hand, the tension between cybernetic thinking and dialectical materialism, either as the state's official philosophy or as philosophical method; on the other hand, the tension between the scientific reception and the political reception of cybernetics, in the situation where some of the scientists who developed cybernetic theories and described themselves as 'cyberneticists' were scientific workers holding high functions in the Party.

It is often repeated that cybernetics, together with advancements in mathematics from the 1930s, were firmly rejected by the propaganda in the Soviet Union under the Stalinist era.[2] As Slava Gerovitch points out, 'in 1954 the Short Philosophical Dictionary [still] defined cybernetics as a "reactionary pseudoscience" and "an ideological weapon of imperialist reaction"'.[3] The status of cybernetics radically changed after Stalin's death in 1953 and with the beginning of Nikita Khrushchev's era. As Gerovitsh continues:

2   Benjamin Peters, *How Not to Network a Nation: The Uneasy History of the Soviet Internet* (Cambridge, MA: The MIT Press, 2016), 30–32.
3   Slava Gerovitch, *From Newspeak to Cyberspeak: A History of Soviet Cybernetics* (Cambridge, MA: The MIT Press, 2002), 4. This dictionary was translated into Polish and published a year later.

By the late 1950s, cybernetics was recognized as an innocent victim of political oppression and 'rehabilitated' along with some of the political prisoners of the Stalinist regime. Soviet cybernetics emerged as a movement for radical reform of the Stalinist system of science. It gained wide popularity, and in the early 1960s it was written into a new Party Program and hailed as a 'science in the service of communism'. By the late 1960s, however, cybernetics began to lose intellectual content and turn into a fashionable trend.[4]

It is within this historical context, as pertaining to the Eastern bloc, that cybernetic thinking is brought to the fore in the Polish People's Republic, both in scientific and political circles. Moscow's political shadow notwithstanding, the Polish reception of cybernetics followed its own, intellectually independent path, although it still took place in a world where, just like in the whole Eastern bloc, research activities received very little financial support.[5]

In 1954, 'Dialogi o cybernetyce' (Dialogues on cybernetics), a fifty-page article by Stanisław Bogusławski, Henryk Greniewski and Jerzy Szapiro, was published in the journal *Myśl filozoficzna* (Philosophical thought), the main Polish philosophical journal of the Stalinist period.[6] Although the article was published in the section 'The Ideological Face of Imperialism', its aim was to thoroughly assess the meaning of Wiener's book, rather than to reject cybernetics as a 'pseudoscience'. The authors appreciate Wiener's contribution to the mathematical analysis of the processes of automatic regulation, but are rather reluctant to subscribe to the growing popular belief that cybernetics is a ground-breaking scientific theory with great philosophical implications. More importantly, they point out that the advancements in cybernetics in relation to the transmission of information and computer programming are compatible with the Marxist conceptual apparatus.

4   Ibid., 4.
5   Piotr Sienkiewicz and Jerzy S. Nowak. 'Sześćdziesiąt lat cybernetyki i polskiej informatyki' (Sixty years of cybernetics and polish computer science), *Zeszyty Naukowe Warszawskiej Wyższej Szkoły Informatyki*, 3(3): 9–24.
6   Stanisław Bogusławski, Henryk Greniewski and Jerzy Szapiro, 'Dialogi o cybernetyce' (Dialogues on cybernetics), *Myśl filozoficzna* (Philosophical thought) 4 (1954): 158–212.

It would be difficult, and not very productive, to draw a sharp line between 'ideology' and 'science' in this stance related to Wiener's book. The 'Dialogues on cybernetics' rather shows how scientists could live, publish, and communicate under the real socialism.

In his 1964 lecture titled 'Cybernetics and the Dialectic Materialism of Marx and Lenin', the German philosopher and logician Gotthard Günter points out that 'there is no doubt cybernetics has since about 1960 arrived in Marxist countries in full splendor'.[7] Cybernetics was not considered a threat to the official philosophical doctrine but, on the contrary, an opportunity to re-examine certain positions of Marxism-Leninism from a different angle. At the same time, communist propaganda in Poland made cybernetics a synonym for rationalization and technoscientific progress. Służewiec, the former industrial area in Warsaw, even saw the creation of Cybernetics Street, not to mention Computer Street, Progress Street, Rationalization Street and Invention Street, in accordance with the Six-Year Plan, that is, the centralized plan adopted in 1950 which concentrated on developing the heavy industry sector in the Polish People's Republic. Incidentally, Służewiec's former factories have today been replaced by the headquarters of transnational companies, and the area has been transformed into one of the biggest office basins in Europe—but those streets still exist.

Putting aside this ideological drift of cybernetics, it is remarkable how many academics and engineers, particularly those working in technological universities, were attracted by cybernetic ideas. In 1962, the Polish Cybernetics Society was founded on the initiative of the mathematician and logician Henryk Greniewski, the economist Oskar Lange, and the mathematician Stanisław Turski. The Society had branches in several Polish cities and counted more than 1000 members ten years later. A press note on the foundation of the Society was published in *The New York Times* in June 1962. It is worth quoting as it shows the nature of the tension between science and politics that conditioned the reception of cybernetics in the Polish People's Republic:

7   Gotthard Günther, 'Cybernetics and the Dialectic Materialism of Marx and Lenin' in *Computing in Russia: The History of Computer Devices and Information Technology Revealed*, ed. Georg Trogemann, Alexander Y. Nitussov and Wolfgang Ernst (Braunschweig: Vieweg Verlag, 2001), 317–32.

Fig. 2: Article from *The New York Times*, 3 June 1962, p. 16; transcribed by the author.

Cybernetics Society Is Formed in Poland in a Policy Reversal

Warsaw, May 27. A Polish cybernetics society was founded last week in Warsaw.

In scientific circles the event, coinciding with the tenth anniversary of the Polish Academy of Sciences, was regarded as a success of the progressive scientific spirit in Poland.

Cybernetics deals with comparative studies of the control system formed by the nervous system and brain and mechanico-electric communications systems, such as computers. In Eastern European scholarly circles it is symbolic of all that was missing in the Stalin era.

[...] The spectacular development of data processing and computing techniques has persuaded Communist authorities to take the new science seriously. But scholarly sources report that it is still treated gingerly in orthodox quarters.

The same is said to be true of econometrics, the analysis and evaluation of massed data by means of special statistical methods and devices, and also of linear programming researchers and advanced sociological theory.

The works of post-war Polish sociologists, heavily influenced by methods developed in the United States, are being translated and read in the Soviet Union. But they are not yet published there, according to authoritative informants.

Economics and other social sciences are still regarded as 'sensitive subjects' in Eastern Europe because they unavoidably touch on political matters. New ideas in these disciplines also disturb Communist theorists, who are expected to believe that the Marxist dialectic explains everything about human society.

Prof. Adam Schaff of Warsaw University, who is regarded as the voice of Polish science in top Communist party circles, seeks to define the line between freedom and political 'responsibility' for his colleagues.

He has just published a criticism of what he calls the 'mania' in Poland for poll-taking, market research and other forms of modern sociological inquiry. Six months ago, addressing Communist sociologists in Prague, Professor Schaff said that as serious scientists they had no choice but to make use of the new techniques developed in the West.

In learned circles Professor Schaff's seeming about-face was read as a warning that the present progressive mood in Polish science was outrunning its political possibilities.

However, Wladyslaw Bienkowski, a former Minister of Education and once an intimate of Wladyslaw Gomolka, the Communist leader, responded with a stinging rebuttal.

'Social practice is impossible without information,' he wrote. He attacked 'one-sided propaganda' as archaic. 'Practical men need empirical information in order to act,' he said.

M. Bienkowski concluded with the advice to 'some professors' that it would be wiser to come to terms with sociology.

The advice was well-regarded among leaders of Polish science who attended the tenth anniversary celebration of the Academy of Sciences.

However, M. Gomolka sounded a different note. He said the Communist party expected scientists to shape their research programs to the policies laid down at a Central Committee meeting in March, at which a big leap forward in industrial technology was demanded.

'Absolute priority must be given to the kind of research that plainly points to economic benefits,' he said.

Cybernetics and, more generally, the nascent information science, were at the same time dismissed and felt to be a necessity. On the one hand, the self-perpetuating propaganda machine still found the diffusion of cybernetics and 'Western' innovations an uncomfortable match with the ideological version of Marxist doctrine. On the other hand, cybernetics as 'the new science' was believed to be able to optimize the socialist planned economy in accordance with some elementary economic principles.

Oskar Lange's Economic Cybernetics

In this respect, Oskar Lange's theory of economic cybernetics is of crucial importance. A researcher in mathematical economics, a member of the Central Committee of the Polish United Workers' Party, and the first president of the Polish Cybernetic Society, Lange (1904–1965) developed a theoretical model of a socialist economy, taking into account some mechanisms of the market but refuting the narrow idea of the self-regulating market. Contrary to Friedrich Hayek and the Austrian school of economics, Lange contended that it was fully possible to monitor supply and demand in a centrally-planned economy. While his book *On the Economic Theory of Socialism* (published in 1938 during a stay in the USA), he puts Marxian economics and neoclassical economics together, his *Introduction to Economic Cybernetics* (1965) was meant to combine cybernetics and economics to defend the state-planned economy:

> From the very onset of the development of the political economy, economists were engaged in problems which we define today as cybernetic problems. They were dealing with the processes of regulation and control of processes consisting of mutually related elements before such problems appeared in other fields of study—in technology and biology—and long before they were formulated in general theoretical terms in a new science—cybernetics.[8]

Just as Hayek uses the armamentarium of cognitive sciences to make the idea of the self-regulating market natural and universal,[9] it can be argued that Lange uses the armamentarium of cybernetics to develop a model of socialist economy and to reframe cybernetic thinking with a view to support the dialectical processes of development as pertaining to dialectical materialism. Drawing on 'the scientific socialism of Marx and Engels' and Keynessian state-administrated capitalism, Lange

8   Oskar Lange, *Introduction to Economic Cybernetics*, trans. Józef Stadler (Oxford: Pergamon Press: 1970), 1.
9   Matteo Pasquinelli, 'How to Make a Class: Hayek's Neoliberalism and the Origins of Connectionism', *Qui parle* 30, no. 1 (2021), 161.

rejects the idea of the market as a self-regulating system. He argues that 'scientific socialism was the first to expand the principle of conscious management of social processes as its basic historical task'.[10] It is then possible for him to use the concepts such as regulation, management, and stability in different philosophical and political settings. In a nutshell, grounding in dialectical materialism his original description of what a cybernetic system looks like, he offers an abstract model of the effective model of a socialist economy.

From an economic point of view, the relevance of Lange's approach to cybernetics consists in his demonstration that economic models based on cybernetic thinking can be effectively used for analysing the dynamics of the economic processes. In this respect, his economic cybernetics is also a cybernetic economics. From a philosophical viewpoint, however, the concept of the whole is central to this approach, but reconsidered in strict relation to the dialectical processes of its development. According to dialectical materialism, Lange says, there are material systems, and their elements are linked by cause-and-effect chains. To understand how these systems operate, it is necessary to distinguish their properties from the properties of the elements they consist of. In other words, these systems have their own regularities of operation that cannot be fully explained by the laws of operation of the particular elements. Lange defines these systems as wholes. Explaining the philosophical assumptions behind his approach to economic cybernetics, he offers a wide range of examples of such wholes; chemical compounds in relation to the physical aggregates of elements, living matter in relation to physical and chemical systems, animal organisms in relation to individual cells of living matter, psychic processes in relation to the biological properties of the organism, finally social formations in relation to the biopsychological properties of human organisms. What is new in this rather typical cybernetic vision of wholes and of their primacy over their elements, is Lange's contention that all changes within wholes have a dialectical character. Therefore, another key element to understanding the effective maintenance of the proper operation of the whole is the notion of contradiction. Contradictions, Lange argues, appear in each system constituted as a whole and their appearance causes a transformation that leads to the disappearance of the resulting contradictions. This transformation breeds new

10   Oskar Lange, *Introduction to Economic Cybernetics*, 2.

contradictions that consequently bring about a new transformation in and of the system. In a nutshell, the systems constituted as wholes are subject to permanent change. All these changes take place in a specific direction, which means that they constitute a process of development; specific wholes combine into more complex systems, and these systems acquire new properties that they did not have before.

In his approach to the system, Lange seeks to overcome mechanicism and 'metaphysical finalism'. By the latter he means any system of thought requiring a reference to the substance—such as the life force, élan vital, the soul, or the spirit of a nation or of an epoch—assumed decisive for the emergence of the wholes with their new properties. Mechanistic approaches also fail to explain this emergence, as they are based on the belief that a whole is a simple sum of all its parts. Put simply, if mechanism misidentifies the wholes with their properties, finalism tends to explain them by referring to entities whose existence cannot be empirically proved. By challenging these two explanations, Lange's economic reinterpretation of cybernetics intended to enable an understanding of the whole in light of the process of dialectical development. It was also meant to resituate dialectical materialism and to provide what was known as the scientific socialism of Marx and Engels with an up-to-date scientific foundation stemming from statistics and mathematical economics, but accompanied by a deeper historical and socio-philosophical reflection that was directly related to the place where he chose to live.

From a 'philosophy of contemporary existence' to a theory of everything

The first issue of the quarterly *Postępy cybernetyki* ('Progress in cybernetics', published by the Polish Cybernetics Society (PCS) from 1978 to 1993), still had much to do with the tension between the cybernetic understandings of the system and the socialist reality, even though the latter was no longer that of the 1960s, when the PCS was founded. Under the rule of Edward Gierek, the First Secretary and the leader of the Polish People' Republic between 1970 and 1980, known for opening the country to new Western ideas and loosening censorship, Poland underwent massive industrialization, which substantially improved living and working conditions. The title of the quarterly was a verbatim repetition of the *Proceedings of the First International Congress of Cybernetics* published in 1969 in London.[11]

The aim of the quarterly was 'to publish the results of theoretical research, experimental research and theoretico-experimental research in the field of technological, biological, medical and social cybernetics'.[12] The editorial committee also welcomed 'articles including thorough analyses related to issues of control, coordination and management in physical, biological, medical, economic, sociological and pedagogical processes'.[13] Topics could be suggested either by the editorial committee or by the state institutions and authorities.

In the opening article, titled 'Cybernetics as a Philosophy of Contemporary Existence',[14] the minister of communication, Edward Kowalczyk, said:

> If anyone reflects on the development of human living conditions on earth, they must notice that, with the growing number of the world's inhabitants, with the increase in social consciousness and with the extended impact of economic activity on the natural environment, there is an urgent need to look at the ensemble of relations taking place in human society at a general scale.
>
> The need to ensure equal conditions for social existence, to use natural resources in a more rational way, to stop the process of environmental degradation and to ennoble interpersonal relations at various scales of this problem requires methods of thinking and acting that combine so-called common sense, which is inherent to

11   John Rose, the editor of this peculiar publication admits that some 'somewhat fatuous contributions were included in order to bring to the surface certain undesirable accretions'. He adds that 'a mature science has to live and cope with those who are trying to jump on the bandwagon and use it as a vehicle for their exuberant claims'. Quoted in Young, 'Machine Intelligence', 261.
12   Edward Kowalczyk, 'Cybernetyka filozofią współczesnej egzystencji' (Cybernetics as a philosophy of contemporary existence), *Postępy cybernetyki* (Progress in cybernetics) 1 (1978): 7–10. All translations from Polish are my own.
13   Ibid., 6.
14   This title directly refers to the paper delivered by Louis Challier at the previously mentioned congress of cybernetics; Challier described cybernetics as the 'science of sciences and the safeguard of men'. Cited in John F. Young, 'Machine Intelligence', *Nature* 230 (26 March 1971): 261.

> human beings, with scientific problem solving and scientific tasks. Such methods are offered by cybernetics.[15]

Kowalczyk's call for rethinking the socialist economy can be interpreted as a grave concern about the large-scale ecological devastation caused by state socialist productivism (which, incidentally, did not differ much from its capitalist counterpart, criticized by the degrowth movement under the name of 'growthism' today), if not as a veiled critique of the system prioritizing the increase in steel and coal production with no attention for what is defined today as 'external cost'.

Some context is needed to understand the high hopes, at the time, for cybernetics, as 'the new science', to offer scientific problem solving methods with a view to overcoming this productivist fever and the crudeness of communist thinking. Cybernetics was expected to produce a change in scientific practices, understood not only as the production of knowledge, but also as 'an immediate productive force', especially through a better understanding of nature and a new understanding of the system.[16]

In a way, cybernetics could be read as a new kind of humanism, which seemed to challenge Marx's theory of the mode of production—which was considered the key factor in creating social relations and raising social consciousness, and the central idea to his humanism. The truth, however, is that by the end of the 1970s, cybernetics was already becoming a theory of everything and losing its theoretical relevance. There was a growing tendency to take cybernetics for the new philosophy that could describe all social, cultural, biological and psychological phenomena by means of simple models. Consider Marian Mazur, specialized in electrothermics, and the author of a theory of autonomous systems and of the qualitative theory of information,[17] who tried to explain the functioning of the psyche through a cybernetic typology of what he called 'the character' (1976).[18] Under the pretext that it is possible to 'organize' human characters according to

15   Kowalczyk, *Progress in Cybernetics*, 7.
16   Ibid., 8.
17   Marian Mazur, *Cybernetyczna teoria układów samodzielnych* (A Cybernetic theory of autonomous systems), (Warsaw: PWN, 1966).
18   Marian Mazur, *Cybernetyka i character* (Cybernetics and character), (Warsaw: PWN, 1976).

their 'parameters', Mazur defined cybernetics as 'a psychology for the twenty-first century'. Another example is Jan Trąbka, a neurologist who developed an original neuropsychiatric explanation of consciousness through cybernetics but ended up combining neurocybernetics, gnosis, and chaos theory.[19]

All in all, instead of becoming 'a philosophy of contemporary existence' for a better organized socialist world, cybernetics got absorbed by automatic control and robotics on the one hand and by informatics on the other, long before the fall of socialism, as a system but also as a political force.[20] Contemporary complex systems and their industrial applications largely correspond to the theoretical assumptions of the first cybernetics, although their architects might be unfamiliar with the history of cybernetics and its promises, which had spread over the world and taken quite unexpected local forms.

It can therefore be said that the reception of cybernetics in Poland took place in two fields independent of each other; in what is now referred to as STEM (science, technology, engineering and mathematics), where cybernetic methods were successfully introduced, and in the field of SHS (social and human sciences), where cybernetics sometimes inspired too-far reaching extrapolations under the pretext of seeking to overcome the specialization of science and to unify scientific methods. Commenting on these extrapolations, Sienkiewicz and Nowak point to 'the glaring examples of 'cybernetization' of the human and social sciences'.[21] Nevertheless, they suggest that the fascination about cybernetics might ultimately have triggered the development of many disciplines in the field of mathematics and engineering.

19   Jan Trąbka, *Mózg a świadomość* (The Brain and consciousness) (Kraków-Wrocław: Wydawnictwo Literackie, 1983).
20   As André Gorz famously put it after the fall of the Berlin Wall, commonly associated with the fall of the Eastern bloc, 'as a system, socialism is dead. As a movement and an organized political force, it is on its last legs. All the goals it once proclaimed are out of date. The social forces which bore it along are disappearing'. Gorz, *Capitalism, Socialism, Ecology*, trans. Chris Turner (London: Verso Books, 2012), 6.
21   Piotr Sienkiewicz and Jerzy S. Nowak, 'Sześćdziesiąt lat cybernetyki i polskiej informatyki' (Sixty years of cybernetics and polish computer science), *Zeszyty Naukowe Warszawskiej Wyższej Szkoły Informatyki* 3, no. 3 (2009): 13.

From the pre-cybernetic era to contemporary digital automata and beyond

Is there anything we can learn from the Polish (mis)understandings of cybernetics when addressing the question as formulated by Yuk Hui: How might the cybernetic movement contribute 'to the new form of thinking that is urgently needed to understand and reorient our digital earth'? Bronisław Trentowski, the Polish romantic and liberal philosopher who introduced the word cybernetics into the Polish language in 1843, and who developed a pre-cybernetic approach to cybernetics, can help with this task.

Born in 1809, Trentowski is known for his attempt to build a 'national philosophy'. He subscribes to the Polish messianist movement and to the struggle for the national independence from the period when the Polish territory was split between Prussia, the Habsburg monarchy and Russia.[22] Trentowski developed his messianist national philosophy through a contentious dialogue with German idealism, especially through a critical engagement with Hegel's speculative philosophy. He introduced the term *cybernetyka* ('cybernetics' in Polish) in the book with the translated title, *The relation of philosophy to cybernetics as the art of governing a nation*. In this book cybernetics is defined as 'a difficult art of governing the nation' and is intimately bound to philosophy.[23] Philosophy, Trentowski says, 'relates to cybernetics in the field of politics as much as philosophy relates to theology in the field of religion'.[24] Just like religion is the source for philosophy and theology, 'politics is the always fresh source for philosophy and cybernetics'.[25]

Trentowski borrowed the term *cybernetyka* from French physicist André-Marie Ampère, recognized as the founder of electro-dynamics, who used the neologism *cybernétique* ('cybernetics' in French) in 1834 in his classification of the sciences. By cybernetics, Ampère meant the art of government; he considered cybernetics as a part of his political

22   See the section 'Polish Messianism' in the Wikipedia entry
'History of philosophy in Poland', https://en.wikipedia.org/wiki/
History_of_philosophy_in_Poland#Polish_Messianism.
23   Bronisław Trentowski, *Stosunek polityki do cybernetyki, czyli sztuki rządzenia narodem* (The relation of philosophy to cybernetics as the art of governing a nation) (Poznań: Księgarnia Jana Konstantego Żupańskiego, 1843), 9, https://kpbc.umk.pl/dlibra/doccontent?id=258132.
24   Ibid., 194.
25   Ibid., 12.

theory. When Wiener used the term cybernetics in 1948, with reference to its Latin form, *gubernator* (the root of the English word 'governor')—he was unaware of the fact that it had been already used in that context.[26] In *The Human Use of Human Beings*, he says: 'I found later that the word had already been used by Ampère with reference to political science, and had been introduced in another context by a Polish scientist, both uses dating from the earlier part of the nineteenth century'.[27]

Trentowski takes over Ampère's idea that cybernetics is to a nation what strategy is to an army, and extends this thought within his own philosophical project. He builds his political philosophy on the distinction between radicalism and historicism. The radical stance translates into revolutionary methods and tends towards the deification of the human self in a world where human institutions—such as state, language, and religion—are subject to permanent change. By contrast, the historicist stance is based on belonging to a tradition; it rejects revolution and comes from the idea of a transcendent god.

Trentowski's reasoning is dialectical. He argues that there is a constant contradiction between these two stances and that their tension makes constant progress possible. Put simply, radicalism, as a thesis, represents a tendency towards the future and fosters new ideas, whereas historicism, as an antithesis, is the conservative force that counters the change. If historicism compels radicalism to give up new ideas that go too far, radicalism remains progressive because it compels historicism to give up the most obsolete ideas. Trentowski considers political philosophy in terms of a synthesis. The function of political philosophy would be to develop a critical look at the unilateralism related both to radicalism and historicism.

Neither a radicalist nor a historicist, Trentowski seems to suggest that it is necessary to manoeuvre between these two extremities depending upon a given situation.[28] It is precisely in this context that he introduces the term cybernetics, and discusses the relation between

26   Flo Conway and Jim Siegelman, *Dark Hero of the Information Age: In Search of Norbert Wiener, the Father of Cybernetics* (New York: Basic Books, 2005), e-book.

27   Norbert Wiener, *The Human Use of Human Beings: Cybernetics and Society* (London: Free Association Books, 1989), 15.

28   Distinguishing between tyranny, aristocracy, a republic and constitutional monarchy in relation to the question of political freedom, Trentowski advocates for the constitutional monarchy, where the ruler is not a tyrant but respects the people and is able to govern them, which amounts to dealing with all parties disputing each other.

cybernetics and philosophy. He uses the term 'cybernet', that is, 'a good ruler'. In his view, cybernetics refers to a practical action depending upon circumstances, whereas philosophy offers general principles. If philosophy tends to work out a synthesis on a theoretical and conceptual level—taking into account radicalism and historicism—cybernetics appears as something more pragmatic; it is supposed to manoeuvre within these two extremities as pertaining to real political conflicts. Because human reality is subject to perpetual change and constantly forms itself, to govern a nation means to act in a dynamic situation. This is why philosophy is necessary, Trentowski seems to suggest, as it offers concepts that make it possible to understand these dynamics. Discussing the function of cybernetics in relation to philosophy, Trentowski defines the cybernet as a 'birth attendant'; cybernetics assists the formation of the nation or, in more general terms, the formation of humanity. In a nutshell, cybernetics pragmatically helps to bring the best philosophical ideas to the political fore, whereas philosophy shows the space of possibilities and paves the way towards the future. This is not to say that philosophy prevails over cybernetics, because cybernetics is responsible for making real decisions here and now and, in this respect, is even more important than philosophy. However, it is still the task of philosophy to show the best way toward the future.

In this respect, Trentowski's conservative take on dialectics might be refreshing today, if we only put aside his penchant for constitutional monarchy, which does not seem to have much relevance today. His pre-cybernetic approach to cybernetics encourages us to reassess the political significance of cybernetics after cybernetics, when 'to govern' and 'to control' become interchangeable in a social reality potently shaped by digital automata (large language models, commonly referred to as artificial intelligence, or AI). These automata are no longer cybernetic, as they are based on the mechanisms of learning, rather than on the mechanisms of self-regulation. If Trentowski is right in saying that politics is 'the always fresh source'[29] for philosophy and cybernetics (as a difficult art of governing a nation), this means that the question about philosophy after artificial intelligence as a technology simulating cognitive processes will not let us progress far, until we reclaim the positive meaning of self-governance in relation to nations,

---

29   Trentowski, *Stosunek polityki*, 12.

territories, regions, groups and individuals, challenging the idea of 'autonomous' technology.

We lose the ability to think and act on our own if we do not know how to govern ourselves, and we lose this *knowledge* not because digital automata count much faster than we do, but because we do not know the rules of their algorithms as real autonomous and embodied subjects, but rather as abstract 'minds' considered the property of the physical wired brain processing information. If we selectively read Trentowski from the vantage point of the era of AI, whose builders and ideologues tell us that it is 'unstoppable',[30] the relation of philosophy to cybernetics would mean this: It is the task of philosophy to address the question of the subtle yet fundamentally political difference between automation and autonomy; it belongs to cybernetics to anticipate the moment when learning digital automata become ungovernable and to reverse or stop their development, instead of falling prey to the 'this is unstoppable' ideology.

'I am compelled to say that it is a very slight hope', Norbert Wiener said, responding to a common belief shared by his followers, who hoped that cybernetics was the way to better understand humans and society.[31] 'The devaluation of the human brain' bound to the industrial revolution has been going beyond the limits of what Wiener perhaps could imagine.[32] What is at stake here, however, is not the limits of imagination, but the condition of possibility of political life. This is why it is useful to step back from the current computational mania and to revisit the political meaning of cybernetics in the pre-cybernetic era, with a view to developing a political philosophy of the learning post-cybernetic digital automata, able to address the questions that too many contemporary AI philosophers do not touch with a ten-foot pole.

In this respect, Oskar Lange's forgotten attempt to put cybernetics and dialectical materialism together, still has a potential to highlight the political meaning of cybernetics. The intention is not to go back to the old discussion between the proponents of the planned economy and the market system, but rather, to question the limit beyond which

---

30   Sam Altman, 'Moore's Law for Everything', 16 March 2020, https://moores.
samaltman.com/.
31   Doug Hill, 'Foreword', in Norbert Wiener, *Cybernetics or Control and
Communication in the Animal and the Machine* (Cambridge, MA: The MIT Press, 2019), x.
32   Wiener, *Cybernetics*, 40.

computational technology becomes ungovernable. As Gotthard Günther pointed out: 'It is true that dialectic materialism has been used as a tool by one of the most powerful political movements in history but it is ludicrous to believe that it has been invented only to serve extraneous economic or social force'.[33] Socialist scientists and philosophers did not try to show that cybernetics complies with dialectical materialism only because ideological pressure made them do so. Even though this ideological pressure did exist, and in spite of Moscow's political shadow, they knew that the basic assumptions of dialectical materialism, which deals with non-formal problems, cannot be dismissed by any scientific statement coming from the formal sciences. This is because the theory of dialectics, as Günther has it, 'is [of] a higher logical order than any formal-mathematical logic a particular scientific discipline may apply'.[34] We should therefore ask, with a view to a cybernetics for the twenty-first century, how a reconsideration of the theory of dialectics might overcome the classic two-valued logic in logical positivism, which destroys the very notion of subjectivity and can pose a threat to human autonomy when applied to learning digital automata.

Note

This project has received funding from the European Commission as part of the H2020 MSCA-RISE programme under grant agreement No. 101007915. This project has received funding from the Polish state budget under the program 'International Co-Financed Projects'.

33   Günther, 'Cybernetics and Dialectic Materialism'.
34   Ibid.

Reference

Altman, Sam. 'Moore's Law for Everything'. On Sam Altman's website. 16
     March 2020. https://moores.samaltman.com/.
Bogusławski Stanisław, Henryk Greniewski and Jerzy Szapiro 'Dialogi
     o cybernetyce' (Dialogues on cybernetics). *Myśl filozoficzna*
     (Philosophical thought) 4 (1954): 158–212.
Gerovitch, Slava. *From Newspeak to Cyberspeak: A History of Soviet
     Cybernetics*. Cambridge, MA: The MIT Press, 2002.
Conway, Flo and Jim Siegelman. *Dark Hero of the Information Age: In
     Search of Norbert Wiener, the Father of Cybernetics*. New York:
     Basic Books, 2005.
Gorz, André. *Capitalism, Socialism, Ecology*. Translated by Chris Turner.
     London: Verso Books, 2012.
Günther, Gotthard. 'Cybernetics and the Dialectic Materialism of Marx
     and Lenin'. In *Computing in Russia: The History of Computer Devices
     and Information Technology Revealed*, edited by Georg Trogemann,
     Alexander Y. Nitussov and Wolfgang Ernst. Braunschweig: Vieweg
     Verlag, 2001.
Hill, Doug. 'Foreword', pp. ix–xix. In Norbert Wiener, *Cybernetics
     or Control and Communication in the Animal and the Machine*.
     Cambridge, MA: The MIT Press, 2019.
Kowalczyk, Edward. 'Cybernetyka filozofią współczesnej egzystencji'
     (Cybernetics as a philosophy of contemporary existence). *Postępy
     cybernetyki* (Progress in cybernetics) 1 (1978): 7–10.
Lange, Oskar. *Introduction to Economic Cybernetics*. Translated by Józef
     Stadler. Oxford: Pergamon Press, 1970.
Lem, Stanislaw. *Summa Technologiae*. Translated by Joanna Zylinska
     (Minneapolis: University of Minnesota Press, 2013.
Mazur, Marian. *Cybernetyczna teoria układów samodzielnych* (A cyber-
     netic theory of autonomous systems). Warsaw: Państwowy Instytut
     Wydawniczy, 1966.
———. *Cybernetyka a charakter* (Cybernetics and character). Warsaw:
     Państwowy Instytut Wydawniczy, 1976.
Pasquinelli, Matteo. 'How to Make a Class: Hayek's Neoliberalism
     and the Origins of Connectionism'. *Qui parle* 30, no. 1 (2021). doi
     10.1215/10418385-8955836.

Peters, Benjamin. *How Not to Network a Nation: The Uneasy History of the Soviet Internet*. Cambridge, MA: The MIT Press, 2016.

Rose, John, ed. *Proceedings of the First International Congress of Cybernetics*. London: Gordon & Breach, 1969.

Sienkiewicz, Piotr, and Jerzy S. Nowak. 'Sześćdziesiąt lat cybernetyki i polskiej informatyki' (Sixty years of cybernetics and polish computer science). *Zeszyty Naukowe Warszawskiej Wyższej Szkoły Informatyki* (Scientific Notebooks of Warsaw School of Computer Science) 3, no. 3 (2009): 9–24.

Supiot, Alain. *The Spirit of Philadelphia: Social Justice Against the Total Market*. Translated by Saskia Brown. London: Verso, 2012.

Trentowski, Bronisław. *Stosunek polityki do cybernetyki, czyli sztuki rządzenia narodem* (The relation of philosophy to cybernetics as the art of governing a nation). Poznań: Księgarnia Jana Konstantego Żupańskiego, 1843. https://kpbc.umk.pl/dlibra/doccontent?id=258132.

Trąbka, Jan. *Mózg a świadomość* (Brain and consciousness). Kraków: Wydawnictwo Literackie, 1983.

Wiener, Norbert. *Cybernetics or Control and Communication in the Animal and the Machine*. Cambridge, MA: The MIT Press, 2019.

———. *The Human Use of Human Beings: Cybernetics and Society*. London: Free Association Books, 1989.

Young, John F. 'Machine Intelligence'. *Nature* 230 (16 March 1971): 260–61.

Zylinska, Joanna. 'Translator's Introduction', pp. xi–xxi. In Stanislaw Lem, *Summa Technologiae*. Minneapolis: University of Minnesota Press, 2013.

A Brief History of Chinese Cybernetics

Dylan Levi King

To open a Chinese-language work on urban management or artificial-intelligence-augmented planning is to encounter a cybernetic world that is both familiar and unfamiliar. The transliterated names of American and European theorists and thinkers will soon become recognizable, but they will sit alongside names—Chinese, of course, but also foreign figures—mostly unknown outside of the Chinese-speaking world, as well as concepts that do not have an obvious correlative in translation. This world is not often represented in English-language accounts of cybernetics.

Beginning from the foundation of the American scientists and mathematicians who were involved in the wartime establishment and post-war promotion of the field,[1] and continuing through the transdisciplinary fragmentation of the 1960s and 1970s, popular histories of cybernetics may have room for experiments beyond the industrialized West, but, despite Chinese engagement with cybernetics in theory and practice since the 1950s, these works do not offer serious treatments of Chinese cybernetics.[2] Chinese experiments with and applications of cybernetics seem to represent a scholarly lacuna in English. Since cybernetics has been embedded so deeply in Chinese popular, scientific, and political thought, scholarly work on other topics has

1   Yehuda Rav, 'Perspectives on the History of the Cybernetics Movement: The Path to Current Research Through the Contributions of Norbert Wiener, Warren McCulloch, and John von Neumann'. *Cybernetics and Systems* 33, no. 8 (2002): 779–804, is typical of histories of the field in starting with Norbert Wiener (1894–1964), since he coined the term 'cybernetics'. The other key figures are Warren McCulloch (1898–1969), pioneer of neural modeling, mathematician John von Neumann (1903–1957), and Claude Shannon (1916–2001), the theorist who gave us what we now call information theory (he is kept out of the title of the article but given equal standing in the text).

2   Ronald R. Kline's *The Cybernetics Moment, or Why We Call Our Age the Information Age* (Baltimore: Johns Hopkins University Press, 2017), for example, mentions cybernetic experiments in the Soviet Union and Chile, but China is only referred to in passing as a Cold War rival of the United States. The same is true for Thomas Rid's *Rise of the Machines: A Cybernetic History*. (New York: W.W. Norton & Company, 2017). These are popular works on the subject, not necessarily pitched at an academic readership, but there is little scholarly work to fill the gap.

touched on the expanded uses of control theory,[3] but there are few accounts of Chinese cybernetics that spread across disciplines and time periods.[4]

This begs the question: Is there something called 'Chinese cybernetics', a discrete technical practice, or should we understand it as merely a department of Western cybernetic thought? To make a pitch based solely on novel terminology and unfamiliar thinkers will not be enough to convince either the sceptic or those who might be open to considering the uniqueness of Chinese cybernetics. This essay is, rather than a definitive answer to the question, simply an invitation to go a few layers deeper; to scan through the recent history of cybernetic thought and consider the implications of its role in Chinese politics and culture (and also to think about the influence of Chinese politics and culture on cybernetic thought).

My account of Chinese cybernetics begins in familiar territory. The figure of Qian Xuesen, who laboured alongside his fellow cyberneticists in the American defence establishment, will be our guide. He will take us from early cybernetic experiments in rocket guidance and firing controls, back to China, where his involvement in the state scientific apparatus and close contact with the leadership of the Communist Party of China reveals the cybernetic basis of events as diverse as the Great Leap Forward, the management of marketization during the Reform and Opening, the 1983 Strike Hard Campaign, and the introduction of restrictive family planning policy.

Unwrapping Qian's theoretical contributions to cybernetics in the form of systems engineering, metasynthetic wisdom, and open, complex, giant systems, provides an entry point to unfold what seems to be a distinctly Chinese form of cybernetic thought and conception of cybernetics. Qian's detour into parapsychology is sometimes dropped from other accounts of his life, perhaps out of a sense of

---

3   I am thinking here of books by Susan Greenhalgh and Xiao Liu. In *Just One Child: Science and Policy in Deng's China* (Berkeley: University of California Press: 2008), Greenhalgh introduces the idea of 'sinified cybernetics', which I am expanding on here, in the book's chapter on missile scientist and population control planner Song Jian. Xiao Liu's *Information Fantasies: Precarious Mediation in Postsocialist China* (Minneapolis, University of Minnesota Press, 2019) covers at length the adoption of information theory in the culture fever 'wenhuare' of the 1980s.

4   At present, the most ambitious and focused account of Chinese cybernetics can be found in Wang Hongzhe and Jiang Yuan, 'Seeking for a Cybernetic Socialism: Qian Xuesen and the Transformation of Information Politics in Socialist China', *CAC Editorial* 1 (2019): 127–53.

embarrassment, but it is included here as it provides important insights in to his later work. The account closes with the state's response to the COVID-19 pandemic, which offers an opportunity to see Chinese cybernetics in an advanced state. It also provides an opening to evaluate the successes and failures of Chinese cybernetics since the 1950s.

A Chinese Norbert Wiener?

Cybernetics in China does not begin or end with Qian Xuesen. There is a prehistory, of course, that includes Li Yurong, the brilliant mathematicians of Tsinghua, who welcomed Norbert Wiener to the country in 1936;[5] one could even count the engineers of clockwork devices in pre-modern China as part of this history. Qian, however, is a key figure, given that he was present at the wartime moment in American cybernetics and carried his version of that particular technical practice back to China.

Born in 1911, Qian was the son of a provincial official who took up a post in the government of the Republic of China. Qian went to the capital's top schools. His first love was locomotives, followed by an interest in aeroplanes. In 1935 he received a Boxer Indemnity Scholarship funded by the US government, and jumped at the chance to study aeronautical engineering. After a brief stint at MIT, he left for the West Coast to join Caltech's Guggenheim Aeronautical Laboratory and work under theoretician Theodore von Kármán.

Those who recall their time with Qian in Pasadena and Cambridge describe him as a genius. He rubbed shoulders with luminaries like Jack Parsons, who would fall to the occult, and Frank Malina, who would be lured away by utopian communism. Qian, meanwhile, cut a conventional figure. He held himself aloof from worldly affairs. He was an engineer; he built what he was asked to build, without too much concern for what uses it might be put to. He worked as diligently for Franklin Roosevelt and Harry Truman as he did—once the Americans ejected him—for Mao Zedong and Deng Xiaoping. In 1945, he met Wernher von Braun in Bavaria; they spoke about wind tunnels.[6] The only reason the US generals trusted a 'resident alien' to come along on the Nazi debrief

5   Wei Hongsen, 'Norbert Wiener at Qinghua University', in *Chinese Studies in the History and Philosophy of Science and Technology*, ed. Dainian Fan and Robert S. Cohen (Dordrecht: Springer, 2013), 447–51.
6   Iris Chang, *Thread of the Silkworm* (New York: Basic Books, 1999), 112.

was that he was disinterested, but not disloyal. In his five years working with the highest levels of military clearance, there was never even a rumour of espionage.

In 1949, the FBI checked up on Qian. Their job was to smear him as a communist, but they could not find much. With Caltech professors, finding a cause was usually easy enough; attendance at the wrong Young Democrats function or a favourable opinion of Stalin expressed to a friend would suffice. Qian, though, spent his free time at home with his wife and young son, and was not known for sharing political remarks of any sort. Caltech chemist Gustav Albrecht admitted in an FBI interview that he tried to sell his Chinese colleague on the Soviet worker's utopia, but recalled Qian reacting with a 'typical aloof oriental attitude'.[7]

His work with the government was itself a twist of fate. Within a year of Qian's arrival, late in 1936, the military and their contractors turned up at Caltech, answering the call to discreetly ensure the country was on a par with the German military. When war was declared, funding poured into Guggenheim Aeronautical Laboratory at the California Institute of Technology (GALCIT) from the military, and his work was deemed indispensable to the American war effort. Qian found himself among the scientists and strategists who had, in the final years of the war, worked on crafting military-industrial policy for future conflicts. He worked with von Kármán on an ambitious classified report for the Army Air Forces Scientific Advisory Group; titled *Toward New Horizons*, it extrapolated a radical vision of what aerial warfare might look like decades in the future. He had access to classified defence projects, a seat on the US Air Force Scientific Advisory Board, and a gig consulting on the Manhattan Project.

The agents tailing Qian as he meandered around Pasadena in his Buick could not have known much about this classified work. Their job was to rebalance the post-war political order; Hoover and McCarthy had begun rooting out suspected communists and their sympathizers. At Caltech, the investigation focused on Sidney Weinbaum, a member of the Jet Propulsion Laboratory. A Ukrainian Jew who had fled the Bolsheviks in the 1920s, Weinbaum was accused of having concealed his membership of the Communist Party of the United States (CPUSA) to receive clearance for wartime defence contracts. Weinbaum and Frank Malina were comrades, and it was Malina who had introduced Qian

---

7   Federal Bureau of Investigation, 'Tsien Hsue-Shen' FOIPA No. 1126972-000, 26.

to Weinbaum.[8] It was the sort of connection McCarthy's agents were trained to sniff out.

After the FBI knocked on his door in the summer of 1950, Qian tendered his resignation to Caltech and made ready to return to China. Even his FBI files detailed that he was never a fellow traveller, but he could predict the treatment he would receive regardless. When the Immigration and Naturalization Service got wind that Qian was planning to leave, they detained him based on testimony from informants that he had joined CPUSA in 1938. Qian and his family were kept in legal limbo for five years. The Americans feared that Qian would carry his knowledge of ballistic missiles off to China or the Soviet Union, so they wanted to put him on ice until his knowledge became obsolete. But his knowledge of American defence technology—probably less sophisticated than that already possessed by the Soviet's People's Commissariat for Internal Affairs (NKVD)—was secondary to his abilities. During the years of quasi-house arrest, he began a dive into the novel field that would undergird his work in decades to come: cybernetics.

He had first been exposed to Wiener's theories of cybernetics in his aerospace work. It was how missiles were guided: a controller receives information about velocity and pitch, sends information to servomechanisms to make changes, and then receives updated information in a feedback loop. *Engineering Cybernetics*, a book Qian wrote during his detention and published in 1954, theorized control of complex and interrelated systems. His conception of engineering cybernetics, or systems engineering (*xitong gongcheng*) as it came to be known, was not merely an application of cybernetics to engineering, but an engineering science that subsumed control theory altogether.[9]

In the end, his limbo was resolved when the Americans traded Qian in a prisoner exchange in late 1955. One of the greatest minds of the US defence establishment was swapped for eleven pilots captured by the People's Liberation Army in Korea.

8   Chang, *Silkworm*, 82.
9   While this term, 'systems engineering', has some overlap with the engineering management field of systems engineering, it has come to mean something closer to what is referred to in English as 'systems cybernetics', which refers to the marriage of control theory, second-order cybernetics, systems theory, and information theory. In Angela Xiao Wu's look at communication theory in China ('Journalism via Systems Cybernetics, The Birth of the Chinese Communication Discipline and Post-Mao Press Reforms', *History of Media Studies* 2 (2022)), she suggests that the terms 'systems engineering' and 'systems cybernetics' can be used interchangeably.

Advising a nuclear China and the Great Leap Forward

Qian Xuesen's return to China was as unwittingly well-timed as his arrival at Caltech. The ideological reform movement that targeted previous returnees had died down. The Science Planning Commission of the State Council made use of his assistance in putting together a twelve-year programme for scientific development.[10] Qian knew that China's priority had to be nuclear weapons and a ballistic missile to deliver them. He told the leadership that they needed two bombs—the atomic bomb and the intercontinental ballistic missile—and one satellite. The Soviet Union had supported the construction of a reactor in Gansu to enrich uranium, and eventually gave tentative support for a weapons programme. They passed along rockets, as well as plans for their first-generation RDS-1 nuclear warhead.[11] Soviet engineers had used plans lifted by communist agents from the same Anglo-American programme that Qian had consulted on.[12] Soviet support soon dried up, however. The Second Taiwan Straits Crisis in 1958 rattled Nikita Khrushchev. With visions of Chairman Mao sending a Tupolev bomber equipped with a doomsday device over Taipei and triggering Armageddon, he ordered a pause on nuclear assistance.[13]

To take up the slack, the Chinese government sanctioned trial-and-error approaches. The efforts of Qian and his colleagues were successful; the first bomb went off in 1964. That was not yet enough. Two years later, they strapped a nuclear warhead to a Dongfeng-2 medium-range ballistic missile, launched it from a pad in Inner Mongolia, and struck a test site in Xinjiang, a testament to the skill of Chinese

10   Qian was nominally in charge of aeronautical work at the Institute of Mechanics, but his advisory work took precedence. Many of Qian's recommendations were contained in a text he submitted to the Science Planning Commission of the State Council, outlining proposals for building a national aerospace industry, but he consulted on other aspects, as outlined in Zhang Jiuchun and Zhang Jiuchun, 'Guihua kexue jishu, 1956–1957 nian kexue jishu fazhan yuanjing guihua de zhiding yu shishi' (Planning science and technology: the formulation and implementation of the 1956–1957 long-range plan for scientific and technological development), *Zhongguo kexueyuan yuankan* 34, no. 9 (2019): 983. His ideas for the plan went far beyond the modest suggestions of Chinese and Soviet experts. He had a direct hand in writing ballistic missiles, computers, semiconductor technology, wireless control systems, automation, and atomic energy into the plan; see He Zuoxiu, 'Qian Xuesen yu shi'er nian kexue guihua' (Qian Xuesen and the twelve-year programme for scientific development), *Kexue shibao* (Science times), 19 September 2011.
11   Shen and Xia, 'Between Aid and Restriction', 97.
12   Pondrom, *The Soviet Atomic Project*, 224.
13   Shen and Xia, 'Between Aid and Restriction', 110.

control theorists.[14] Qian's role in helping China develop the bomb is still widely celebrated, but concurrent events would serve to give him a black mark in the history books.

The Great Leap Forward was underway at the same time. Today, it is not a period typically associated with scientific progress, but at the time, the Leap was tied to the technological Marxist utopianism of the Twelve-year Plan, faith in the potential of central industrial planning, and, through Qian, cybernetic projects. The Great Leap Forward was based on two central projects: mass mobilization for industrial progress, and optimization of agricultural production. Its industrialization efforts proceeded from the idea that bottlenecks could be eliminated with mobilization. The Great Leap Forward's agricultural schemes, meanwhile, drew on scientific theories; Chinese agronomists devised 'deep ploughing', while experiments in animal husbandry were underwritten by Trofim Lysenko's genetic theories.[15]

In a 1958 article, Qian proposed a series of advances that he believed could be made in agriculture within the next ten years. The future, he said, would see artificial weather modification, industrial processes introduced to farming, biomass fuel solving the energy shortages, a healthier diet via advances in algae farming, and a systemic understanding of solar energy boosting agricultural productivity.[16] The article closed with a diagram drawing on Qian's ideas about systems engineering. He illustrated agriculture as a complex, holistic system, with solar energy connected through agriculture and industry to food, culture, and clothing. It is clear that Qian saw the Great Leap Forward as a potential revolution in the application of technology—including cybernetics and systems theory—to economic, social, and cultural problems.

The realities of the Great Leap Forward are now infamous. In the countryside, Lysenkoist schemes led to chronic soil infertility, and crops were occasionally left to rot on the field. Peasants starved on

14   Minor, 'China's Nuclear Development Program', 573.
15   For a discussion of those theories as deployed by Chinese agronomists, see Zhu Xianling, Ding Zhaojun and Hu Huakai. 'The Deep Plowing Movement of the "Great Leap Forward"'. In *Agricultural Reform and Rural Transformation in China since 1949*, edited by Thomas DuBois and Huaiyin Li, 74–100 (Leiden: Brill Academic, 2016)
16   Qian Xuesen's 1958 article for *Science for the Masses (Kexue dazhong)* is titled 'Looking ten years into the future—after the outline for development of agriculture is realized' ('Zhanwang shi nian—nongye fazhan gangyao shixian yihou'. The title of the article makes clear that these were predictions for the future, but this aspect was downplayed when it was reprinted.

collective farms. It is also obvious now that Qian, despite being occasionally pressed into catching flies and digging latrines, did not have access to a full picture of what was going on. In Beijing, Qian instead watched computers arriving from the Soviet Union and Chinese scientists taking their first steps toward reverse engineering these machines.[17] He even helped send mathematician Hua Luogeng to introduce critical path organizational techniques to factories and farms as part of a short-lived science of operations research and linear programming movement.[18] The interest in and application of operations research, points to another technical characteristic of the Great Leap Forward period, which was seeking solutions to practical issues in agriculture, or other aspects of state planning, through the marshalling of statistics in new computer systems. While this fell by the wayside during the Cultural Revolution,[19] the approach—seeking statistical rationality and rationales—appeared again in later systems engineering experiments.

It was the start of a pattern that would play out repeatedly throughout Qian's career in China; from his place at the centre, the political structure appeared to have a level of organization and capacity that simply did not play out in the rest of the country. Moreover, the main force guiding how scientific proposals were interpreted and carried out was not the voice of Qian or his colleagues, nor sophisticated cybernetic feedback loops, but Maoist political discipline. To Qian, the centralization of agricultural production did not mean cadres demanding unfeasible quotas, but a rational system to facilitate early experiments in fertilizer distribution, and in the use of advanced weather forecasting to direct nationwide crop planting. Qian found himself dragged into the propaganda effort when major newspapers printed a misleading excerpt from an article he had written about ten-year prospects for agricultural reform.[20] They selectively clipped a line stating that

17   Audette, 'Computer Technology in Communist China, 1956–1965', 657.
18   Fu, 'Yunchouxue zai Zhongguo de zaoqi chuanbo (1956–1965)' (The early spread of operations research in China (1956–1965)), 1. For a less technical discussion of operations research and linear programming during the Great Leap Forward, cf. Swetz, 'The 'Open-Door' Policy and the Reform of Mathematics Education', 463–65.
19   Hudeček, 'Hua Loo-Keng's Popularization of Mathematics and the Cultural Revolution', 88.
20   Wang, 'The Making of an Intellectual Hero', 358. For Chinese-language discussion of the controversy that still surrounds Qian and the Great Leap Forward see 'Qian Xuesen lao xiansheng ji buxu wenguoshifei, ye buxu daoqian' (Respected

productivity had not yet reached its possible 'ideal' peak and spun it into the ongoing campaign for cadres to be more ruthless in their enforcement of The Leap policies. As a result, he came to be forever associated in the minds of some with the excesses of the period.[21]

Within a year, the policies of The Leap began to be ignored by commune cadres, and then officially reversed by the central authorities. The operations research specialists went back to work in the defence industry. Officials abandoned schemes for the centralization of agricultural planning and cybernetic management. Control over agricultural policy was ceded to the pragmatists led by Liu Shaoqi and Deng Xiaoping. Their agricultural policy was one of decentralization, with farmers allowed to do what they liked once state quotas were filled—a policy not suited to central planning, cybernetic or otherwise. But the pragmatist programme did not last much longer than The Leap. Within a year of Liu and Deng returning to prominence, the Socialist Education Movement kicked into high gear. The pragmatists were tarred as 'right-deviationists'. Experimentation was out of fashion.

The importance of Qian to the defence programme and the support of Zhou Enlai sheltered him from the worst of it.[22] He managed to dodge the fate of criticism, struggle sessions, and hard labour met by many of his colleagues during the Cultural Revolution. When an armed struggle broke out between technicians and scientists at the Seventh Ministry of Machine Building—which served as the headquarters of the ballistic missile programme—he had the luxury of staying home.[23] Publicly, he went silent in these years. Qian's name appeared only sporadically in the newspapers, announcing political appointments or attached to advances in the space programme. In his collected writings there is a gap between a 1965 article on space exploration and a formulaic September 1976 memorial to Chairman Mao.[24]

teacher Qian Xuesen has no need to conceal his errors nor ask for forgiveness) and Li, 'Shuohua shangren' (Hurting people with his words by supporting the Great Leap Forward: another side of Qian Xuesen).

21   Becker, *Hungry Ghosts*, 77.
22   I. Chang, Thread of the Silkworm, 248.
23   Hua, 'Wenge zhong de Qian Xuesen', 12.
24   The first was the 1965 article 'Dui suowei "renlei lvxing de jixian" de yijian' (Opinions on the so-called limits of human travel) in a popular scientific magazine; the second was 'Zhongshen bu wang Mao zhuxi de qinqie jiaohui' (Always remember Chairman Mao's instructions), which appeared in *Renmin ribao* (People's daily).

Cybernetics and opening up

By the time Qian Xuesen returned to the public eye in the late 1970s, he had turned again to the promise of cybernetics. State cybernetics projects had never been possible before. Political instability pre-empted any attempts to overcome China's limited computing power; antagonism toward any ideas associated with the Soviet Union, the standard-bearer for socialist cybernetics, made the idea politically dangerous. By 1978, though, Deng had tamed the chaos.

Qian went to work spreading the gospel of systems engineering. He worked with his protegé, the Soviet-educated missile guidance genius Song Jian, on a revised edition of *Engineering Cybernetics*. The new release took into account developments since 1954 in information theory, control theory, systems theory, operations research, and management science. In a 1978 article for state media, Qian described systems engineering as the 'technology of organizational management' (*zuzhi guanli de jishu*).[25] In Qian's conception, systems engineering was a system that sat above applied science (*jishu kexue*), encompassing cybernetic theory, information theory, systems theory, and operational research, and foundational science (*jichu kexue*), built from systematics (*xitongxue*).[26] He touted it as a holistic and comprehensive method to chart and optimize the relationship of elements within a complex system. He advocated for systems engineering to regulate nationwide industrial and agricultural production.

His timing was impeccable. Deng Xiaoping and his loyalists were already laying the groundwork for the theoretical modifications that would be the dawn of a new age of scientism. In March of 1978, Deng proclaimed in a speech for the National Conference on Science that science and technology were among the primary productive forces and that the goal of his socialism was to develop those forces.[27] This was a major repudiation of the Maoist line upheld by the Gang of Four,

25   Qian, 'Zuzhi guanli de jishu—xitong gongcheng' (A technology for organizational management—systems engineering).
26   This was outlined in a 1986 speech for a seminar on systems engineering. See Qian, 'Wo dui xitongxue de renshi licheng' (My journey of understanding with systems theory).
27   M. Chang, 'The Thought of Deng Xiaoping', 381.

which held that the development of productive forces—labour, the machinery of production, and human expertise—was not desirable without changing the social structure created by production itself. If the economic relationships were undesirable, so was development itself, and any pragmatic argument in its favour made you a political enemy. The economic base of productive forces remained subordinate to the relations of production, which were themselves subordinate to the superstructure, made up of politics, law, culture, and scientific thought.

Deng reversed this to say that the productive forces, including scientific inquiry and technological progress, were what drove society. The productive forces could be developed without concern about the relations of production, and scientific progress could be liberated from the constraints of ideology. A series of books and articles followed, with theorists advancing the idea that science and technology could be considered philosophical systems that did not need to be subordinated to political theory.[28] Deng called on 'mental workers who serve socialism' to return to work and contribute to building the nation.[29]

28   The theoretical direction of these works often came from the Chinese Dialectics of Nature Research Association, proposed by Chinese Academy of Sciences members in 1977, then founded at the direction of Deng Xiaoping in 1978. A sinified dialectics of nature became the language with which to formulate a new philosophy of technology. The group relaunched *Newsletter of Dialectics of Nature* (Ziran bianzhengfa tongxun) as a forum for philosophical discussion of science and technology. The journal, which had not been published since 1966, did not abandon a Marxist materialist foundation but ventured a philosophy of technology that allowed, after Deng Xiaoping's ruling of it as a primary productive force, independence from—or even supremacy over—politics. The Chinese Dialectics of Nature Research Association's publication became a forum for thinkers like Yuan Deyu, who published his landmark 'Technology is an independent object of study' ('Jishu shi yige duli de yanjiu duixiang') in the journal in 1982. Throughout the early 1980s, other journals, conferences, and research associations were launched to host discussions of the philosophy of technology. Cybernetic thought infected many of these discussions, as Academy of Sciences members absorbed ideas from lectures given by Qian at conferences and the Central Party School between 1979 and 1982. For an overview of these works on the philosophy of technology, see Gao and Zou, 'Philosophy of Technology in China'. For Qian's role in the immediate post-1978 writing on the philosophy of technology, see Wei, 'Qian Xuesen goujian xitonglun de jiben shexiang' (Qian Xuesen's basic considerations in the construction of systems theory), and 'Fenxiang yi Qianxuesen zhidao women jinxing xitonglun yanjiu de ruogan wangshi' (Recalling some past events in Qian Xuesen's leadership in conducting systems research).
29   Deng, 'Zai quanguo kexue dahui kaimushi shang de jianghua' (Speech at the opening ceremony of the National Conference on Science).

Calculating the one-child policy

The depoliticized mood was right and Qian Xuesen had the theoretical tools, but finding the computers to run these projects on was still a problem. In his 1978 article, Qian concluded with a note that any attempts to actually implement systems engineering would require 'incredibly powerful computers'. Only a handful of computers in the country fit that description; several dated Soviet mainframe computers and indigenous derivatives,[30] IBM supercomputers illegally acquired by the People's Bank of China,[31] Control Data Corporation (CDC) mainframes purchased in the late 1970s through European middle-men, and—after the Sino-American détente—supercomputers purchased directly from Universal Automatic Computer (UNIVAC) and IBM.[32] The defence industry, and in particular the Seventh Ministry where ballistic missile guidance systems were designed, had both computers and cybernetics experts.

The number of prominent Chinese cyberneticists had grown by this time; researchers like Song Jian, Chen Hanfu, Guan Zhaozhi, Yang Jiachi, Li Guangyuan, Han Jingqing, and Guo Lei had kept pace with their foreign peers. They had managed to come up with parallel advances in ballistic missile guidance and fire-control systems. But their research was restricted to the military and the space programme, while Soviet, American, and British cyberneticists had been called on to apply their ideas to economic planning and organizational management.

1978 not only brought and end to Cultural Revolution strife and Maoist political discipline, and a rehabilitation of scientific expertise, but also sharp cuts to the defence budget. This meant that defence scientists suddenly had to justify their relevance. They found their cause in the prospect of cybernetics for planning social systems.

In late May of 1978, a delegation of Chinese cyberneticists—this included Yang Jiachi, Chen Hanfu, and Song Jian—visited Helsinki for the Seventh Triennial World Congress of the International Federation of Automatic Control.[33] It was the first time since 1964 that a Chinese delegation had attended, and they discovered what they had been missing out on.

30   Audette, 'Computer Technology in Communist China, 1956–1965', 660.
31   Wang Hongzhe, 'Manchang de dianzi geming' (The long electronic revolution: the computer and red China's technological governance, 1955–1984), 288.
32   Maier, 'Computer Science and Information Technology in the People's Republic of China', 374.
33   Greenhalgh, 'Missile Science, Population Science', 258.

At the congress Song Jian made the acquaintance of Huibert Kwakernaak, a Dutch cyberneticist that had fallen under the influence of the Club of Rome, a trans-national anti-natalist alliance founded by Italian industrialist Aurelio Peccei and British former Organisation for Economic Cooperation and Development (OECD) science policy advisor Alexander King. Kwakernaak's 1977 paper 'Application of Control Theory to Population Policy' makes reference to Edward Goldsmith's population alarmist and anti-industrialization tract from 1972, *A Blueprint for Survival*, as well as to *Mankind at the Turning Point: The Second Report to The Club of Rome* by Eduard Pestel and Mihajlo D. Mesarović.[34] Song Jian took note of the idea of combining cybernetics and population control.

Three decades of communism in China had not extinguished the anti-natalist tendency that had consumed the elite since the New Culture Movement at the close of the Qing Dynasty (1644–1911).[35] Pro-natalist policies only held sway for a few years in the 1950s before the party answered the calls of the All-China Women's Federation to provide contraception.[36] After 1978, population panic came back in full force, with a number of journals and conferences launched.[37] It seems clear from the way that Song Jian writes about population growth that he was scientifically convinced, but also viscerally disgusted by surplus humanity:

> In 1957, Mao Zedong said ironically: 'In terms of child births, human beings seem to be least capable of controlling themselves and there does exist a situation of anarchism...' ... In 1964, seven years after Mao's remarks, the second census showed an increase of another 100 million, making a total of 700 million. Soon the 'Cultural Revolution' came. By 1969, even before people could extricate themselves from chaos and agony, an increase

34   Kwakernaak, 'Application of Control Theory to Population Policy', 359, 377.
35   For an account of Republican Era (1912–1949) family planning in theory and practice, see Mirela David, 'Free Love, Marriage, and Eugenics' and 'Female Gynecologists and Their Birth Control Clinics'.
36   White, *China's Longest Campaign*, 23.
37   Population control thinking among scientists and other members of the elite went into hibernation in Maoist China. Ma Yinchu, who attempted in 1957 to introduce what he called *xin renkoulun* (new population theory) was attacked as a Malthusian and supporter of eugenics. He was rehabilitated in 1979, just before family planning policies were introduced.

of another 100 million people was recorded. By 1974, the total reached 900 million. During that time, people lived in confinement, yet they were completely free to indulge themselves in reproductive capability.[38]

He recalls from his 1978 visit that he was 'extremely excited' and 'determined to try' new cybernetic methods for population control. He did not have access to anything as sophisticated as the global simulations commissioned from MIT for *The Limits to Growth*, so he began by plotting population growth on Seventh Ministry computers using data pulled from state databases. He gathered cybernetics experts from within the Seventh Ministry and the larger military-industrial ecosystem and began applying ideas from Qian's systems engineering. Many of them came from the limited collection of cybernetic population scholarship he brought back from Helsinki, which included Kwakernaak's paper, as well as J. H. Pollard's *Mathematical Models for the Growth of Human Populations* and A.J. Coale's *The Growth and Structure of Human Populations: A Mathematical Investigation*.[39]

His work involved finding 'the feedback mechanism of [the] population system', its parameters, and how to achieve optimal control.[40] His conclusion, based on a model that took into account 'studies of natural resources, the level of socioeconomic development, living standards, and ecological equilibrium' was that the target population for China should be seven hundred million. The only way to get there within a decade was by restricting all women to a single child. Once he had a sound mathematical model, Song Jian, the cyberneticists, and Qian went to state planners with a plan to apply systems engineering to the problem of population growth. It was easy to sell those planners on the conclusions arrived at by their model.[41] The alternative would be runaway population numbers, impeding modernization and economic growth. China began to implement the one-child policy in 1980.

38   Song, 'Systems Science and China's Economic Reforms', 2.
39   These are among the works mentioned in Song Jian's early work on cybernetic population planning, including Song, 'Cong xiandai kexue kan renkou wenti', Song and Yu, 'On stability theory of population systems and critical fertility rates', and Song, Kong, and Yu, 'Population System Control'.
40   Song, Kong, and Yu, 'Population System Control', 12.
41   Greenhalgh, 'Missile Science, Population Science', 243.

What happened next was a chaotic social experiment that exposed just how hard it was to build a cybernetic political apparatus, especially one functioning on the level of a great power numbering hundreds of millions. As with The Leap, there was an extreme dichotomy between the level of institutional control that scientific planners assumed, as opposed to what the institutions were actually capable of. On the ground, enforcement varied widely between localities, with some jurisdictions following the rules to the letter and others comparatively lax. In some areas, women were forced into having abortions or to use of contraceptives like IUDs. Some women opted to give birth to 'black children'—unregistered, hidden, or adopted out—with many unable to gain the household registration (*hukou*) that would allow them access to schools, medical services, or good jobs.[42] They slipped through the cracks of a system that could not actually enforce its prerogatives, nor update effectively in response to feedback.

The violence and coercion needed to carry out the one-child policy might be enough to conclude that it was a failure, at least from a humanitarian point of view. But perhaps things look different from the perspective of the family planning officials in the landlocked central province of Shaanxi, or from that of a demographer, isolated in his office in Beijing. Did they see the number of births go down? Yes. The total fertility rate declined.[43] However, despite the population panic that seized Song Jian and state planners, China's total fertility rate had already peaked somewhere between ten and fifteen years prior.[44] It is hard to isolate how much of the decline was wrought by increasing urbanization, rising prosperity, and an enforced end to the communal lifestyles of the work unit and commune. The contributions of the one-child policy to keeping birth rates low were just one factor in a mess of statistical noise. Nevertheless, the party faithfully adhered to the one-child policy with only slight modifications for the next thirty-five years. They did so even as China's fertility rate rapidly declined, dropping

42   For two discussions of this problem, nearly three decades apart, see Jowett, 'China: The One, Two, Three, Four and more Child Policy', and Vortherms, 'China's Missing Children'.
43   Jiang and Liu, 'Low Fertility and Concurrent Birth Control Policy in China', 556.
44   Whyte et. al, 'Challenging Myths about China's One-Child Policy', 153. Given the lack of reliable demographic data for the 1960s and 1970s, a rough range is offered.

below replacement in 1990,[45] and continued to fall thereafter—on par with Asian neighbours with no equivalent policy.

Despite a ban on sex-selective abortions, this rule was often skirted.[46] Even with the addition to the census of the millions of children that went unregistered under the one-child policy, China was left with a massive gender disparity.[47] If this was systems engineering applied to governing a great power, it was a failure. Cybernetic regulation of a system requires accurate sensors. Regulating family planning required a large amount of accurate and comprehensive data, but, as the millions of unregistered births showed, the sensors were broken.

Likewise, effectors in the system were not reliable. In the case of the 'black children', mothers knew they could escape surveillance by simply giving birth in another jurisdiction, or perhaps paying a bribe. The existence of a child might be noted in the databases of some state organs but not others. Now that the population problem has changed to a lack of births, and the system's goal was to boost them, the ineffectiveness of the effectors is even more apparent. There are no known control signals to send into the system to coax fertility to increase. Later relaxations to the one-child policy had nothing to do with the changes in fertility rate, but were the result of particular groups or regions demanding leniency.[48] All this only played out in the decades after the proposals of Song and his colleagues had been adopted; in the meantime, the cyberneticists were expanding their reach ever further.

Systems engineering and reform

Soon after his political victory with the one-child policy, Song Jian was called on to apply his systems engineering expertise to the task of reforming state price controls. Even as China's economy opened up, the prices of over a hundred products and commodities were not allowed to float, but had their price set by the state. His team, made up of some of the same cyberneticists from the population scheme, established a

45   Ibid, 146.
46   Hesketh, Li, and Zhu, 'The Consequences of Son Preference and Sex-Selective Abortion in China and Other Asian Countries', 1374.
47   Shi and Kennedy, 'Delayed Registration and Identifying the 'Missing Girls' in China', 3.
48   Short and Zhai, 'Looking Locally at China's One-Child Policy', 375; Liu, 'The Quality–Quantity Trade-Off', 568.

model for the gradual relaxation of that control. Prices for more than two hundred items in forty-five categories were fed into a model:

> 114 equations, among them 19 equations in time series of dynamics, 43 for state description, and 52 for equilibrium. There are defined 142 structural parameters, including 43 endogenous and 20 exogenous variables and three types of policy control variables: purchasing and retailing prices, rate of wage increases, and taxation. The interdependent relationships among different variables constitute a large-scale dynamic system. Having reached stable operation, the system now is permanently resident in a large computer database and ready for running at any time.[49]

Song Jian called for more. In a landmark 1984 article in *People's Daily*, 'Systems engineering and the new technology revolution' (*Xitong gongcheng he xin jishu geming*), he laid out a vision for systems engineering to take the place of all decision-making processes.[50] In the ideal scenario, the government would create a central authority to manage the entire cybernetic apparatus and train specialized technicians to staff it. The leadership was open to these ideas. Song Jian was steadily promoted. In 1985, he was put in charge of the State Science and Technology Commission and was appointed to the State Council a year later.

Cybernetic ideas began to spread to an increasingly wide audience. The reformist think tanks developed by Politburo Standing Committee members Hu Yaobang and Zhao Ziyang promoted systems engineering too. Even before Song Jian's price control modelling, He Weiling, a member of the influential China Rural Development Issues Research Group, started publishing works calling for cybernetic thought as a way to revamp state planning and make it compatible with private markets.[51] He co-authored two books on the topic with Deng Yingtao, son of the reform skeptic Deng Liqun: *Jingji kongzhilun*

49   Song, 'Systems Science and China's Economic Reforms', 1–7.
50   Song, 'Xitong gongcheng he xin jishu geming' (Systems engineering and the new technology revolution), 5.
51   Gu, 'Cultural Intellectuals and the Politics of the Cultural Public Space in Communist China (1979–1989)', 404.

(Economic cybernetics) and *Dongtai jingji xitong de tiaojie yu bianhua* (The adjustment and evolution of dynamic economic systems).

Jin Guantao, affiliated with the *Journal of Dialectics of Nature*, had a surprise hit with *Kongzhilun yu kexue fangfalun* (Cybernetics and scientific methodology), co-authored with cyberneticist Hua Guofan in 1983, introducing cybernetics to a popular audience, and inviting contemplation of methodological implications that he would make use of in a work published a year later, with his wife, Liu Qingfeng: *Xingsheng yu weiji—lun Zhongguo fengjian shehui de chao wending jiegou* (Prosperity and crisis: on the ultrastable structure of Chinese feudal society). This book applied systems engineering and computer modelling to Chinese history and was widely read among intellectuals.[52] Jin's methods and his conclusion—a conception of China as an 'ultrastable system—spread to the popular press and helped spark a 'three theories'—information theory, systems theory, control theory or cybernetics—fever among the Chinese intellectual elite and consumers of middlebrow popular science magazines.[53]

Apart from population planning and price controls, the most consequential early adoption of systems engineering turned out to be within the Public Security Bureau (PSB). Through the late 1970s and early 1980s, there were widespread concerns that urban crime in the wake of Reform and Opening had made the cities less safe.[54] The PSB began to establish what they called 'comprehensive management of public security'.[55] This was an idea fortified with ideas from Qian's own conception of the more general social systems engineering (*shehui xitong gongcheng*) and the more specific legal systems engineering (*fazhi xitong gongcheng*), essentially applying his ideas on systems engineering to law enforcement.[56]

52   '*He shang* and the plateau of ultrastability', 6.
53   Wang and Jiang, 'Seeking for a Cybernetic Socialism', 150; Liu, 'Ershi shiji Zhongguo kexuezhuyi de liang ci xingqi' (The two rises of scientism in China), 44.
54   According to a PSB study, panic about street crime was almost unanimous in urban centers. For reporting on PSB polls see Ge, *Di-er deng gongmin: gongheguo di-yi ci yanda* (Second-class citizen: the Republic's first strike hard campaign), 15, and Tanner, 'State Coercion and the Balance of Awe', 97.
55   Hoffman, 'Programming China', 6.
56   For an account of legal systems engineering in theory and practice, see Xiong, 'Fazhi xitong gongcheng yu shehui xitong gongcheng' (Legal systems engineering and social systems engineering).

The PSB began experimenting with systems engineering methodology in the 1983 Strike Hard (*yanda*) campaign, launched to counter a wave of street crime and gangsterism.[57] A beat cop in Beijing's Chaoyang District could feed information about sources of social disorder back to his station, where the chief could organize a pre-emptive strike or launch a deterrence campaign.[58] That information—names of offenders still at large, possible accomplices, intelligence on the methods used by criminal elements—could be sent further up the PSB chain of command, then distributed back again. The mission statement of the Strike Hard campaign lays it out like this:

> The practical experience of recent years proves that only through organization on multiple fronts, a concerted policy of executing legal measures in a manner that is 'hard, fast, and sweeping', and unforgivingly striking against criminal elements can we deter crime, educate and save young people that have lost their way, and better carry out comprehensive management of public security. … We must take a sweeping approach to rounding up criminal elements that have not yet made themselves known, as well as criminals that have already offended.[59]

The chaotic Tiananmen Square protests of 1989 helped to spur massive investment and collaboration with multinational firms to equip the fragmented police system with computer network technology. By 1994, before widespread consumer access to the internet, the PSB started to be knit together through what would become known after 1998 as the Golden Shield project (*jindun gongcheng*), which had access to telecommunications data, customs records, and tax information through rudimentary networked government programmes.[60]

---

57   The logic of various forms of 'comprehensive management' (*zonghe zhili*) is explained in Yan, ''Yanda' xingshi zhengce de lixing shendu' (A rational review of 'strike hard' on crime policy).

58   Tanner, 'State Coercion and the Balance of Awe', 97; Wong, *Police Reform in China*, 98; Trevaskes, 'Severe and Swift Justice in China', 24.

59   Zhong-gong zhongyang, 2011.

60   Wong, Police Reform in China, 273; Tai, 'Casting the Ubiquitous Net of Information Control', 240.

The present-day programme of advanced information technology, artificial intelligence, multiple surveillance networks, and big data integration has many sources, not all of them indigenous. But the debt owed to Qian's theories of legal systems engineering is acknowledged by thinkers in the field.

A detour into the metaphysical

As he entered his eighties, Qian Xuesen embarked on a period of theorization that created the foundation for the next generation—the present generation—of systems cybernetics in China. He proposed a complete reorganization of human thought that managed to integrate extrasensory perception, an alternative scientific method, and a cybernetic theory of everything.

In the late 1980s, Qian had already organized information theory, systems theory and control theory under systems engineering. He proposed a more general classification of science and technology into a dozen departments, including mathematics, systems science, the arts, and somatic science. Each department was linked to the foundation layer of Marxist philosophy through bridges; social science, systems science, and cognitive science, for example, were linked to Marxism through, respectively, historical materialism, systems research, and epistemology. Each department could also be classified by theoretical foundation, technical basis, and applied technology.[61] This was an attempt to break out of scientific reductionism by bringing the social sciences and natural sciences together. Qian also included within his reorganization space for somatic science (*renti kexue*)—more directly translated as 'human body' science—which included paranormal phenomena like extrasensory perception and telekinesis.[62] Qian's detour into metaphysical investigation is crucial to his thought in the 1980s and 1990s, but, like his contributions to the Great Leap Forward, were usually elided or misunderstood.

The final years of the Cultural Revolution saw the official rehabilitation of traditional Chinese medicine and the emergence of folk healers promoting exceptional abilities in *qigong*, a method of cultivating,

61   Qian, 'Wo dui xitongxue de renshi licheng' (My journey of understanding with systems theory).
62   Qian, Yu, and Dai, 'A New Discipline of Science', 5.

managing, and projecting *qi*, or vital force. During Reform and Opening the tension between these pseudoscientific phenomena and the new scientism had to be resolved—and it was Qian and scientists at the Institute of Mechanics that led the way. As early as 1978, *qigong* masters were invited to the institute to test what was going on physically when they cast their blasts of *qi*. In 1979, Qian took notice of a story circulating in the national media about a boy in Sichuan that could hold an envelope up to his ear and read letters written on a card inside, and began backing experiments with what was called 'extraordinary function' (*teyi gongneng*).[63] From his position within the scientific establishment, particularly his posts at the National Association for Science and Technology and Commission for Science, Technology and Industry for National Defence, Qian enthusiastically promoted research into somatic science.[64]

Qian's interest in the extraordinary abilities of *qigong* became slightly suspect within China after the vicious reaction in the early 1990s to the popular explosion of affiliated new religious movements, including Falun Gong, and their penetration into elite Party circles. A vigorous sceptic movement did not have much time for Qian's attempts to prove telepathy was real (in addition to those experiments, he also wrote frequently about UFOs). But he was not alone; the 1980s saw many attempts to connect advances in quantum theory with the paranormal, as Qian and other somatic science researchers did, and his interest in telepathy and telekinesis was shared by the CIA and Sony's parapsychology-focused Extra Sensory Perception and Excitation Research (ESPER) Lab.

For American intelligence and Japanese researchers, as well as Qian, research into parapsychology was conducted for potential application in control systems. Extrasensory perception held promise as a means of human interface with digital, wireless information systems. In her chapter on Qian in *Information Fantasies*, Xiao Liu writes, 'The two strands [extrasensory perception and wireless technology] converged around the cybernetic logic of incorporating humans into the real-time information circuits'.[65]

63   Qian Xuesen's inquiries into these 'extraordinary functions' was controversial at the time and has remained a curiosity to later commentators. For an account of Qian and his paranormal investigations, see Zhang, 'Qian Xuesen ceng yi dangxing danbao, renti teyi gongneng shi zhende'.
64   Ownby, Falun Gong and the Future of China, 63–64.
65   Liu, Information Fantasies, 40.

The interest in somatic science and extraordinary functions is what pushed Qian to attempt to rewrite scientific thought in his model of qualitative-to-quantitative meta-synthesis. What he proposed was a method of synthesizing qualitative and quantitative observations. This was an attempt to unify the natural and social sciences, since his model of analysis included social phenomena, qualitative experience, and scientific method. In the context of somatic science, an observation—a man can, by applying touch, soften the metal stem of a spoon to the point that it can easily bend—is made based on subjective experience, which is then integrated with quantitative data (the quantitative data will not necessarily support or prove the qualitative observation). This subverted the scientific method of hypothesis, experimentation, analysis, and conclusion. Qian explained this idea in a 1993 paper co-authored with Yu Jingyuan of the Institute of Information and Control and Dai Ruwei of the Institute of Automation:

> Empirical hypotheses (judgment or conjecture) are put up which cannot be proved by rigorous scientific methods. ... Their accuracy can be checked on models built from empirical data and reference material, with hundreds and thousands of parameters. ... Through quantitative calculation and repeated collation, a conclusion is finally reached. This conclusion is the best to be found at this stage of knowledge of reality. This is quantitative knowledge arising from qualitative understanding.[66]

Qian came up with a model to implement this new method, which he called, in his own English translation, the 'Hall for Workshop on Meta-synthetic Engineering'. A proposition is fed into the model, then integrated with quantitative data, interdisciplinary expert opinion, and information analysis software or other artificial intelligence.[67] He termed the knowledge created through this qualitative-to-quantitative method

66   Qian, Yu, and Dai, 'A New Discipline of Science', 5.
67   Gu and Tang, 'Some Developments in the Studies of Meta-Synthesis System Approach', 173–74; Tang, Li, and Liu, 'State-of-The-Art Development of Complex Systems and Their Simulation Methods', 275–278; frequent Qian collaborator Dai Ruwei explains the idea at length (and the uses it can make of artificial and human intelligence) in ''Renji jiehe' de dacheng zhihui' (The great wisdom of 'human-machine' hybrids).

'meta-synthetic wisdom'—sometimes described as 'great wisdom', or *dacheng zhihui*.[68] This was the only knowledge capable of grasping what Qian called 'open, complex, giant systems'.

To understand all of these ideas together, Qian suggested the human body as an example. It is an 'open' system, since it exchanges energy, information, and material with the outside world; it is a 'complex' system because of the level of complexity found not only in its basic composition but also within its subsystems; and it is 'giant' because of the number of subsystems it contains. To return to the proposition of someone bending a spoon, meta-synthetic wisdom is produced through integrating quantitative physical data, contributions from experts in—taking Qian's own list—'physiology, psychology, Western medicine, traditional Chinese medicine, Qigong, psychokinesis, etc.', and analysis with information and computing technology.[69] Since the human body is an open system, the analysis must also take into account ideas from physics, political science, and ecology.

The Hall for Workshop on Meta-synthetic Engineering, meta-synthetic wisdom, and open, complex, giant systems are concepts invisible in English, except in the occasional machine-translated academic paper, but they have become as influential in Chinese high-tech social governance discourse as Qian's work from the 1970s and early 1980s.[70] The idea of synthesizing human and artificial intelligence lends itself particularly well to and informs thinking on smart cities, the 'urban brain', and AI- and surveillance-enabled urban management.[71]

What Qian's theories provide, beyond another take on systems cybernetics, is a way to integrate the immaterial within hard systems. Just as telekinesis can be integrated into a study of the human body, concepts like spiritual civilization can be reconciled with analysis of

68   For one of the few descriptions in English of this idea, see Liu, *Information Fantasies*, 83.
69   Qian, Yu, and Dai, 'A New Discipline of Science', 5.
70   For examples of these ideas in modern management science, see Guo, Liu, and Guo Qin, 'Research on the Hall for Workshop of Meta-Synthetic Engineering for Solution to Complicated Problem of Strategy Decision', and Tang, Li, and Liu, 'State-of-The-Art Development of Complex Systems and Their Simulation Methods'.
71   For an example of Qian's idea of *dacheng zhihui* applied to urban planning and smart cities, see Song, Zhu, and Tong, 'Qian Xuesen dacheng zhihui lilun shijiao xia de chuangxin 2.0 he zhihui chengshi' (Looking at Innovation 2.0 and smart cities from the perspective of Qian Xuesen's great wisdom).

social systems. Qian's theories reinforced the party's guiding ideological principles of the Three Represents, elevated to official ideology in 2002, the Scientific Outlook on Development, made official in 2007.

The balance of science and power

When the Chinese state made its turn to systems cybernetics a little more than four decades ago, they started from zero. Theoretical guidance for engineers plotting population trajectories on defence industry computers was minimal. The technological tools for the public security system's comprehensive management lagged behind the theory by ten or fifteen years. When Qian died in 2009, his theoretical future of virtual reality information interfaces and guidance by artificial intelligence-augmented meta-synthetic knowledge, was still mostly speculative.

Theory and technology have advanced. Investment in so-called fourth industrial revolution technologies for governance has increased. The re-centralization of state power since 2011 is made possible by, and is in service of, advances in big data, surveillance, and artificial intelligence. Unlike in Qian's time, research and development is not restricted to state institutions but can be devolved to tech giants. Firms like Alibaba are building the cybernetic future; Hikvision develops the technologies required for the social credit city. Advances in Tel Aviv, Toronto, or Tsukuba can be purchased or pirated, and marketing cybernetic governance tools tested in China is a profitable side-line.

Looking back across the last half century, though, the success of China's cyberneticists is unclear; at worst, the programmes were total failures with a massive human cost. The whole logic of cybernetics had been that the system would be able to update in response to the local information that policies and officials encountered. This simply did not happen.

Political attempts at cybernetic planning, both in China and elsewhere, have rarely overcome the problem of limited sensors and weak effectors. This was the case with the one-child policy. Obtaining granular nationwide fertility information is theoretically possible, but to pull it off would require mass mobilization and unanimous participation, or a technological solution so invasive and coercive that it would be easier to grow people in pods. Building in tolerance for unregistered births will necessarily be speculative. Once the numbers are out by millions, monitoring is no longer effective, and if the numbers start coming down rapidly—as the nationwide fertility rate did around 1997—only accurate sensing would allow for adjustment. The system suffered, too, from weak effectors. Distributed enforcement of the one-child policy across local governments and agencies led to uneven enforcement. The effect of the one-child policy on the birth rate was likely negligible, compared to other factors, like urbanization.

Now, as state planners see plummeting birth rates and hope to induce families to welcome up to three children, the same issues remain: it is possible to obtain information, although confirming its accuracy is difficult; and sending information back into the system to affect change is unreliable. The obsession with statistics and models looks similar to the Great Leap Forward and Song Jian's cybernetic family planning solutions. But unlike those periods, we are in a state where mobile internet technology and surveillance are ubiquitous, artificial intelligence has entered the scene, bureaucratic information sharing has improved, and there are mechanisms to integrate private with government data. This has not sharpened sensors so much as inundated them. Even with high-quality data and enormous computing power to sort through it all, there remains the problem of figuring out how to find the key signals, and what to do with them.

The summertime lockdown in Shanghai is the most obvious recent example of these failures. An investigation by city health officials concluded that the Omicron variant of the Coronavirus had been allowed to spread from a quarantine hotel in the Xujiahui Residential District because of negligence by health officials. By that point in the pandemic, a later investigation concluded, many staff members were only going through the motions. The virus was spread from asymptomatic travellers through the hotel's ventilation system, then made the jump to sanitation workers. It was not noticed until the standard testing regime in neighbouring districts identified a spike in cases. When the health system began picking up positives during their routine tests, phone screens across the city turned yellow and red, confining people to their residential compounds or homes. By the 5th of April, twenty-five million people in the city were under some form of lockdown.

Surveillance had been compromised by human negligence. Health code applications developed by Tencent, Alibaba Group, and a handful of other firms gave the government powerful tools to watch over the state of affairs, but they differ from contact tracing in most countries, in that they do not rely on a Bluetooth ping but pull data from a central server running algorithms to determine the likelihood of exposure to confirmed or suspected cases. When it was reliable, it only prompted the algorithm to respond according to its zero-Covid programming— people exposed to the virus, whatever their symptoms, social obligations, mental state, or access to the necessities of life, must be completely isolated. The sensors trained on a narrow slice of public health seemed to have given local authorities tunnel vision.

As food shortages and mass disapproval mounted, and the effects of paralyzing the third largest city in the world worked through into the national and global economy, the problem for authorities became how they might extricate themselves from the situation. In the end, they did not. As with the one-child policy, irrational and ineffective policies were left to drag on.

While every effort has been made since the beginning of Reform and Opening to isolate and elevate science and technology, and bend it to fit the political model, criticism of systems cybernetics has become nearly impossible. Science and technology provide legitimacy, and it has accrued not to the pilots at the controls of the vast machine, but to the engineers and navigators, and to the algorithms themselves.

Reference

Audette, Donald G. 'Computer Technology in Communist China, 1956-1965'. *Communications of the ACM 9*, no. 9 (September 1, 1966): 655–61. https://doi.org/10.1145/365813.365816.

Becker, Jasper. *Hungry Ghosts : Mao's Secret Famine*. New York: Henry Holt, 1998.

Chang, Iris. *Thread of the Silkworm*. New York: Basic Books, 1999.

Chang, Maria Hsia. 'The Thought of Deng Xiaoping'. *Communist and Post-Communist Studies* 29, no. 4 (1996): 377–94. https://doi.org/10.1016/s0967-067x(96)80022-5.

Coale, Ansley Johnson. *Growth and Structure of Human Populations: A Mathematical Investigation*. Princeton: Princeton University Press,1972.

Dai Ruwei. '"Renji jiehe" de dacheng zhihui' (The great wisdom of 'human-machine' hybrids). *Moshishibie yu rengongzhineng* (Pattern recognition and artificial intelligence) 7, no. 3 (1994): 181–90.

David, Mirela. 'Free Love, Marriage, and Eugenics: Global and Local Debates on Sex, Birth Control, Venereal Disease and Population in 1920s-1930s China'. Doctoral dissertation, New York University, 2014. https://www.proquest.com/openview/63919370a5ed17e85e841c-6b76eff8fa/1.

———. 'Female Gynecologists and Their Birth Control Clinics: Eugenics in Practice in 1920s–1930s China'. *Canadian Bulletin of Medical History* 35, no. 1 (2018): 32–62. https://doi.org/10.3138/cbmh.200-022017.

Deng Xiaoping. 'Zai quanguo kexue dahui kaimushi shang de jianghua' (Speech at the opening ceremony of the National Conference on Science). Zhongguo gaige xinxiku (Chinese reform database). 12 December 2003. http://www.reformdata.org/1978/0318/5158.shtml. The original speech was delivered on 18 March 1978.

Ding Liting. 'Qian Xuesen lao xiansheng ji buxu wenguoshifei, ye buxu daoqian' (Respected teacher Qian Xuesen has no need to conceal his errors or ask for forgiveness). *Aisixiang*, 3 March 2011. http://www.aisixiang.com/data/39328.html.

Federal Bureau of Investigation. 'Tsien Hsue-Shen'. FOIPA No. 1126972-000. https://archive.org/details/fbi-file-tsien-hsue-shen/FBIFile_Tsien_Part1/. Released under FOIPA on 15 November 2009.

Field, Stephen. '*He shang* and the plateau of ultrastability'. *Bulletin of Concerned Asian Scholars* 23, no. 3 (1991): 4–13. https://doi.org/10.1080/14672715.1991.10409710.

Fu Ge. 'Yunchouxue zai Zhongguo de zaoqi chuanbo (1956–1965)' (The early spread of operations research in China (1956–1965)). *Xibei daxue xuebao (ziran kexue ban)* (Journal of Xibei University (natural sciences edition)) 37 no. 5 (2007): 857–60.

Gao Dasheng and Zou Tsing. 'Philosophy of Technology in China'. In *Philosophy of Technology: Practical, Historical and Other Dimensions*, edited by Paul T. Durbin, 133–51. Dordrecht: Springer Dordrecht, 1989.

Ge Fei. *Di-er deng gongmin: gongheguo di-yi ci yanda* (Second-class citizen: the Republic's first strike hard campaign). Chengdu: Chengdu press, 1992.

Goldsmith, Edward and Robert Allen. *A Blueprint for Survival*. Bari: Laterza, 1972.

Greenhalgh, Susan. 'Missile Science, Population Science: The Origins of China's One-Child Policy'. *The China Quarterly* 182 (June 2005): 253–76. https://doi.org/10.1017/s0305741005000184.

———. *Just One Child: Science and Policy in Deng's China*. Berkeley: University Of California Press, 2008.

Gu, Edward X. 'Cultural Intellectuals and the Politics of the Cultural Public Space in Communist China (1979–1989): A Case Study of Three Intellectual Groups'. *The Journal of Asian Studies* 58, no. 2 (1999): 389–431. https://doi.org/10.2307/2659402.

Gu Jifa and Tang Xijin. 'Some Developments in the Studies of Meta-Synthesis System Approach'. *Journal of Systems Science and Systems Engineering* 12, no. 2 (2003): 171–89. https://doi.org/10.1007/s11518-006-0128-4.

Guo Jing, Liu Desheng and Guo Qin. 'Research on the Hall for Workshop of Meta-Synthetic Engineering for Solution to Complicated Problem of Strategy Decision'. *Applied Mechanics and Materials* 198–199 (2012): 586–90.

He Weiling and Ding Yingtao. *Jingji kongzhilun* (Economic cybernetics). Chengdu: Sichuan renmin chubanshe (Sichuan people's press), 1984.

———. *Dongtai jingji xitong de tiaojie yu bianhua* (The adjustment and evolution of dynamic economic systems). Chengdu: Sichuan people's press, 1985.

He Zuoxiu. 2011. 'Qian Xuesen yu shi'er nian kexue guihua' ('Qian Xuesen and the twelve-year programme for scientific development'). *Kexue shibao* (Science times). 19 September 2011. https://news.sciencenet.cn/htmlnews/2011/9/252518.shtm.

Hesketh, Therese, Li Lu and Zhu Wei Xing. 'The Consequences of Son Preference and Sex-Selective Abortion in China and Other Asian Countries'. *Canadian Medical Association Journal* 183, no. 12 (2011): 1374–77. https://doi.org/10.1503/cmaj.101368.

Hoffman, Samantha. 'Programming China: The Communist Party's autonomic approach to managing state security'. *Merics* website. 12 December 2017. https://merics.org/en/report/programming-china.

Hua Xinmin. 'Wenge zhong de Qian Xuesen'. *Ji yi* 3 (2008): 1-19.

Hudeček, Jiří. 'Hua Loo-Keng's Popularization of Mathematics and the Cultural Revolution'. *Endeavour* 41, no. 3 (2017): 85–93.

Huibert Kwakernaak. 'Application of Control Theory to Population Policy'. In *New Trends in System Analysis: International Symposium, Versailles, December 13-17, 1976*, edited by Alain Bensoussan, 357–78. Heidelberg: Springer Heidelberg, 1977.

Jowett, John A. 'China: The One, Two, Three, Four and more Child Policy'. *Focus* 41, no. 2 (1991): 32.

Jiang Quanbao and Liu Yixiao. 'Low Fertility and Concurrent Birth Control Policy in China'. *The History of the Family* 21, no. 4 (2016): 551–77. https://doi.org/10.1080/1081602x.2016.1213179.

Jin Guantao and Hua Guofan. *Kongzhilun yu kexue fangfalun* (Cybernetics and scientific methodology). Shanghai: Kexue puji chubanshe (Popular science press), 1983.

Jin Guantao and Liu Qingfeng. *Xingsheng yu weiji—lun Zhongguo fengjian shehui de chao wending jiegou* (Prosperity and crisis: on the ultrastable structure of Chinese feudal society). Changsha: Hunan renmin chubanshe (Hunan people's press), 1986.

Kline, Ronald R. *The Cybernetics Moment, or Why We Call Our Age the Information Age*. Baltimore: Johns Hopkins University Press, 2017.

Li Lu. 'Shuohua shangren, chuipeng Dayuejin, bu yiyang de Qian Xuesen' (Hurting people with his words by supporting the Great Leap Forward: Another side of Qian Xuesen). *Aisixiang*, 12 December, 2011. https://www.aisixiang.com/data/47506.html.

Liu Haoming. 'The Quality–Quantity Trade-Off: Evidence from the Relaxation of China's One-Child Policy'. *Journal of Population Economics* 27, no. 2 (2013): 565–602. https://doi.org/10.1007/s00148-013-0478-4.

Liu Qingfeng. 'Ershi shiji Zhongguo kexuezhuyi de liang ci xingqi' (The two rises of scientism in China). *Ershiyi shiji* (Twenty-first century) 4 (1991): 32–47.

Liu Xiao. *Information Fantasies: Precarious Mediation in Postsocialist China*. Minneapolis, MN: University of Minnesota Press, 2019.

Maier, John H. 'Computer Science and Information Technology in the People's Republic of China: The Emergence of Connectivity'. In *Advances in Computers*, edited by Marshall C. Yovits, 363–442. New York: Academic Press, 1988.

Mesarović, Mihajlo D. and Eduard Pestel. *Mankind at the Turning Point: The Second Report to the Club of Rome*. New York: Dutton, 1974.

Minor, Michael S. 'China's Nuclear Development Program'. *Asian Survey* 16, no. 6 (1976): 571–79. https://doi.org/10.2307/2643520.

Ownby, David. *Falun Gong and the Future of China*. Oxford: Oxford University Press, 2010.

Pollard, John Hurlstone. *Mathematical Models for the Growth of Human Populations*. Cambridge: Cambridge University Press, 1973.

Pondrom, Lee G. *The Soviet Atomic Project*. Singapore: World Scientific, 2012.

Qian Xuesen. 'Dui suowei "renlei lvxing de jixian" de yijian' (Opinions on the so-called limits of human travel). *Ziran bianzheng fa yanjiu tongxun* (Newsletter of dialectics of nature) 3, 1965.

———. 'Zhanwang shi nian—nongye fazhan gangyao shixian yihou' (Looking ten years into the future—after the outline for development of agriculture is realized). *Kexue dazhong* (Science for the masses), 1958.

———. 'Zhongshen bu wang Mao zhuxi de qinqie jiaohui' (Always remember Chairman Mao's instructions). *Renmin ribao* (People's Daily), 16 September 1976.

———. 'Wo dui xitongxue renshi de licheng' (My journey of understanding with systems theory). In *Xitong kexue jinzhan* (The progress of systems science), edited by Guo Lei, 2–17. Beijing: Kexue chubanshe

(Science publishing), 2017. This was a speech delivered on 7 January 1986 for a seminar on systems engineering.

———. 'Zuzhi guanli de jishu—xitong gongcheng' ('A technology for organizational management—systems engineering'). *Wenhuibao* (Wenhui daily), 27 September 1978.

Qian Xuesen, Yu Jingyuan and Dai Ru-wei. 'A New Discipline of Science: The Study of Open Complex Giant System and Its Methodology'. *Chinese Journal of Systems Engineering and Electronics* 4, no. 2 (1993): 2–12.

Rav, Yehuda. 'Perspectives on the History of the Cybernetics Movement: The Path to Current Research Through the Contributions of Norbert Wiener, Warren McCulloch, and John von Neumann'. *Cybernetics and Systems* 33, no. 8 (2002): 779–804. https://doi.org/10.1080/01969720290040830.

Rid, Thomas. *Rise of the Machines: A Cybernetic History*. New York: W.W. Norton & Company, 2017.

Shang Zhicong, Tian Xiteng and Yan Wenyu. 'The new civic epistemology of data proof: A case study of knowledge disputes in the formulation of China's fertility policy'. Cultures of Science 6, no. 1 (2023): 98–112. https://doi.org/10.1177/20966083231164845.

Shen Zhihua and Xia Yafeng. 'Between Aid and Restriction: The Soviet Union's Changing Policies on China's Nuclear Weapons Program, 1954–1960'. *Asian Perspective* 36, no. 1 (2012): 95–122. https://doi.org/10.1353/apr.2012.0003.

Shi Yaojiang and John James Kennedy. 'Delayed Registration and Identifying the "Missing Girls" in China'. *The China Quarterly* 228 (November 2016): 1–21. https://doi.org/10.1017/s0305741016001132.

Short, Susan E. and Zhai Fengying. 'Looking Locally at China's One-Child Policy'. *Studies in Family Planning* 29, no. 4 (1998): 373. https://doi.org/10.2307/172250.

Song Gang, Zhu Hui and Tong Yunhai. 'Qian Xuesen dacheng zhihui lilun shijiao xia de chuangxin 2.0 he zhihui chengshi' (Looking at Innovation 2.0 and smart cities from the perspective of Qian Xuesen's great wisdom). *Bangong zidonghua* (Office automation) 17 (2014): 7–13.

Song Jian. 'Cong xiandai kexue kan renkou wenti' ('Examining the population problem from the perspective of contemporary science'). *Guangming ribao* (Guangming daily), 3 October 1980.

———. 'Systems Science and China's Economic Reforms'. *IFAC Proceedings Volumes* 18, no. 9 (1985): 1–7.

———. 'Xitong gongcheng he xin jishu geming' (Systems engineering and the new technology revolution). *Renmin ribao* (People's Daily), 5 September 1984.

Song Jian and Yu Ching-Yuan. 'On stability theory of population systems and critical fertility rates'. *Mathematical Modelling* 2, no. 2 (1981): 109–121.

Song Jian, Kong Deyong and Yu Jingyuan. 'Population System Control'. *Mathematical and Computer Modelling* 11 (January 1988): 11–16. https://doi.org/10.1016/0895-7177(88)90443-8.

Swetz, Frank. 'The "Open-Door" Policy and the Reform of Mathematics Education in the People's Republic of China'. *Educational Studies in Mathematics* 8, no. 4 (1977): 461–78.

Tai, Zixu. 'Casting the Ubiquitous Net of Information Control: Internet Surveillance in China from Golden Shield to Green Dam'. In *ICTs for Mobile and Ubiquitous Urban Infrastructures: Surveillance, Locative Media and Global Network*, edited by Rodrigo Jose Firmino, Fabio Duarte, and Clovis Ultramari, 237–55. Hershey: Information Science Reference, 2011.

Tang Yiming, Li Lin and Liu Xiaoping. 'State-of-The-Art Development of Complex Systems and Their Simulation Methods'. *Complex System Modeling and Simulation* 1, no. 4 (2021): 271–90. https://doi.org/10.23919/csms.2021.0025.

Tanner, Murray Scot. 'State Coercion and the Balance of Awe: The 1983–1986 "Stern Blows" Anti-Crime Campaign'. *The China Journal* 44 (July 2000): 93–125. https://doi.org/10.2307/2667478.

Trevaskes, Susan. 'Severe and Swift Justice in China'. *The British Journal of Criminology* 47, no. 1 (2006): 23–41. https://doi.org/10.1093/bjc/azl032.

Vortherms, Samantha A. 'China's Missing Children: Political Barriers to Citizenship through the Household Registration System'. *The China Quarterly,* January 2019, 1–22. https://doi.org/10.1017/s0305741018001716.

Wang Hongzhe. 'Manchang de dianzi geming: jisuanji yu hongse Zhongguo de jishu zhengzhi, 1955–1984' (The long electronic revolution: the computer and red China's technological governance, 1955–1984). Doctoral dissertation, The Chinese University of Hong Kong, 2014.

Wang Hongzhe and Jiang Yuan. 'Seeking for a Cybernetic Socialism: Qian Xuesen and the Transformation of Information Politics in Socialist China'. *CAC Editorial* 1 (2019): 127–53.

White, Tyrene. *China's Longest Campaign: Birth Planning in the People's Republic, 1949–2005.* Ithaca, NY: Cornell University Press, 2019.

Whyte, Martin King, Wang Feng and Cai Yong. 'Challenging Myths about China's One-Child Policy'. *The China Journal* 74 (2015): 144–59. https://doi.org/10.1086/681664.

Wang Ning. 'The Making of an Intellectual Hero: Chinese Narratives of Qian Xuesen'. *The China Quarterly* 206 (June 2011): 352–71. https://doi.org/10.1017/s0305741011000300.

Wei Hongsen. 'Fenxiang yi Qian Xuesen zhidao women jinxing xitonglun yanjiu de ruogan wangshi—chentong daonian jing'ai de Qian lao' (Recalling some past events in Qian Xuesen's leadership in conducting systems research). Qinghua xiaoyou wang (Qinghua University alumni online), 9 November 2009. https://www.tsinghua.edu.cn/info/1856/74106.html.

———. 'Norbert Wiener at Qinghua University'. In *Chinese Studies in the History and Philosophy of Science and Technology*, edited by Dainian Fan and Robert S. Cohen, 447–51. Dordrecht: Springer Dordrecht, 2013.

———. 'Qian Xuesen goujian xitonglun de jiben shexiang' (Qian Xuesen's basic considerations in the construction of systems theory). *Xitong kexue xuebao* (Systems science journal) 21, no. 1 (2013): 1–8.

Wong, Kam C. *Police Reform in China*. Boca Raton: CRC Press, 2011.

Wu, Angela Xiao. 'Journalism via Systems Cybernetics: The Birth of the Chinese Communication Discipline and Post-Mao Press Reforms'. *History of Media Studies* 2 (2022). https://doi.org/10.32376/d895a0ea.182c7595.

Wu, Serena Weiying. 'Information Anxieties: Popular Imaginations of Information in Post-Mao China'. *Intercollegiate U.S.-China Journal* 2 (2022).

Xiong Jining. 'Fazhi xitong gongcheng yu shehui xitong gongcheng' (Legal systems engineering and social systems engineering). *Xitong gongcheng lilun yu shijian* (Systems engineering in theory and practice) 31, no. 1 (2011): 187–94.

Yan Li. "Yanda' xingshi zhengce de lixing shendu' (A rational review of 'strike hard' on crime policy). *Aisixiang*, 21 June 21 2012. https://www.aisixiang.com/data/54597.html.

Zhang Jian. 'Qian Xuesen ceng yi dangxing danbao, renti teyi gongneng shi zhende' (Qian Xuesen used the party spirit to affirm that paranormal abilities were real). Pengpai xinwen (The paper), 25 July 2015. https://www.thepaper.cn/newsDetail_forward_1356238.

Zhang Jiuchun and Zhang Baichun. 'Guihua kexue jishu: 1956–1957 nian kexue jishu fazhan yuanjing guihua de zhiding yu shishi' (Planning science and technology: the formulation and implementation of the 1956–1957 long-range plan for scientific and technological development). *Zhongguo kexueyuan yuankan* (Journal of the Chinese Academy of Science) 34, no. 9 (2019): 982–91.

Zhu Xianling, Ding Zhaojun and Hu Huakai. 'The Deep Plowing Movement of the "Great Leap Forward"'. In *Agricultural Reform and Rural Transformation in China since 1949*, edited by Thomas DuBois and Huaiyin Li, 74–100. Leiden: Brill Academic, 2016.

Why Did Cybernetics Disappear from Latin America? An Incomplete Timeline

David Maulén de los Reyes

Two principal changes of paradigm took place in cybernetic history; these were first-order cybernetics in the early 1940s, and second-order cybernetics in the 1970s.[1] The first paradigm to consider was formulated by Mexican neurologist Arturo Rosenblueth, working with the famous mathematician Norbert Wiener (Fig. 3) and the engineer Julian Bigelow. They collaborated in the United States in the 1930s and early 1940s. After Rosenblueth returned to Mexico in 1944 to a new research institution, the Department of Physiology of the National Institute of Cardiology (INC), he invited Wiener to join him. Between 1945 and 1949 he was visited for periods of research and exchange by his teacher

Fig. 3: Arturo Rosenblueth and Norbert Wiener in the National Cardiology Institute (Instituto Nacional de Cardiología), Mexico City, 1945. Archive National Cardiology Institute Library, Mexico.

1   First-order cybernetics arose in the 1940s and refers to the first-order prediction and design of behaviour and interaction in machines and living beings. This approach was directed by a specialist, or a group of specialists, combining the sciences of communication, administration and organization, neurology, civil engineering, and communication theory, among others. Second-order cybernetics, which was already mentioned in Arturo Rosenblueth, Norbert Wiener and Julian Bigelow's 'Behavior, Purpose and Teleology', *Philosophy of Science* 10, no. 1 (1943): 18–24, would become part of an important discussion by the late 1960s. It consists of a process that is no longer unidirectional, from a sender to a receiver. In second-order cybernetics the receiver is also part of the process design, which is a more heterarchical cybernetic concept.

Walter Cannon, and by the precursors of cybernetics; Walter Pitts, Oliver Selfridge and Norbert Wiener.

They began to talk about first-order cybernetics, especially in what Wiener called the 'first paper': 'Behavior, Purpose, Teleology' published in 1943.[2] Wiener followed this with *Cybernetics: Or Communication and Control in the Animal and the Machine* in 1948, written while he was visiting scholar at the Instituto Nacional de Cardiología de México (National Institute of Cardiology of Mexico). Wiener said: 'All I said in the book (in the basic principles) was in this paper first'. This is the first moment in the history of cybernetics in Latin America. The second moment came in the late 1960s, when the anthropologist Margaret Mead began to talk about the 'cybernetics of cybernetics', that is, second-order cybernetics. The practical experiences of British cybernetician Stafford Beer, in Chile in the 1970s, are a concrete presentation of the ideas of second-order cybernetics. In the 1970s Mead noted that these ideas had already been discussed thirty years earlier; but the concepts began to be implemented during the 1970s. This is the basic original structure from 1943 (Fig. 4).

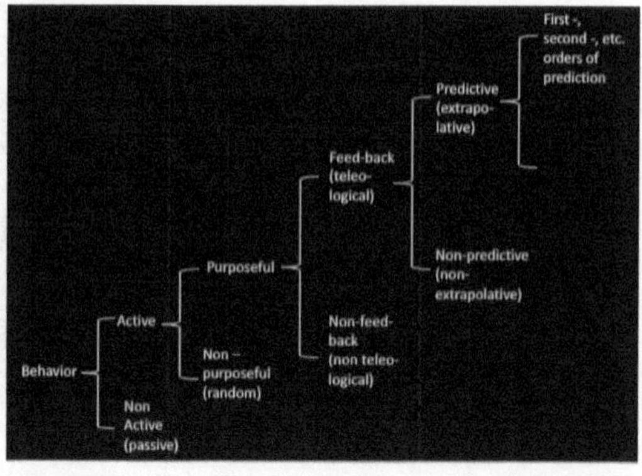

Fig. 4: First-order, second-order, and so on, of behaviour prediction explained by Arturo Rosenblueth, Norbert Wiener and Julian Bigelow in 'Behavior, Purpose, and Teleology', 1943. Diagram by the author.

A timeline for cybernetics in Latin America presents itself as an incomplete structure—a timeline in progress. In the present case, I will try to formulate a specific methodology for talking about the history of technology, design science and especially cybernetics in which the

2   Rosenblueth, Wiener and Bigelow, 'Behavior, Purpose and Teleology'.

equivalences between biological behaviour and technical physical behaviour are investigated from a multidisciplinary framework. This will
involve an interpretation of the sociology of symbolic production, the
retrospective vision of a timeline where it is possible to identify the
epistemologies that formulate or motivate the creation of interfaces
or devices. The device is a conceptual and practical mechanism. It is
neither only material, nor only conceptual, but both simultaneously:
it consists of the relationship between the technician and the person
who receives the inputs, the information. Sometimes, under special
circumstances, the devices or mechanisms transform into institutions,
or into social representational systems. Symbolic production would
change the behaviour of communities, but this is exceptional. One
example is when a paradigm shift occurs; first-order cybernetics in
the 1940s and second-order cybernetics in the 1970s changed human
behaviour, therefore cybernetics is a definition of behavioural design
into some kind of environment. In the 1940s, it was more unidirectional,
while in second-order cybernetics it was more heterarchical and less
centralized. This entire small localized process was located in the global process, and simultaneously in a dialogue with the global process,
with effects playing out back and forth between both sides.

'Why did cybernetics end in Latin America?' is an open question,
given that for many people cybernetics ended in the 1970s, when state
development models stopped predominating as a national government
model. One primary example, Cybersyn in Chile during the 1970s, was
the last step in this period of development by the State. When present-
ing this question to other countries, some stated that they continued
to try to work on cybernetics in the 1980s. This question is an open
research opportunity for anyone interested in writing a new history of
this field. The crossed timelines in the diagram are models of learning,
models of participation, and models of organization. These three elements will produce a fourth element: the action.

The first step, or first paradigm, is in the 1943 paper by Wiener,
Rosenblueth and Bigelow mentioned above, where they sketch out a
structure of behavioural design. In an interdisciplinary network and environment framework, they show different environmental design steps,
including the first (and second, and third) orders of behaviour prediction. The name 'first-order' arose from the fact that it was the first order of behaviour design, going unidirectionally from the technician to
the people. In second-order cybernetics, the people who receive this

design have also been part of the design formulation process, and they have made decisions on the result. This methodology, which has also received the name co-op design, is based on an evolved conception of feedback. However, second-order cybernetics only entered the history of cybernetics in a practical way during the late 1960s. The initial statement came from 'Behavior, Purpose, and Teleology'. The idea of feedback came from neurological studies. In 1942, while Rosenblueth was in the United States, his teacher sent him to give a lecture at the Josiah Macy Foundation[3] about feedback and circular causality. At this time, the Macy Conference did not yet exist as an institution of cybernetics in the United States, but the lecture was attended by, among others; Warren McCulloch, Margaret Mead, Gregory Bateson, and other important cyberneticians of the 1950s. Mead remembered and wrote about this thirty years later. As previously noted, though, Rosenblueth went to Mexico in the 1944 to work in a national public neurological research institution, on the condition that he could invite his teachers Walter Cannon and Norbert Wiener. Wiener lived part-time in Mexico in the 1940s while working at this institute. They continued discussing the same topics, leading to Wiener writing his famous book *Cybernetics: Or the Control of Communication in Animals and Machines*.[4] The Mexican publisher Enrique Freyman, residing in Paris at the time, spurred on publication by promising Wiener that he would publish the book upon completion through his publishing house Hermann (later they associated with The Technology Press, predecessor of MIT Press, and Wiley publishing house). At the same time, within this new framework in Mexico, Rosenblueth invited Ramón Alvarez-Buylla, a Spanish scientist who lived in Mexico and did neurological research in the USSR, to collaborate with them. Álvarez-Buylla was a disciple of the precursor of cybernetics Pyotr Anokhin, author of the theory of the functional system. They continued the research in Latin America. They conversed in French and English, but Rosenblueth insisted that they write in Spanish, in order to build a research environment in the region. They led the Department of Physiology of the Center for Research and

3   Regarding this historic juncture in 1942, I recommend reviewing Ruth Guzik's research, e.g.: 'Relaciones de un cientifico mexicano con el extranjero: El caso de Arturo Rosenblueth' (Relations of a Mexican scientist with foreigners: The example of Arthur Rosenbleuth), *RMIE* 14, no. 40 (2009): 43–67.
4   Norbert Wiener, *Cybernetics: Or Control and Communication in the Animal and the Machine* (Cambridge, MA: MIT Press, 1948).

Advanced Studies (CINVESTAV), an important neurological research institute since the 1960s, as it still is today.

At this point, we can begin to discuss devices. The design and management of behaviour within a state framework began with the president of Guatemala, Jacobo Arbenz, as far back as the early 1950s. Arbenz contracted an engineer from New Zealand, William Phillips, who invented a new computer that worked with water instead of electricity, named the Monetary National Income Analogue Computer (MONIAC), used in the Guatamalan National Central Bank. This system allowed users to visualize the future of the national economy on screens with a greater or lesser amount of water in glasses, and was one of the first experiments with the cybernetic control of a national economy.[5]

Another important part of the history of cybernetics in Latin America is related to the Hochschule Für Gestaltung (HfG, the School of Design) in Ulm, Germany, in the 1950s. It presented some similarities and several crucial differences with the Dessau Bauhaus (1926¬1932). The United States provided 50 per cent of the funding for HfG Ulm in the 1950s, on the condition that the director should not be German. The new director was Max Bill, a former Bauhaus student from Switzerland. Bill set out a new policy that 50 per cent of the students and 50 per cent of the teachers should not be German. The implementation of this decision had unpredictable and remarkable consequences. The change of this very important school in the 1950s and early 1960s had a strong impact on Latin America, India and Japan, when students returned from Ulm to their own countries and created design schools or institutional design production practices, adapting the ideas of the HfG Ulm to their own economic and cultural contexts. One of the first teachers at HfG Ulm was the philosopher Max Bense, director of the Information Department from 1954 to 1958. Bense was a theorist with his own interpretation of first-order cybernetics, which he imparted during his teaching career in HfG Ulm to a large number of Latin American students. The definition Bense gave to cybernetics at this time was derived from Charles Peirce's semiotic theory, from David Birkhoff's

5   After Arbenz nationalized natural resources and commodities and attempted a land reform, his government was interrupted by a military coup. I would like to thank Andrés Burbano for informing me of this case on centralized planning of the economy using a computer, twenty years before the Cybersyn economic predictions.

mathematical theory of aesthetics, from Claude Shannon's information theory, and from Wiener's ideas about first-order cybernetics. Bense even invited Wiener to the school as a guest lecturer in 1955. He worked only briefly in Ulm, and his classes on cybernetics were continued by Horst Rittel from 1958. Rittel is important because with these ideas, he began to talk about systemic design, and translated his ideas of cybernetics into the design process. After Rittel left HfG Ulm in 1963, the last teacher of cybernetics at the school was Abraham Moles.

After Bense moved on from HfG Ulm, he became fascinated with the development of the avant-garde in Brazil. He travelled to Brazil frequently in the early 1960s because he considered avant-garde neo-concrete art to be a kind of mathematical aesthetic theory. Subsequently, in 1966, one of these neo-concrete artists, Waldemar Cordeiro, took up Bense's ideas, and in 1970 began to do 'Arteônica', or electronic art, working with computers, without seeing them as mere instruments. On the contrary, he thought that information technology, as a social and cultural evolution of gestalt theory, was very important for the relationship between human environments and technology, which grew out of Bense's influence and the exchange with Brazilians in the 1960s. Some South American students at HfG Ulm in the 1950s included the Brazilian Alexander Wollner, who studied under Bense. In the 1960s Wollner used some of the Bense's ideas to Escola Superior de Desenho Industrial (ESDI), the famous design school in Rio de Janeiro. Another HfG Ulm student of this time was the Chilean Eduardo Vargas, who also studied under Bense and Rittel, and returned to Chile in 1960. Vargas used models of interactional design and the model of organization, which was taught in HfG Ulm particularly by Bill, applying them for designing self-construction housing co-operatives in the 1960s in the port of Valparaiso. This was a successful interpretation of co-op design, in which he was also influenced by the systemic approach of Christopher Alexander. In 1968, Vargas became the director of the Catholic University of Valparaíso TV channel (UCV TV). Perhaps the most famous case was the German designer Gui Bonsiepe. After studying in HfG Ulm in the 1950s, he became a teacher there during the 1960s. After HfG Ulm closed in 1968, Bonsiepe came to Chile with the help of the International Labor Organization (ILO) and the Import Substitution Program (ISI), under a United Nations (UN) contract, and worked at the National Development Corporation (Corporación de Fomento de la Producción de Chile, CORFO). The UN programmes bringing a strong influence to bear on the Third World to move their economies away from commodities and to focus on industrial technology. The work which Bonsiepe did at CORFO was very important for the well-known Cybersyn project (1971–73). Further influences included the already-mentioned Arteônica by Waldemar Cordeiro, as well as from Tomás Maldonado, an Argentinian teacher in HfG Ulm in the 1950s who became the rector there during the 1960s. They are influences that go in two directions, although the HfG Ulm is the one that influences in a more visible way, also, for example, the ideas of the concrete movement of Argentina and Brazil, influenced in their own way the pedagogy of Maldonado in the HfG Ulm, or in Bense's ideas.

Environment

The environment was an important element of cybernetics in the 1940s, but became even more significant in the 1960s. The word for environment in German, *Umwelt*, has different definitions. It is an important element in cybernetics where human beings, and the relationship between the human being and the different social, technological or cultural environments around them, are the main purpose. Technology is only an interface or device between human beings and environment, not a principal object. This concept of the environment has different roots. For example, Rosenblueth's lecture at the Macy Foundation in New York in 1942, emphasized the importance of technical biological and physical behaviour in the environment. The concept also appeared in the new curriculum of the Architecture School at the University of Chile in 1946. When they interpreted the Bauhaus Dessau curriculum of 1928–1930, they defined three concepts of the environment; technological, social, and natural. During the final period of the HfG Ulm, influenced by Jakob von Uexküll's Umwelt concept, efforts were made to change the HfG Ulm into an institute for environmental design research, ultimately to no avail. Following this episode, Maldonado wrote a book in 1971 about human beings and social changes concerning technology, published in Spanish in Argentina by a publisher created by Maldonado in the 1950s, Nueva Visión or NV (the New Vision).

Network

Argentina saw cybernetics develop through a process similar to that in Mexico. The principal figure in Argentine cybernetics of this period is Manuel Sadosky, who was an important mathematical and computing teacher in the 1950s and formed a group of scientists from various fields. He began to write about cybernetics in 1951. Following this phase, between 1955 and 1966 he began to research computing in the main public state university, the Universidad de Buenos Aires (UBA), with a cohort of scholars including Rolando García, Ernesto García Camarero, Pedro Zadunaisky, Sigfrido Mazza, Julián Aráos, Mario Gradowczyk, Oscar Maggiolo, Amilcar Herrera, Hugo Scolnik and Oscar Varsavsky. Together with Hernán Rodriguez Campoamor, Sadosky wrote *Psychology and Cybernetics*, published in Buenos Aires in 1958, raising a critique of the technozoism of the concept 'electronic brain'.[6] Technozoism is a philosophical position configured by those cyberneticists who support the existence of thinking, sensitive or emotional automatons or mechanisms.[7] This occurred almost simultaneously with Rosenblueth publishing a paper on the same topic, which is cited critically by Argentine authors. During this period in national universities in South America, including Chile and Argentina, the common process to study computing was to begin by doing classes within the universities, then go abroad to do research, followed by buying computers to bring to South America for research purposes. These actions led many participants to desire to produce such devices for themselves in the future. In 1961 work began at UBA with a famous computer imported from the UK and named Clementina. The enthusiasm for solving problems from public and social life, as well as private enterprise, through mathematical models, even led to the creation of programming that expanded the original capacity of the Ferranti Mercury or Clementina computer. One of the main objectives, in addition to education, was to create a national agency or national state company dedicated to computing. However, a military intervention in 1966 led to the work at UBA being closed down. At this juncture, the scholars decided that rather

---

6   Hernán Rodríguez Campoamor and Manuel Sadosky, *Psicología y cibernética* (Psychology and cybernetics) (Buenos Aires: Siglo XX, 1958).
7   Ibid.

than going to Europe or the United States, they would remain in South America. Some of the Sadosky cohort went to Chile, others went to Peru, and still others went to Venezuela and Brazil. Oscar Varsavsky left Argentina and ultimately taught at the Popular Participation Study Center (CENTRO) with scientists from Brazil in 1974. There Varsavsky, with the support of the United Nations Development Program (UNDP), could explain his Numex mathematical model, while Carlos Senna also taught the Viable System Model (VSM) used with Cybersyn in Chile.

Sadosky could not continue to work at the university after 1966, but he continued working as a private technician. He moved across the River Plate to the Department of Computing at the University of the Republic in Uruguay. Here we can see an example of this network. Amilcar Herrera came from the Sadosky cohort in Argentina to the National University of Chile, and edited a publication about the future of technology and society with different scholars from Latin America, followed by a return to Argentina in 1971. At this time, he did not go to Buenos Aires; rather, he came to the well-known semi-private Fundación Bariloche in the Andean resort city of the same name. Herrera was accompanied by a fellow Argentine scholar from the Sadosky's group, Hugo Scolnik, who collaborated with him on a very complex model for the future based on data processed by the computer center created in Bariloche. The model was called 'Latin American World Model' (Modelo Mundial Latinoamericano or MML). Scientists such as Graciela Chichilnisky participated in this approach. Decades later, beginning in 1997, she would promote the Kyoto protocol, extending the 1992 United Nations Framework Convention on Climate Change (UN-FCCC). The MML came from a critical answer to the model 'The Limits of Growth' formulated by scientists at the Massachusetts Institute of Technology (MIT), which stated that within forty to fifty years the earth could no longer support humanity with the same growth model as in the early 1970s. However, the Argentinian scientists and scholars at the Bariloche Foundation thought that the MIT model was incomplete and lacking in complexity, which led them to create the MML. It states: 'We answer North American computing with South American computing'. The fruit of their efforts was a model with four zones in the world and five main factors, which they considered more complex than the MIT model, and became very well known in Austria. The International Institute for Applied System Analysis (IIASA) Colloquium presented this model in 1974. It was translated into German, English and French, but after the Argentine military coup of 1976, the work of the Bariloche Foundation stopped. Despite this, in 1978 the UN invited the authors of the MML from Bariloche to formulate a new model for calculating basic needs. Figure 5 shows one of the models they did for the future of Globality in the early 1970s.

Fig. 5: Fundación Bariloche computing centre, and a visual representation of the Latin American World Model (MML) developed and disseminated between 1972 and 1976. Photos and diagram courtesy of Dr Hugo Scolnik.

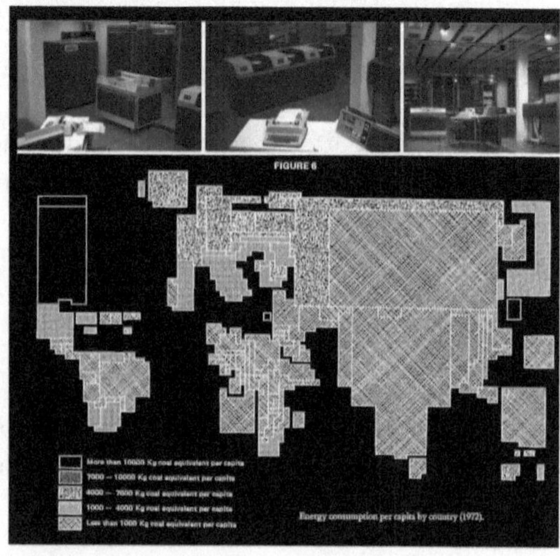

Second-order

To understand second-order cybernetics, especially in the 1960s or 1970s, we must understand its concept of heterarchy. The word 'cybernetics' was coined in 1947 by Arturo Rosenblueth and Norbert Wiener, and originally came from the Greek word 'κυβερνητική', around the fourth century BC, which is also the root of government, organization, management, and so on. In the 1960s, British cybernetician Stafford Beer used the word 'heterarchical', meaning a decentralized model wherein people who received the design can decide for themselves.

As a South American reference, we can see that in the Chilean context of the 1920s, the movement of the active school raised a concept of heterarchy similar to that of second-order cybernetics. To elaborate further, in the 1930s the same teachers from the active school movement made graphic visual designs in which they proposed public schools as the nodes of a system of social organization that would administer the territory in a decentralized and participatory manner. This approach highlights the importance of first having a type of decentralized epistemology, where decisions about the use of technology follow after achieving this epistemology. This knowledge was already clearly stated in Chile in 1936, several decades before Beer used the concept of heterarchy at CORFO in 1971. This epistemology from the active school with each part of the system can also make decisions for itself. Here is the heterarchical model (Fig. 6):

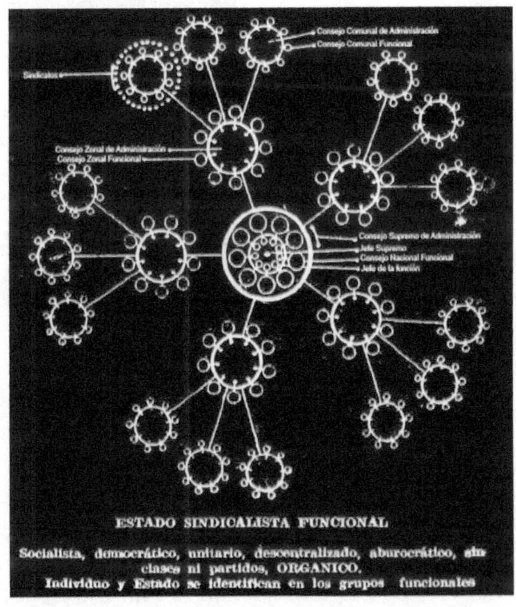

Fig. 6: The decentralized administration approach to educational reform of the active school in Chile in 1928, and its projection into the territory, is the first great reference for the local heterarchy. In 1936 the 'nerve group' in Curicó (Chile) published a visualization of these ideas. Diagram courtesy of Leonora Reyes Jedlicki.

After the end of World War II, there was a second great example before Beer worked in CORFO, when he discussed the VSM as an interpretation of second-order cybernetics. This model has three basic elements; human beings, nature and the social environment, and technology. During the 1940s at the new School of Architecture at the University of Chile, we can see the three factors in the new curriculum for design and architecture studies; human beings (H), nature (N), and materials (M). The material gives rise to technological devices, nature provides environmental concepts, and from the human being comes biology (Fig. 7).

Fig. 7: The human being, nature (the natural and social environment), and material (technology) were the three basic elements of the new curriculum of the School of Architecture, University of Chile, from 1946 to 1963. Redrawn by the author from the original, the handwritten version was published in the magazine *Arquitecturay Construcción*, Chile 11 (1947). The original image, drawn by Tibor Weiner, Abraham Schapira and Jorge Bruno González, was presented and explained by bio-architecture professor José Garciatello at the sixth Pan-American Congress of Architecture at the National University of Engineering (Universidad Nacional de Ingeniería, UNI) Lima, Perú in 1947.

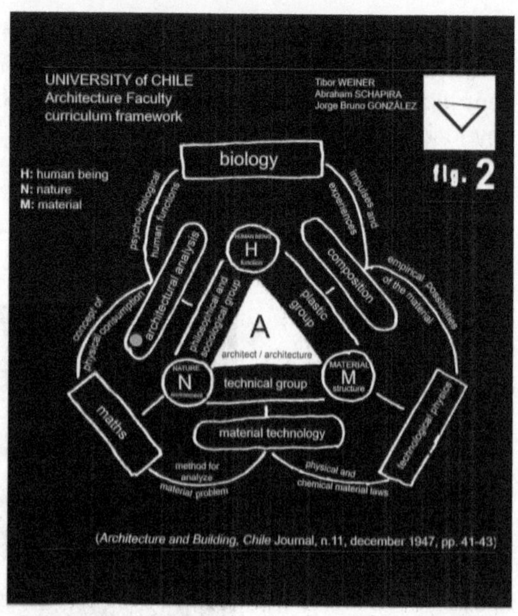

Since the 1940s, Chilean design students in the National Architectural School had to study biology for the design of architecture and urban planning, and also worked within a heterarchical model. They tried to change the institutional direction of common space design for planning during the 1950s and 1960s. This meant that once the cybernetic project under Beer actually began in the 1970s, there was already twenty years of experience within the national institution for public development with such ideas, which we can also call second-order cybernetics, or at least VSM. When considering the concept of environment in the architectural studies programme in the late 1940s, it is possible to recognize how they were discussing the concept of environment and nature, environment and technology, environment and human biology, psychology, community, and other factors, well over twenty years before the arrival of Beer in 1971. This concept was further developed in the 1950s with the notion of designing a city as a living system, which changed urban planning laws in the 1960s and created a framework for the next cybernetic work at the National Development Agency. An example is the bio-architecture studies from Chile in the 1940s, where housing is a cell in a biological system (Fig. 8).

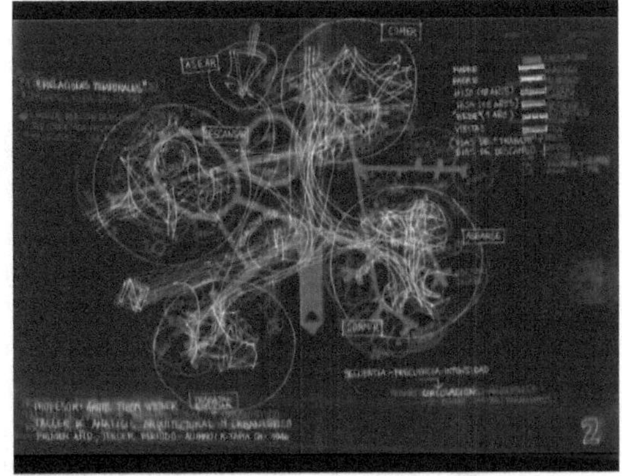

Fig. 8: Diagram of 'the basic molecule of inhabiting' within the concept of 'the city designed as a living organism'. Drawing by Ricardo Tapia-Chuaqui in Tibor Weiner's workshop, at the University of Chile in 1946. Image courtesy Tapia-Chuaqui/Hola family, Beatriz Mella and Alejandro Crispiani.

During the 1930s, when Rosenblueth was working with Wiener in the United States, he helped Latin American scholars. One such case was the Chilean Joaquin Luco, who studied with Wiener and Rosenblueth in 1937 and 1938, and upon returning to Chile in the 1950s founded the new Department of Neurological studies at Catholic University Medicine Faculty. The Chilean biology scholar Mario Luxoro was similar, since he studied electrophysiology and electron microscopy and got a PhD from MIT in 1957. Upon returning to Chile, Luxoro created a cellular physiology laboratory (Montemar) in 1965, the same year that he helped create the Faculty of Sciences at the University of Chile.

Francisco Varela, one of the co-authors of the autopoiesis theory of 1970, was a student strongly influenced by Luco at the Catholic University School of Medicine in 1964. He continued his studies at the new Faculty of Sciences at the University of Chile from 1965 to 1967, where he met Humberto Maturana and where he returned to in 1970 to become a professor after earning his PhD at Harvard.

During the same timeframe, to continue considering the impact of a possible VSM on architecture and state-led urban planning, the model of the city designing system in the 1960s in Chile used the same framework from the 1940s. This presented the same epistemology of the active school for the territory, determining that it should be a system with an organic, dynamic structure with decentralization in each part of the system. There would be no centralized model, and each part would make its own decisions for working. This fundamental epistemology for second-order cybernetics is not unidirectional or centralized.

Maturana was another notable exemplar of the proto-cybernetic Chilean scientists who studied in the United States in the mid-twentieth century and invested in the development of an organic state. Maturana studied at MIT between 1958 and 1960. With the support of Heinz von Foerster, he began to work on the problem of how computing can approximate neurological or biological systems.

Chile had a similar history to Argentina; in 1958 at National University (later as University of Chile), Guillermo González did digital computing with the name COMEX for experiments at the school. They created a department of computing at the National University with scientists such as Carlos Martinoya, who in 1958 had proposed to transform the Laboratory of Servomechanisms of the Faculty of Engineering into a computer centre. Martinoya was an engineer who also studied visual perception and biology, and began to teach in the Faculty of Sciences in the 1960s, at the time Varela was a student there. In Santiago, Efraín Friedman was the director of the Computing Centre at the University of Chile when they began to study using a German ER-56 computer nicknamed Lorenz. This centre wanted to work on computing parallel with what was happening in Argentina with the Sadosky group at the same time. In the 1960s, the engineering faculty at University of Chile dedicated 25 per cent of their curriculum for engineers to the humanities and social sciences. In 1968, CORFO created the National Company of Computing (ECOM). Personnel from the computing department at the University of Chile went to CORFO to sign the national cooperation for development. When Friedman came from the University of Chile to this place, the framework came from CORFO and the National Computing Company, along with the Institute for Technology Research supported by the UN at first, followed by support from the Chilean government.

Figure 9 records a very notable moment; it originally came from a book made by a teacher at the Technical State University (Universidad Técnica del Estado, UTE).

Fig. 9: 'Elements of computation', a manual for teaching programming to high school students developed by professors at the Technical State University (Universidad Técnica del Estado, UTE) Inés Harding and Jaime Michelow in 1972, published by the University of Chile in 1973.

At this institution in the early 1970s, professors Jaime Michelow and Inés Harding created a teaching programme for national secondary school education, where public school students had to learn to write programmes. In this public school teaching guide made by Michelow and Harding, we can see the only IBM 360 unit the national computer company had, as well as how they taught students to programme.

This brings us to perhaps the most famous moment in the history of Chilean cybernetics, when CORFO contracted Beer, who had worked in England in the 1960s. When CORFO hired Beer in 1971, his company Sigma had already advised Chilean Customs at the port of Valparaiso in the use of its new computer implemented in 1960. Beer worked as a business advisor during the 1950s and 1960s, specializing in management, at a time characterized by labour governments, large state-owned steel and coal companies, and union involvement in decision-making. The following note was made by Stafford during his second Chilean period (1971–73): 'If the gov is the people' (Fig. 10). Beer explained many times the impact of his first meeting with President

Salvador Allende in 1971, who had also studied medicine. Beer always remembers that when he was going to explain that System 5 of the VSM was the decision space where he, 'comrade President', would be, Allende interrupted him and said: 'System 5, the decision space, where the people will be'. This was a way of interpreting Beer's 'heterarchy' in a radical way.

Fig. 10: 'If the gov(ernment) is the people', post-it note written by Stafford Beer, placed on top of his personal folders and files on the Cybersyn project (Chile 1971–73) donated to Liverpool John Moores University. Courtesy of The Stafford Beer Archive at Liverpool John Moores University Special Collections & Archives.

The idea of the decentralized system for second-order cybernetics is that each part of the system made self-management decisions, which was a principal cybernetic goal. This arose in part from a different national production model, because the Workers' United Center of Chile (Central Unica de Trabajadores, CUT) made a new deal with the government in the 1970s for greater decentralisation in production organisation. In 1939 the government and national agencies began to create national enterprises and companies with CORFO. By the early 1970s, though, this tactic changed as the government bought out private industries which they deemed strategic for the country, leaving them with management responsibilities in many industries. This need led them to hire Beer, with the expectation that he could teach them how to manage all these national industries with the second-order cybernetic model.

Usually when the socialist cybernetics of the Cybersyn project are mentioned, it is associated with the socialist cybernetics of the

USSR or GDR of that time. In general, Soviet cybernetics of the 1960s and 1970s had more influence in Cuba, and marginally more in Mexico, Venezuela, Argentina, and even Brazil.

After some research about cybernetics in socialist Germany, its connections with Latin America are not yet clear.[8] In this sense, Cybersyn was a type of socialist cybernetics of its own interpretation, because it was not exactly the same approach that Beer could apply in England. Fig. 11 shows a model by Beer in CORFO in 1973, and first appeared in the bulletin of the Institute of Technological Research (Intec) belonging to CORFO.

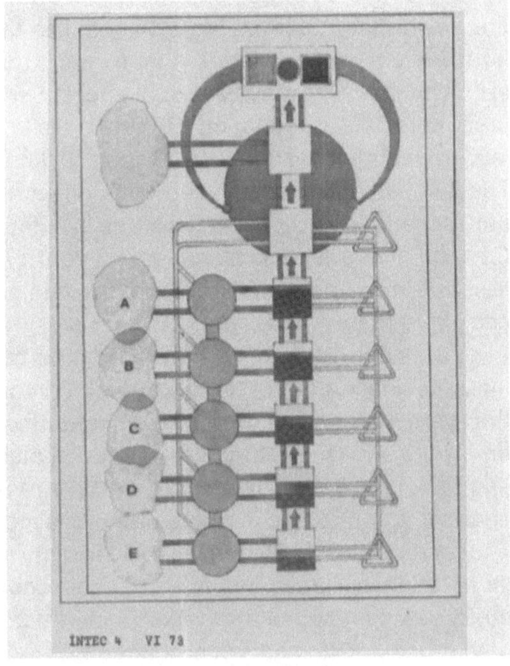

Fig. 11: Stafford Beer's viable system model (VSM), inspired by the central nervous system, applied in the Chilean Cybersyn project between 1971 and 1973. Published in INTEC CORFO's Bulletin 4 (1973), courtesy of Fernando Portal Archive. Image redrawn form the original by the author.

8   Unlike the link with GDR cybernetics, obviously Cuba had a very strong relationship with the USSR cybernetics, especiallý in the early 1970s. The difference between these two types of 'socialist cybernetics' seems to be that in the case of the USSR, the cybernetic administration would correspond specifically to specialized technicians, whereas the objective of Cybersyn was that the workers, and even the general population as in the Cyberfolk (a subproject of Cybersyn), would manage the system themselves. I thank Slava Gerovitch for this last specification.

Beer's VSM is made up of six parts (environment, System 1, System 2, System 3, System 4, and System 5), and CORFO baptized it as the Synco in 1972. As Corfo was the one that coordinated all state companies, Intec also worked within this scheme.

The diagram in Fig. 11 may be the first drawing of the system used in CORFO and its subsidiaries such as INTEC or ECOM; it was made in 1972. The circle with the letters A, B, C, D, E represents the external social and natural environment. The structure with the arrows is a metaphorical approximation of the spinal column and nervous system. The organs outside (the skin) and inside the human body are System 1 and System 2—the devices and interfaces. Information that comes from the environment across the skin come to the organs of the system, both System 1 and System 2. It then enters the spinal column and travels along the narrow system to the neck. Systems 1, 2 and 3 are in the present tense. The function of System 1 is implementation, its administrative entity is the unit, and its stage in data processing is data entry. The function of System 2 is coordination, its administrative entity is the department or division, and its stage in a data process is storage. The function of System 3 is management control, its administrative entity is sub-management, and its stage in a data process is pre-processing and exploration.

The neck is System 4, where we have the cerebellum, the neurological management of the body, and it then goes to the brain where the system makes the decisions, constituting System 5. The System 4 time-horizon is the future, its function in management is intelligence and foresight, its administrative entity is research, development and analysis, and its stage in a data process is modelling and visualization. The time horizon of System 5 is uncertainty in the present and future, its function in management is political-regulatory, its administrative entity is the management or board of directors, its type of stage in a data process is the start of production.[9]

With this model of the neurological system, Beer translated these concepts to national industrial management. Another example of the heterarchical system appears in Fig. 12. Chile is strip, or ribbon, and has had a centralized model dating to colonial times (1500–1800). With the

---

9   I am especially grateful for the assistance from Rodrigo Fernández Albornoz in synthesizing the viable system model clearly, along with his valuable professional experience.

organic model from the 1960s and 1950s, we can see Santiago in the centre of the country. However, with Arica in the far north and Punta Arenas in the far south, we can see other operational cells of the systems.

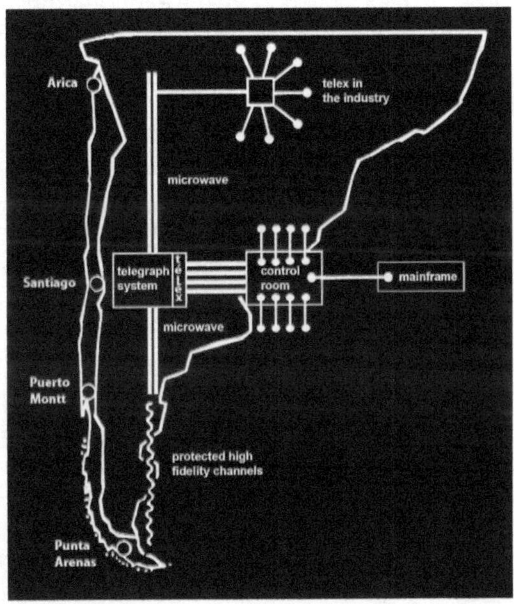

Fig. 12: General decentralized structure from the extreme north to the extreme south of Chile, for state industry administration through real-time data transmission and economic-productive variable predictions. Redrawn from an original drawing by Stafford Beer published in the Chilean magazine *Qué pasa*? (September 1973).

In 1968, Gui Bonsiepe came from HfG Ulm to Chile with the support of the International Labour Organization of the UN after studying first-order cybernetics with Max Bense and Horst Rittel. With this background, Bonsiepe arrived at the national agency CORFO in Chile in 1968 as advisor, and after 1970 was rehired by the government of Chile to coordinate the industrial design produced by CORFO. Two other designers, who were former students of the HfG Ulm, came to work with Bonsiepe at the National Institute for Development of Technology (IN-TEC CORFO) in this second stage; Werner Zempt and Michael Weiss. Bonsiepe and his team manufactured the Cybersyn project devices for Beer, while also applying his background from first-order cybernetics to perform his own interpretation between first-order cybernetics and the ideas of Beer's second-order cybernetics during the same time. The important paradigm shift implemented by Bonsiepe while working with CORFO was the interface concept. Interaction design was crucial in a project about second-order cybernetics, because the design of the interaction is very close to behavioural design with these two definitions of first and second order cybernetics. Bonsiepe tried to operate this very complex system from the economy, politics, and management.

Bonsiepe focused on aesthetics and interaction design while working on Cybersyn (the name is a contraction of cybernetic synergy; it was also known as the Synco project), concentrating on digital and analogue interfaces in both two and three dimensions with the concept of interaction interface. The visual information design which they created offered some examples of the devices created for Cybersyn. Within this project, there was another project named Checo (Chilean economy) focusing on prospectives of stability, which Beer developed based on Ashby's idea about calculating variability. These applied ideas mean that 'variety alone absorbs variety'.[10] That is, the disturbances which a system presents to another system (variety) can only be reduced or eliminated through the same or greater variety. At that date it was common for economic forecasts (foresight) to be made with information several months back, in this project (Checo) it was done with information in real time. For that, Ashby's theory of the required variety was used, to evaluate the elements that were necessary, or were not necessary, to make this future prediction of the economy and make decisions in the present with this information, especially with the network of state company connections.

The group Bonsiepe led in the same agency did the screens in which it was possible to see a display of data on the future of the economy, and the different factors of the country's productive chain, with the production of these complex economy models and variability. In this story, it is also important to remember that in the early 1950s there was a precedent of Checo in Guatemala with the MONIAC (Fig. 13), whose implementation was attempted in a project for natural resource nationalization under a social democratic government interrupted by a coup d'etat in 1954.

---

10   Beer describes the influence Ross Ashby had on him in *Diagnosing the System for Organisations* (London: John Wiley, 1985).

Fig. 13: The MONIAC computer designed by the New Zealand economist William Phillips, used by the Central Bank of Guatemala in the early 1950s (a computer that worked with water). It is a distant antecedent of the Checo (Chilean economy) project. Checo was a component part of the 1971–73 Chilean Cybersyn project. The computer in the picture is the version of the MONIAC used by Phillips at the London School of Economics (LSE) in 1958. Courtesy LSE Library.

In Guatemala, there was an attempt to perform prospectives (projection of possible future scenarios, especially economic ones) and economic management with computing in the national bank for a social-democratic government. Checo continued this trend twenty years later with greater complexity. At the same time, with the same model of natural resource nationalization, and promotion of the technology industry that would create added value through decentralized models of administration, decision-making, and interaction, they began to design, develop and manufacture the devices in the same country. For instance, the cheaper TV prototype ANTU was used in the Cybersyn project Cyberfolk. Cyberfolk was a Cybersyn sub-project that consisted of real-time decision-making, in which city residents could vote online on the decisions of their municipal council, which also had an eye on producing technology within the same country where it was used. The Industry of Radio and Television (IRT), an agency associated with CORFO, produced different electronic devices for information technology and interaction design during these years. All of this industrial production ended in 1973 (Fig. 14).

Fig. 14: Antu television manufactured by the defunct National Radio and Television Company (IRT-CORFO) in Arica, Chile, between 1971 and 1973. It was used in the closed circuit of the Cyberfolk project, which consisted of the inhabitants of the cities of Mejillones in the north of Chile and Tomé in the south of Chile being able to use the Antu television installed in their homes to watch meetings of the municipal councils within their two respective cities. When the council was about to make a decision, the residents of each city could vote directly on these decisions via remote control while watching on closed-circuit TV. Part of the Cybersyn-CORFO project. Photo courtesy of Sebastián Concha, Arica City Museum.

At the same time, it must be noted that the Cybersyn project was not the only second-order cybernetic project in Chile, since second-order cybernetic projects were part of the spirit of the Unidad Popular era (1970–73). For instance between 1971 and 1972, the National Ministry for Urban Planning and Housing (MINVU) designed and built a crucial building for the UN conference about third world development (UNCTAD III), completed in ten months. Normally at that time, such a building would take three years, but they did it in ten months using the prospective (predictive) system with computing, before April 1972, with a Critical Path Method (CPM) model and with programmes evaluation and review technique (PERT) model. Prospective is a management concept used in Cybernetics, designating prediction of behavior.

This took place in a heterarchical way, with the engineers teaching the workers how to introduce information every day, and how to do the prospective planning for the construction one day in the week. Another example was at the National Technology University (UTE), where Jaime Michelow taught. Between 1968 and 1973 they worked on a similar system for a decentralized university management system through a telex network coordinated by a central computer in the different regions of the country with schools belonging to the UTE. These examples illustrate how second-order cybernetics had a lot of resonances in this historical moment, where there was a great deal of thought given to managing computing in a more effective and decentralized way.

We now come to considering the devices themselves. Before the neoliberal policies that began in the 1970s in Chile, the UN supported the development of technology and design education as a tool to support third world economies. One of the exceptional cases was the agreement of the HfG Ulm with UNESCO in 1965. At the same time, many governments of Central American and South American countries in general also supported these policies of their own technological development in different ways (Argentina, Chile, Mexico, and Cuba, for example). These are the devices made in Latin America in the early 1970s, such as those of the National Development Agency where Bonsiepe and other designers were working with young Chilean young Cyberners; they could manufacture calculators, tools, and radio devices.

They tried to move into computing, but the institution's work was stopped with the military coup in Chile in 1973. But, at the same time, Sadosky was working as a private citizen after being barred from university employment, which led him to make calculator tools in Argentina—the famous Cifra 311—and another Argentina technician, Juan Salonia and Héctor Muller, separately worked on the creation of computers in Córdova city in 1976. At the same time in Chile and as a side story, José Vicente Asuar created the compute Comdasuar in 1978. Asuar was a musician and became one of the first electronic musicians in Chile in the 1960s, but he was an engineer as well. Asuar worked in the University of Chile until the military coup in 1973, after which he created a computer for technological music in his home due to being banned from university work.

On the other side of the continent, for example, the creation of the CID-201 computer was very important, at the University of Havana, Cuba in 1970; in the 1980s, the Mexican commercial computer Printaform, by Jorge Espinoza-Meireles, was very successful.

Another remarkable parallel story is that of Hellmuth Stuven, an engineer with MINVU, who wrote the cybernetic programme for building construction in Chile for UNCTAD III in 1972. He went into exile in Denmark during the 1970s and early 1980s, after which he worked on the design and production of the personal computer named Thor.

In a context similar to the rest of Latin America, in which the production of their own technology is not common, but with specific conditions that are slightly different from those of Chile, Argentina or Mexico, in Cuba during the late 1960s and early 1970s, there was obviously a strong influence from Soviet cybernetics, but it was not only the reference. Cuban specialists also discussed Wiener and Rosenblueth as major referents for first-order cybernetics in the 1940s—they wrote about this. Cuba founded a cybernetics institute in 1971, where the research Beer produced was extensively discussed. During this time, Cuba produced some devices as well, such as the Silna 999 analogue computer in 1968, and the CID-201 computer in 1970.

In Mexico, one pioneer in teaching architecture with computers in the 1970s was Alvaro Sanchez, who aimed to apply systemic design and systemic cybernetic theory in architecture, and in 1977 published the book *Sistemas Arquitectónicos y Urbanos. Introducción a la teoría de sistemas aplicado a la arquitectura y a la planificación urbana* (Architectural and Urban Systems. Introduction to systems theory applied to architecture and urban planning). Then, in 1983, Meireles began to implement personal computers in his Mexican enterprise Printaform.

The Chilean military coup of 1973 made a clear before-and-after line on the national development model. By 1975, the model was strictly free trade, and the wide range of state programmes stopped. For example, in that period, the ECOM and INTEC disappeared, and since 1980, CORFO, according to the new constitution, would never create state companies and industries again. Although the change to the neoliberal model was later in other Latin American countries, it also stopped technological and computer development and production projects in Mexico and Argentina in the 1990s.

Another famous reference during this timeframe was the autopoiesis model of the already mentioned biologists Maturana and Varela, as presented in their 1972 book, *On Machines and Living Beings.*[11] Beer was very interested in this model, considering that autopoiesis could be used in social models and management, although Varela and

11   Francisco Varela and Humberto Maturana, *De máquinas y seres vivos* (On machines and living beings) (Santiago de Chile: Editorial Universitaria, 1972).

Maturana were not sure about this utilization. Autopoiesis took its model from immune system epistemology. Varela explained that the it was not merely for reacting to viruses, since the immune system has its own system for living and working, making it not only a system reacting to external stimulation. It is true that immune systems work with external stimulation, since viruses change continually, but the system does not exist for only this reason. The basic system of the autopoiesis thesis is that the reaction has its own system for living.

By 1974, three years of work had been put into the Maturana and Varela's research project. A screen shows a digital visualization of the autopoiesis model named Proto-bio (meaning 'first life' in ancient Greek), developed by the engineer Ricardo Uribe (Fig. 15). The Proto-bio came from the autopoiesis epistemology, and explained this theory with a moving digital visualization on the first computer they had.

Fig. 15: Digital visualization of the behavior of the principle of autopoiesis by Francisco Varela and Humberto Maturna, produced by Ricardo Uribe under the name of Proto-Bio (first life) in 1974. Illustration made by the author.

One indicator of the interest in cybernetics in South America during this period was the simultaneous translation and publication of Paul Idatte's *Nociones fundamentales de cibernética/Chaves da cibernética* (Fundamental notions of cybernetics) in both Brazilian Portuguese and Spanish in 1972; the Chilean edition was published by the University of Chile. It is very significant that between the 1950s and the 1970s, in Argentina, Chile, Mexico, Venezuela and Brazil, books on cybernetics were translated and published from a very heterogeneous perspective, showing its development not only in the United States, but also its variants, for example in France, England and the Soviet Union. Idatte's publication is a good example of that situation.

From an even more committed point of view, following the September 1973 military putsch in Chile, the Brazilian cybernetician Carlos

Senna, following his work on Cybersyn in Chile, moved on to Peru to collaborate with the Argentinian computer scientist and mathematician Oscar Varsavsky and Darcy Ribeiro, Brazilian specialist in education, sociology and anthropology, with support from the UNDP in a 1974 project in which they taught the VSM and second-order model from union organizations.

During the 1970s, there were at least three important cybernetic models in South America: Beer's VSM, Amilcar Herrera's Latin American World Model (MML) at the Bariloche Foundation, and Varsavsky's Numex model in Peru. With the Numex, in addition to the VSM of Beer, and the MML of Bariloche, we could count an additional model, since the three different models had ongoing discussions with each other to look for novel ways and methods. Varsavsky published several books focused on the social commitment of scientists and cultural and economic development in South America during this period, which came out in Chile, Peru, and Argentina. Another very important agent of change at that time was the Peruvian engineer Francisco Sagasti, who was working on possible technology development in South America in the 1970s. Between 1973 and 1980, Sagasti coordinated the Science and Technology Policy Instruments project, with the participation of Argentina, Brazil, Colombia, Mexico, Venezuela, Peru, Egypt, Yugoslavia, India and South Korea.

Back in South America, the Chilean architect Jaime Garretón published a book in Argentina in 1975 about how to use cybernetics in urban planning, which applied the Claude Shannon model for communication. Meanwhile, the researcher Charles Francois founded an institution in Argentina in 1976, and in 1997, with support from another institute of cybernetics (IAS) in Peru, he published and wrote about the history of cybernetics.

One difficult part of the story of cybernetics in Latin America during this period comes from the systemic theorist Russell Ackoff, who was in Mexico in 1976. He worked extensively with Mexican scholars at the National University (Universidad Nacional Autónoma de México, UNAM). He adapted a model called Inactivism, Reactivism, Prectivism and Interactivism for the Mexican government, but it was impossible to put it into practice. At the same time, in 1979, in Mexico, Ackoff's book *Rediseñando el futuro* (Redesigning the future) was translated and published with the Limusa publishing house (published before by Wiley in English in 1974). In the same context in Mexico, in 1977 and 1982, the Mexican publisher Fondo de Cultura Económica (FCE) translated and published two of Beer's books: *Designing Freedom* and *Decisión y control: el significado de la investigación de operaciones y la administración* (Decision and control: the meaning of operations research and cybernetic management). Then, in 1983, after Ackoff, Beer was contracted to design a second model for the Mexican government with the VSM. Both Ackoff and Beer said that corruption and bureaucracy in Mexico made it impossible to implement these systemic and cybernetic models in the government.

In parallel, when Sadosky had to leave the National University (University of Buenos Aires, UBA) in Argentina in 1966, one of his main breakthroughs came from the department of computing in the university where he went to work in Uruguay (Universidad de la República, UDELAR) until 1973. In Northern Argentina and Southern Brazil, he met the young Uruguayan engineer Victor Ganón for discussions about Beer's second-order cybernetics. Ganón went to study computing management in London between 1974 and 1975, and after the military dictatorship ended in in Uruguay in 1985, he initiated a project to use computing in public administration during the return to democracy in Uruguay, and convinced the President to hire Beer. Beer was very happy and said Uruguay was his 'second Chile', and Ganón became the management chief for the new project. Together, a new cybernetic programme for government management was developed in collaboration with the UNDP and named Cybernetic Uruguay (Urucib). The Urucib programme was created to manage national industries for the government, since national enterprises and companies continued in Uruguay in the 1980s. At the present time (2023), software exports are the third-largest income source for Uruguay. This process began with the locally produced software for Urucib, which was later sold to other countries.

Fig. 16 shows the device made for Urucib by Ganón in the 1980s, for which they also had to produce software. This last element, producing software, made in Uruguay for the Urucib project, and not using an imported one, was a task which Beer initially believed to be impossible.

Fig. 16: Remote control
used to interact with
Uruguay Cibernético at the
Presidential Management
Centre, Uruguay. This device
was a kind of proto-mouse,
for the exclusive use of
the President, which is
why its attached text said:
'Presidential Computer
Attribute'. Images courtesy
of Victor Ganón.

However, the ultimate product was the first software made in Uruguay for export;[12] in the 1990s some other countries purchased the Urucib model for national industry management. The most successful customers were the national government of Nicaragua, and the government of Buenos Aires in Argentina. The Buenos Aires Metropolitan Area has four times the population of Uruguay. The city of Buenos Aires alone has as many inhabitants as Uruguay. In this sense, Urucib was very successful and was the beginning of the long development of computing within a model that, in part, continued to be promoted by the state, but it would also have led to neoliberalism and the efficiency of private companies. In fact, before President Jorge Batlle stopped the Urucib project in Uruguay, Ganón thought that it could be used in the new Southern Common Market Mercosur, created in 1990, as a tool for exchange and management among partner countries. However, the system disappeared from Chile in the 1970s, and disappeared from Argentina, where the government had a national industry working with the University of Chile, in the 1990s. Fig. 17 shows the VSM used by the Uruguayan government in the 1980s. However, it is also important to mention that Urucib has another system element which was not included in the original Beer VSM, the Cyberfilter, which was a new Uruguayan development (1985-90), which improved the first model of the famous Chilean VSM's Cybersyn (1971-73).

12   Chile abandoned this path in the 1970s; however, Uruguay created and sustained a policy over time with support from the government, businessmen, and the Ministry of Public Education. Software exports are now its third source of income, with higher numbers than much larger countries such as Brazil or Argentina.

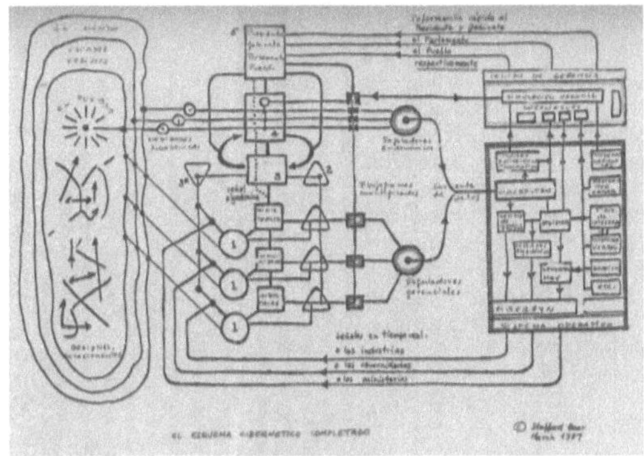

Fig. 17: Complete cyber-
netic scheme for Uruguay
Cibernético, the viable
system model with the
Cyberfiltre, Stafford Beer,
Uruguay 1987. Courtesy Victor
Ganón from Urucib archive
in Montevideo, Uruguay, and
the Stafford Beer Archive
at Liverpool John Moores
University Special Collections
and Archives authorization
of use.

The Cyberfilter continued to be used in Colombia in the late 1990s by Angela Espinosa, who had studied in England until 1995 with Raúl Espejo, one of the scholars from the first period of Cybersyn, who used this model. Espinosa applied it in Colombia (1995-98) at the national audit office. This is notable, because as noted before, Beer and Ackoff deemed the systemic cybernetic model for the government impossible because of the corruption in Mexico. Nevertheless, Espinosa used it to combat the corruption in Colombia in the late 1990s.

In the late 1980s, Varela was working in exile at the National Centre for Scientific Research, and in the United States, MIT took on the ideas from the 1970s about Proto-bio and autopoiesis regarding autonomous self-generating living systems (what is known in cybernetics as recursion). Varela was working on the structural coupling and the origin of meaning in a cellular automation in 1988. From this experience, carried out by Varela with the support of MIT and the CNRS (Centre national de la recherche scientifique), the Bittorio was born.

One practical use of the cellular automaton epistemology in Chile in the late 1980s was developed by Miguel Giacaman, who used the autopoiesis model and the immune system model in a design for anti-virus software or bio-digital architecture, in order to fight the Jerusalem virus in October 1987. Giacaman ultimately named his creation Virus Detection (Vir-Det). This kind of software was always undergoing further development, which meant that it was not only for one kind of virus. The Chilean IBM office bought it in 1994 and changed its name to Oyster (Fig. 18).

Fig. 18: Oyster, an 'eternal' antivirus programme invented by Miguel Giacaman using the logic of autopoiesis and the immune system, originally called Virus Detection (Vir-Det) in the late 1980s. Image capture from a video recording of the production process of the Oyster 2.0 in 1994 for television, made by Pablo Rosenblatt; courtesy P. Rosenblatt.

Continuing along cybernetic lines of thinking focused on the production of communication and information technologies, Giacaman created a Chilean model for the production of Film Master, since it was very expensive at the time to buy film master machines from other countries.[13] This system had major cost advantages, allowing for broader use. In this period, the National Universities (University of Chile and the State Technical University) no longer worked with the national computing industry (ECOM CORFO, 1968–83), the National Technology Development Institute (INTEC CORFO, which existed around the same time as ECOM), or with other national agencies. The past collaboration was what had facilitated projects like Cybersyn, and the formulation of autopoiesis and Proto-bio. All this collaboration disappeared after the 1975 change of economic model. However, from the 1970s Giacaman continued alone (or at least without institutional network support) with epistemological research for the use of technology and science, and was successful in the late 1980s with a kind of cellular automata. From a systemic point of view, Giacaman continued to develop the ideas of Autopoiesis in a practical way, until he managed to structure a paradigm shift in bio-digital architecture, but without the institutional environment of his predecessors, which limited the projection of these discoveries in the long term. For example, in the following years, Chile lost the opportunity to be a pioneer in the global antivirus industry.

13   The film master is the basis for the production and reproduction of digital barcodes.

In the late 1990s, Miguel de Icaza in Mexico created the desk environment for Linux, Gnome. This was followed by a project from the Colombian model of management with second-order cybernetics, created by Raul Espejo, an engineer from the original Cybersyn project in Chile working in England with Espinoza. During the last twenty to fifty years, Uruguay software exports have been an exception in Latin America, given the predominance of revenues from commodities after all the national industries disappeared in the 1970s. Uruguay began to build this capacity in the 1980s, with the outlook common in national development to consider programmes that can run for anything between five and twenty years. Meanwhile, in the local interpretation of neoliberalism, national projects with a timeframe of above two years are not as frequent as they were before. The long-term framework helped give rise to the Ceibal Plan by Nicholas Negroponte to provide every public school student in Uruguay with a computer using the Linux system.

Another approach to cybernetic network frameworks in Latin America was designed in 2013 with the Union of South American Nations (UNASUN), which tried to create a fibre-optic internet in order to create greater independence from US-based networks. However, UNASUN gradually disappeared with the end of the so-called pink wave of governments (with President Correa in Ecuador, Morales in Bolivia, Mujica in Uruguay, and Rousseff in Brazil, to name a few examples), and the independent internet project remained unfinished.

Around 2022, the Syntesis Binational Corporation from Chile and Argentina took a fresh approach to 1970s second-order cybernetics and elaborated their concepts of relational cybernetics. They raised the concept of the environment used (in second-order cybernetics, and even in the first-order cybernetics in the 1940s) as an object outside the body and organism, and said that the environment was not an object or a thing. What they meant is that environment is another kind of natural, social and or cultural identity. According to the Syntesis Binational Corporation, relationships are what need to be designed, not interactions, giving rise to different interpretations of development and sustainability.

This is the final point of this overview. Latin American cybernetics exists inside an organic definition of state and production, but there are two kinds of modernity models, as well as two kinds of cybernetic definitions and praxis. Questions arise within each context. The VSM in second-order cybernetics insists on the need for unique contextual interpretations in order to create management models. The main objective for this type of vernacular or regional cybernetics is the interaction between the human being and the environment, and the different kinds of technologies are the devices, since using technology and producing technology are absolutely different things. This difference arises from contextual variations, as well as the fact that techniques for using technology constitute a type of technology in themselves. In this triangle, different kinds of interpretation for this environment are needed. The open question for us, both within Latin America and outside of it, is about the present use of this story and, as has already happened in the past, about its possibility of being complementary with stories from other contexts; that is, how can we use this past, and look for the possible futures of cybernetics.

Note

A first version of this article was published in *AI & Society* 37, no. 3 (2022): 1293–1.

Reference

Beer, Stafford. *Diagnosing the System for Organisations*. London: John Wiley, 1985.

———. 'The Viable System Model: its provenance, development, methodology and pathology.' *The Journal of the Operational Research Society* 35, No. 1 (January 1984): 7–25.

Guzik, Ruth. 'Relaciones de un cientifico mexicano con el extranjero: El caso de Arturo Rosenblueth' (Relations of a Mexican scientist with foreigners: The example of Arthur Rosenbleuth). *RMIE* 14, no. 40 (2009): 43–67.

Rodríguez Campoamor, Hernán and Manuel Sadosky. *Psicología y cibernética* (Psychology and cybernetics). Buenos Aires: Siglo XX, 1958.

Rosenblueth, Arturo, Norbert Wiener and Julian Bigelow. 'Behavior, Purpose and Teleology'. *Philosophy of Science* 10, no. 1 (1943): 18–24.

Varela, Francisco and Humberto Maturana. *De máquinas y seres vivos* (On machines and living beings). Santiago de Chile: Editorial Universitaria, 1972.

Wiener, Norbert. *Cybernetics: Or Control and Communication in the Animal and the Machine*. Cambridge, MA: MIT Press, 1948.

Life-in-formation: Cybernetics of the Heart

Daisuke Harashima

To reflect on the issues of modern technology and humanity and to realize a better relationship between them, we must fundamentally re-examine today's predominantly mechanistic civilization and overcome its limitations. In this contemporary world of technology, where humans are treated as if they were information processing machines, people's hearts, and the meaning and value of their life, have been alienated and ruthlessly suppressed. Breaking through this difficult situation is an urgent challenge for contemporary thought. To achieve this, a biological informatics that reinterprets information as significance (i.e. meaning and value) for the living being would be welcome. Cybernetics for the twenty-first century should indeed become such an informatics.

The task of cybernetics for the twenty-first century is to recover the meaning and value of life that has been suppressed by the technological condition. But the classical cybernetics proposed in the mid-twentieth century was, on the contrary, precisely the theoretical foundation of that mechanistic information technology. However, as I will explain, a hint to overcome the modern technological condition is hidden within classical cybernetics; it has the potential to open up a biological worldview. What is important for twenty-first century technology, is to carve a path from a mechanistic worldview to a biological worldview from within. Through biological informatics, it involves recovering the meaning and value of life, and saving the hearts of people. I will now proceed to articulate the prospects regarding the initial step in this direction.

First of all, cybernetics for the twenty-first century should focus on life. '生命' (*seimei*) is a Japanese word that means 'life', but we can interpret it literally as 'living a life' (命を生きる, *inochi wo ikiru*). Then, who is living a life? I am living my life, of course. At the same time, however, I feel deep inside myself 'a life is living my life'. When I take care of this feeling of life, I find myself in a peaceful and compassionate mood. An egoistic self descends lower and lower, and a great warmth rises up from within a heart. It is a small heart, yet it is a heart of infinite sadness (かなしみ, *kanashimi*), of sorrow (悲しみ, *kanashimi*) and love (愛しみ, *kanashimi*).[1] Cybernetics for the twenty-first century must be cybernetics of the heart. I learned this notion of cybernetics from two neocyberneticians in Japan: Toru Nishigaki, who founded fundamental informatics, and Nami Ohi, who is researching a developmental model of psychic systems from the standpoint of fundamental informatics.[2]

Looking back, I was brought up with the notion that the twentieth century was a century of war, but the twenty-first century must be a century of peace. Today, it is still up to us to accomplish this, though it may seem like we are moving away from our goal. Cybernetics for the twenty-first century must be a cybernetics of peace too. This does not mean that peace can be achieved if we had some advanced cybernetics

1   In English, 'sadness of sorrow' may sound redundant, and 'sadness of love' may sound contradictory. The Japanese word 'かなしみ' (*kanashimi*) generally corresponds to the English words 'sadness' or 'sorrow', but in reality, this Japanese word is polysemous and can also mean affection or a kind of 'love', although it is not very common in that sense today. The subtle nuances of 'かなしみ' are somewhat expressed by the choice of kanji characters used to write it. Kanji characters frequently used for this are '悲' (*hi*), '哀' (*ai*), and '愛' (*ai*). When written as '悲しみ' or '哀しみ,' it generally means 'sorrow', and there is also a compound word '悲哀' (*hiai*) that specifically means 'sorrow'. The character '悲' represents the feeling of a heart (心, *kokoro*; the lower part of the character) being torn apart (非, *hi*; the upper part of the character), heartbreaking, and the word '悲しみ' is commonly used to express the sadness resulting from experiences of loss. However, '悲' also carries the meaning of compassion. '哀' (*ai*) also means not only sorrow but also compassion. It shares the same sound as '愛' (*ai*), which means love, and the word '哀れみ' (*awaremi*) signifies compassion. The words '悲しみ' and '哀しみ' already have connotations that resonate with compassion and love. In Japanese, the word '愛' is commonly read as *ai* and means love, and occasionally, although not very common, '*kanashimi*' is also written as '愛しみ', signifying affection or a kind of love. In this usage, there is an underlying sentiment that somehow resonates with the sadness or sorrow of '*kanashimi*'. I believe that the emotional state of 'かなしみ' (sadness), which underlies both '悲' (sorrow) and '愛' (love), becomes an important research topic for the twenty-first century cybernetics of the heart. Nami Ohi, mentioned later in this text, is already researching, through a neocybernetics approach, how the sadness of sorrow stemming from experiences of loss can develop into the sadness of compassionate love by recovering its meaning. You might also want to refer to Seiichi Takeuchi, *'Kanashimi' no Tetsugaku* (Philosophy of 'Kanashimi') (Tokyo: NHK Publishing, 2009). As pointed out there, it is worth noting that the Japanese philosopher Kitaro Nishida, in the early twentieth century, argued that the inception of philosophy should not be 'wonder', as philosophers have often stated, but rather it should arise from '悲哀' (sorrow). See also note 34.

2   Toru Nishigaki, *Kiso Jouhougaku I, II, III* (Fundamental informatics) (Tokyo: NTT Publishing, 2004, 2008, 2021); Nami Ohi, 'Imi no kaifuku ni yoru soushitsu-taiken no kachi no hanten: shinteki-system no hattatsu-model' (Meanings recovery enables us to survive loss experiences: a model proposal of psychic systems development process), Shakai Jouhougaku (Socio-informatics) 8, no. 1 (2019): 49–64.

to control our minds, bodies, societies, and environments, so that the world is peaceful; that is the opposite approach to my cybernetics of the heart. What I mean is a process of the growth of the heart, to survive the questions to which we must find answers as we live together, comforting and encouraging each other to live. Can we control such a process of the heart with materialistic or mechanistic technology? I do not think that we can. Then, what can technics do in this process? I hope that honest consideration of these questions will become the ethos of cybernetics for the twenty-first century.

Put plainly, just because we become materially rich does not mean that we also gain spiritual wealth, and vice versa. We must distinguish between these two orders. When the order of the material is applied to the spiritual, the heart is suppressed. However, this was precisely the approach of classical, twentieth-century cybernetics and of modern technology. Reflecting on this, we must reopen the informational or biological possibilities that were latent in classical cybernetics. How can the heart of love and peace be nurtured and realized? This is the question of cybernetics of the heart.

The term cybernetics was coined from the Greek word *kybernete*, to steer, which implies that the purpose of cybernetics was, in the first place, to study how the living being survive in its environment, like a steersman sailing in rough seas. However, cybernetics is usually thought of as the technology to mechanize living organisms, and, in fact, has been applied in just this way under modern technological conditions. But that is not what cybernetics is supposed to be. I would argue instead that cybernetics is a study of living life. In other words, it suggests an approach that opens up a biological worldview from within this modern mechanistic worldview. I hope that cybernetics for the twenty-first century will become steering technics to help us survive our passage of life. It is not technology, but, as I will argue, it is a technics for observing the significance of each individual living system observed from the perspective of a cosmic system of life, corresponding to the significance of everything in a world observed from within each individual living system. Throughout this essay, I will explain what this complex description means.

Classical cybernetics: mechanism and enframing

Cybernetics is an information systems theory founded by Norbert Weiner in the mid-twentieth century, based on which contemporary information technology has been developed. It aimed at an integrated science of the living being and the machine, as indicated in the title of Wiener's book *Cybernetics: Or Control and Communication in the Animal and the Machine.*[3] It is a theory of control and communication for systems to achieve their objectives in their uncertain environments. In other words, it is a mathematical model of how animals do this. A mechanism of feedback allows machines to simulate the purposive behaviours of animals; a system compares a predictive model of its environment with fed-backed information about the consequences of its output, which returns as the next input, in order to optimize its behaviour and get closer to achieving its objectives. A machine equipped with a feedback mechanism is able to adapt to changes in its environment and complete its tasks automatically. It can be said that this machine collects information that is useful for its purpose from its environment. In other words, for the cybernetic system, the world is a world of valuable things, in terms of the usefulness for its purpose.

Here lie two problems of cybernetics: mechanism and enframing (*Gestell*). It is a critical task for cybernetics for the twenty-first century to recognize and overcome both. Mechanists believe that the living being is a machine. Cybernetics blurs the distinction between the living being and the machine from the perspective of mechanistic systems theory; it considers both as feedback machines. Modern science has been divided into two opposing positions on the understanding of life: vitalism and mechanism. Organicism and systems theory have tried to reconcile them. It is said that cybernetics completed this reconciliation in the form of a triumph of mechanism.[4] This aspect of cybernetics as mechanism conceals a crucial possibility for the future of cybernetics: the possibility to open up the mechanistic modern science to a biological perspective. My vision of cybernetics for the twenty-first century is in this direction. I will elaborate on this later.

3   Norbert Wiener, *Cybernetics: Or Control and Communication in the Animal and the Machine* (Cambridge, MA: MIT Press, 1948).
4   Yuk Hui, *Recursivity and Contingency* (London: Rowman & Littlefield, 2019).

But first, let me explain the other issue: enframing. Martin Heidegger used this term to describe the essence of modern technology (*moderne Technik*) in the mid-twentieth century.[5] The essence of technology is to drive human beings to regard the world as an inventory of assets that should be effectively utilized. From this perspective, nature is nothing but a resource to be exploited. According to Heidegger, enframing technology is the result of Western metaphysics since Plato and Aristotle. Cybernetics completed this process. He said that cybernetics is the end of philosophy and the beginning of Western European civilization's world dominance,[6] meaning, the technological dominance of the world. Human beings under modern technological conditions experience the environmental world as a world consisting of useful things.[7] Human beings, who observe the world as a stock of natural resources to be exploited, are themselves living in such a world and are, of course, themselves regarded as human resources to be exploited. This does not mean that there are only useful things in the world, but rather that anything that is not related to the binary choice of useful or useless does not appear within that world. In other words, how the experiential world is constructed is determined in this way by technology of enframing. In this light, the modern information society opened up by cybernetics and the global capitalist system supported by modern technology could be seen as the expected results of human beings driven by the enframing technology. People live their days exploiting themselves as resources, constantly calculating their own usefulness. We can say that cybernetics, with its probabilistic concept of

5   Martin Heidegger, *The Question Concerning Technology and Other Essays*, trans. William Lovitt (New York: Garland, 1977).

6   Martin Heidegger, *On Time and Being*, trans. Joan Stambaugh (New York: Harper & Row, 1972); see also Hui, *Recursivity and Contingency.*

7   I use the term 'environmental world' to indicate that it is a world wherein a living being lives but the life of the living being constructs the world itself. The environmental world is neither the real world that is independent of the living being, nor the ideal world that is created by and within the living being. Second-order cybernetician Heinz von Foerster said that we are living in our environment, but the environment is invented by us. Biologist Jakob von Uexküll's concept of *Umwelt* grasps this well, and it is usually translated into Japanese as 環世界 (*kansekai*) or 環境世界 (*kankyousekai*), which literally means 'environmental world'. See Heinz von Foerster, 'On constructing a reality', in *Understanding Understanding: Essays on Cybernetics and Cognition* (New York: Springer, 2003); Jakob von Uexküll, A Foray into the Worlds of Animals and Humans: With a Theory of Meaning, trans. Joseph D. O'Neil (Minneapolis: University of Minnesota Press, 2010).

information, provided a theory for calculating usefulness. It is important that cybernetics for the twenty-first century rethink the concept of information. I will discuss this in more detail later.

Reflecting on the modern anthropocentrism that led to spiritual decadence and to the environmental crisis, we are seeking new values that reposition human beings in the cosmos. Considering the notion of technology of enframing, however, it seems that modernity, which has been called anthropocentric, in fact has been technologocentric above all.[8] It is as if human beings are miserable machines enmeshed in a gigantic network of machinery spanning the entire universe, bound by mechanical laws and forced to work according to orders to serve the machine. In such a cosmology, the living being is reduced to a set of cybernetic data-processing algorithms; the distinction between the living being and the machine disappears, and the concept of life is eliminated from the theory. Nevertheless, human beings still believe they are doing all of this voluntarily, as if it were anthropocentric. Technological singularity theorists and transhumanists would predict such a technologocentric future as if it were inevitable, and ever more likely to become a reality. However, the cosmology underlying such thinking is, in fact, groundless. Technological universalism is nihilism. As Yuk Hui argues, it is an urgent task for cybernetics for the twenty-first century to relativize the cosmology of modern technology and open up different possibilities.[9]

Although we, modern human beings, seem to be driven by technology at the level of our unconscious self-understanding, something else seems to be at work that has been driving us deeper inside, even deeper than technology. That is life. I argue that life, and making sense of the feeling of life, is the critical step for cybernetics for the twenty-first century. Indeed, technology acts on how our experiential world of significance is constructed, but, at a deeper level, the driving force

8   Heidegger's question concerning technology as enframing (*Gestell*) in the context of critique of Western metaphysics resonates with Jacques Derrida's critique of the logocentrism of Western metaphysics; Jacques Derrida, *Of Grammatology*, trans. Gayatri Chakravorty Spivak (Baltimore: Johns Hopkins University Press, 2016). In view of this, I use the term 'technologocentric' here. Technocentrism does not necessarily means technologocentrism, because technocentrism can have different forms, as Yuk Hui's concept of technodiversity indicates. See Yuk Hui, *The Question Concerning Technology in China: An Essay in Cosmotechnics* (Falmouth: Urbanomic, 2016/2019).
9   Hui, *Recursivity and Contingency*.

behind the construction of the world itself is at work, and that is life. To sense it, to listen to it, to observe it—this is the decisive step for cybernetics for the twenty-first century. In fact, this step was already taken in classical twentieth-century cybernetics, and has gradually been realized in neocybernetics since the late twentieth century. I would like to suggest a vision for cybernetics for the twenty-first century, referring to such new cybernetics, especially neocybernetic thinking in Japan, which I myself have been working on.

A future cybernetics that is not enframing touches something that drives human beings even more deeply than technology. It touches life-in-formation: cybernetics of the heart. Heidegger, against modern technology, invoked the ancient Greek notion of *techne*.[10] Is life here the same as techne, or not? What about, for example, Dao in Chinese thought, or the inhuman in Jean-François Lyotard's sense, as referred to by Hui?[11] There are many to compare. This is an important question, but I have to refrain from going into it at this time. I hope that this life is at least in some small way global, and we can acquire a concept of a global system that values the heart of life-in-formation. There are many issues to be addressed in order to achieve this goal, but in the hope of contributing to such a vision, I would like to start by sharing my views on neocybernetics, especially from the standpoint of fundamental informatics, which has been addressing the question of discovering the biological possibilities latent in cybernetics, which at first glance appears to be extremely mechanistic. Fundamental informatics has also been seeking to contribute to the invention of future technics, respecting the history of Western civilization as the background for modern technology, while reflecting on the understanding of technology in Japan since its modernization, and reconsidering their differences.

As Nishigaki puts forward, if we are to face the question of information technology and human beings, we should not see the computer as mere a tool for computation, but rather see its underlying logic and cosmology of Hellenism and Hebraism; we should not just understand them conceptually, but look into the historical context and civilizational significance; we should see, with the eyes of the heart, the spirit of those who espouse the logos and the heartache of those who need

10   Heidegger, *The Question Concerning Technology*.
11   Hui, *The Question Concerning Technology*; Hui, *Recursivity and Contingency*.

technologies of mobility and ubiquity because of dispersion.[12] The meaning of the same computational machine is quite different when it is an ideal universal logic machine invented out of desperation for help and when it is a convenient calculator that was merely imported. The modern Japanese understanding of technology—which was introduced in the nineteenth century as something universal in a superficial sense through separating it from religion—has not faced such questions at an existential level, and thus has suppressed the hearts of those living in traditional cosmologies until today. There have been many such differences and tragedies on earth. I learned from Hui's cosmotechnics and Nishigaki's fundamental informatics a way to open up richer possibilities for diverse future technics by rethinking technology from a cosmological perspective.

Material observation and informational observation

Let me first review just one important matter regarding the shift from classical cybernetics to neocybernetics that is relevant here: the notion of observation. Weiner's cybernetics developed into a new phase around the 1970s: neocybernetics. It includes Heinz von Foerster's second-order cybernetics, Humberto Maturana and Francisco Varela's autopoiesis, Ernst von Glasersfeld's radical constructivism, at a later stage, Niklas Luhmann's social systems theory, and the recent works of Bruce Clarke and Mark B. N. Hansen, who proposed the term neocybernetics.[13] Toru Nishigaki's fundamental informatics can be also included in neocybernetics.

There are various differences between classical cybernetics and neocybernetics, but the decisive one that I would like to focus on here

12   Toru Nishigaki, 'Saishukougi: La Mancha no Jouhougakusha' (The last lecture: informatics researcher of La Mancha), memorial lecture, The University of Tokyo, 2013.

13   Heinz von Foerster, *Understanding Understanding*; Humberto Maturana and Francisco J. Varela, *Autopoiesis and Cognition: The Realization of the Living* (Dordrecht: D. Reidel, 1980); Ernst von Glasersfeld, *Radical Constructivism: A Way of Knowing and Learning* (London: Routledge, 1995); Niklas Luhmann, *Social Systems*, trans. John Bednarz, Jr. with Dirk Baecker (Stanford: Stanford University Press, 1995); Bruce Clarke and Mark B. N. Hansen, eds., *Emergence and Embodiment: New Essays on Second-Order Systems Theory* (Durham, NC: Duke University Press, 2009).

is that the concept of observation has been deepened. This means that there are two modes of observation in the new systems theory. On the one hand, a system is observed as an object by an observing subject from outside the system. On the other hand, a system is recursively observing itself observing. In classical cybernetics, the observer observes the system objectively from outside. In other words, it observes what input the system receives, how it is processed internally, and what output it produces. In neocybernetics, by contrast, the observer also observes how the system itself observes its own world.

Actually, classical cybernetics was already concerned not with the problem of how to control a system as an object, but how a system itself manages to achieve its goal within its uncertain environment.[14] This suggests that cybernetics can study how the world looks from within the living being, not only by observing it as an object of observation from outside, but also by observing it observing itself and its environment. The development of this biological insight is an important achievement of neocybernetics. The step taken in terms of the notion of observation is expressed simply in von Foerster's term second-order cybernetics, and in the title of his book *Observing Systems*.[15]

We have to note, however, that there is still room for misunderstanding in the concept of second-order observation. That an observing subject observes another system's observation as its object of observation from outside the system means, in a sense, that one is observing the observing system. But that is not what second-order observation means here; it is in fact nothing other than first-order observation redirected to the observation of another observing system. In short, it does not change the mode of observation itself. Observing the world from the perspective of living beings is a different mode of observation.

From the perspective of the living being, its own environmental world is not a world as an object of observation independent of itself as observing subject, but a world observed including the observer itself. The living being constructs its own world through living, while living in it. However, the environmental world is not the same as a world that is constructed idealistically or solipsistically by the subjective consciousness of a living being. Although the lived environmental world is a world that the living being has constructed through its life, it is also

14 Wiener, *Cybernetics*.
15 Heinz von Foerster, *Observing Systems* (Seaside, CA: Intersystems, 1981).

a world in which the living being is always already living as a particular being in the world: the self that exists in the world and the self that constructs the world. This self does not refer to a private, individual, or conscious ego. The being-in-the-world-self and the constructing-the-world-self are identical but different; it is living in a world constructed by itself. This recursive self-productivity and self-referential ambiguity occurs in the lived observation.

The distinction between the two modes of observation is the remarkable shift from classical cybernetics to neocybernetics; observation in which the observing subject objectifies the system as an object of observation, and observation as the living process of construction of its world to live in. By observing the system from both perspectives, it becomes possible to observe the living being as a system in two ways: mechanistically and biologically. In other words, the living being can be observed as an algorithm of data processing and as a lived process of constructing its world. The former observes the inputs, outputs, and internal processing of the system, while the latter observes the world as it is experienced by the living being here and now, constructing the world itself. I call these two modes of observation 'material observation' and 'in-formational observation'.[16] The observation in classical cybernetics, in which a system is observed as an object, is a material observation, or a mechanistic worldview. By contrast, the observation of the construction of the world of the living being is an in-formational observation, or a biological worldview. These two modes of observation are fundamentally different.

Materially open and in-formationally closed system

Rather than simply reject cybernetics, how can we respect the future vision latent in cybernetics itself? Here, I provide a sketch of biological cybernetics, referring to the arguments of Hideo Kawamoto and Toru Nishigaki. Kawamoto introduced autopoiesis theory to Japan, and has continued to explore it in his own unique direction. Nishigaki has

---

16   Daisuke Harashima, 'Kaisouteki jiritsusei no kansatsukijutu wo meguru media approach' (Media approach to observation-description of hierarchical autonomy), in *Kisojouhougaku no Frontier* (The frontier of fundamental informatics), ed. Toru Nishigaki (Tokyo: The University of Tokyo Press, 2018): 137–157.

reconsidered the concept of information from the viewpoint of life, and has founded and continues to explore fundamental informatics. They can both be placed within the theoretical paradigm of neocybernetics. However, it seems to me that they are both somewhat distinct in the way they respect life, compared to other neocyberneticians. Precisely for this reason, I feel a deep sympathy for them, and I think of their works as keys to cybernetics for the twenty-first century. Of course, an important feature of neocybernetics is that it amounts to cybernetics from the perspective of the living being, and it generally involves profound considerations of life. This should give us a clue to the idea of biological cybernetics.

First, let me briefly explain how autopoiesis was introduced to Japan by Kawamoto, for here lies a key point to understand neocybernetics as biological cybernetics. Kawamoto, who translated Maturana and Varela's *Autopoiesis* into Japanese, classified systems theory into three generations in order to contextualize autopoiesis. According to Kawamoto, the first generation is an equilibrium open system of homeostasis, the second is a non-equilibrium open system of self-organization, and the third is an operationally closed system of autopoiesis.[17] Based on Kawamoto's classification, Nishigaki pointed out that the first and second generations are necessary conditions for the living system, but only the third generation is considered a sufficient condition.[18]

Autopoiesis is a theoretical systems model originally proposed by biologists Maturana and Varela as a natural scientific definition of the living being, that is, without presupposing, as some vitalists do, any material components unique to the living being. It did not seek a material component, but an organization—namely a relation among the components of a system—that is unique to the living being. The living being here refers to the biological and life-scientific organism, of which the cell is the smallest unit. Kawamoto's classification of the three generations of systems means that there are three different notions of the organization, and the first and second generations—that is, the homeostasis of equilibrium open systems and the self-organization

17   Hideo Kawamoto, *Autopoiesis: Daisan-sedai System* (The third-generation system) (Tokyo: Seidosha, 1995).
18   Nishigaki, *Fundamental Informatics*, vol. 1, 67.

of non-equilibrium open systems—can be said to be necessary conditions for the living system. But what can be said to be a sufficient condition was only formulated in the third generation: the autopoiesis of operationally closed systems.

We can observe the homeostasis of the first-generation system in, for example, the ability of a living being to keep the condition of its internal environment constant, despite changes in its external environment. However, this ability is not unique to the living being, for we can also observe it in a machine with a feedback mechanism. We can observe the self-organization of the second-generation system in, for example, the morphogenesis or ontogenesis of a living being. However, this is not unique to the living being either, for we can also observe it in non-biological physical phenomena such as crystallization. By contrast, the autopoiesis of the third-generation system is, according to autopoiesis theory, unique to the living being. Autopoiesis means self-production, which is not about self-reproduction or homogenization, but about making oneself by oneself, that is, a recursive self-production process in which the product of the producing process comes back to produce the producing process itself. Autopoiesis theory claims that this is unique to the living being. In autopoiesis theory, a system produced by itself is called an autopoietic system, in contrast with a system produced by others, which is called an allopoietic system. Machines, including any product of modern technology, are allopoietic systems as long as they have external designers who produced them. For example, even though artificial intelligence is capable of machine learning, it is still allopoietic, because its learning methods are determined by its external producers.

In this classification, the first and second generations are both open systems, but the third generation of autopoiesis is an operationally closed system. That the autopoietic system is closed is misleading, if we do not distinguish between the two modes of observation of the material and the informational, because it would be strange, from the physicochemical point of view, for the living being to be a closed system. This is precisely because, as the classification itself indicates, the living being must be an open system, as it is homeostatic and self-organizing. The living being is a materially open system with input and output, as is evident in its metabolism. What does it mean, then, that it is nevertheless an operationally closed system? This is not a contradiction, and we can see the operational closure not through material observation but through informational observation. In short, the living being is a materially open and informationally closed system.

In the case of the first and second generations, when we observe a system informationally, we are actually observing its inputs and outputs, and its internal processing, from outside the system as an object of observation, that is, as an informationally open system. In other words, we are in effect only observing it materially. This is the mechanistic systems theory. However, if we distinguish between material and informational observations, we can see that the living system is both materially open and informationally closed.[19]

What does it mean that a system is informationally closed or open? The informationally closed system is autonomous, because the way it operates is self-produced. By contrast, the informationally open system is heteronomous, because the way it operates is instructed by others. The autonomous operation is internally formed, not instructed from outside, so it is called closed. By contrast, the heteronomous operation is instructed from outside, so it is called open. To put it another way, the informationally closed system autonomously produces its own responses to a given stimulus, while the informationally open system heteronomously responds to an external stimulus.

From informational observation, we see that for closed systems, there can be freedom, contingency, and becoming. Conversely, the operation of the informationally open system is determined, so if there is uncertainty, it is only probabilistic. There may be many possibilities, but there is no pure contingency open to real changes. Open contingency, when described as a system, applies to the informationally closed system.[20]

We can see this in the difference between the regularities of the living being and the machine. We can observe regularity in the behaviour of the living being, not because it moves according to some given rules, but rather because it produces a provisional rule-like pattern as a result of its viable performance. This pattern is the *nomos* of the autonomous system—the pattern is produced as a result of its recursive operation in living through contingency. The generation of

19   Harashima, 'Media approach'.
20   Daisuke Harashima, 'Ikirareta imo to kachi no jikokeisei to jiritsusei no guuzen' (Self-formation of lived meaning and contingency of autonomy), in *Autonomy in the Age of Artificial Intelligence*, ed. Shigeo Kawashima (Tokyo: Keiso Shobo, 2019): 69–94.

patterns in the living being occurs in the reverse order to that in the machine, in which rules are developed from a set of rules predetermined from outside. Seen retrospectively, classical cybernetics is not a study of how to reduce the living being into the machine. Rather it looks at how the living being can reduce its overwhelmingly unpredictable environment into something more consistent, and thus more conducive to its survival, generating mechanical and regular patterns in that environment. This leads to the informational observation of the living being as an autonomous system.

We need to change our perspective from material observation to informational observation in order to observe the operation of the informationally closed system. When we observe a materially open system, we are observing it from outside. By contrast, when we observe an informationally closed system, we are observing it from within its operation itself. To put it more precisely, when we are observing it, there is no inside or outside. That we observe it from within its operation itself does not mean that there is a boundary in time or space that we observe from inside of it. When we separate the inside from the outside, we are already observing it as a materially open system. To explain it metaphorically, when we draw a circle, observing the drawing process from the perspective of the process itself is the observation of the informationally closed system. There is no inside or outside in the process of drawing a circle. It is only as a result of this drawing process that a circle is left, of which we can say that it has an inside or outside. It is, so to speak, a material trace of the process. The observation of the materially open system looks at this trace.[21]

Note that the materially closed system here means that we can observe neither the input nor the output of the system, and it is irregular and unpredictable. However, without the two observations, we cannot discern whether its irregularity and unpredictability are due to the observer's lack of knowledge, or to the autonomy of the system.[22] In other words, we cannot distinguish the irregularity and unpredictability of the machine from that of the living being. For example, artificial intelligence is sometimes unpredictable, even to the people who made it.

21   Kawamoto explains the difference between the open system and the closed system in detail using the metaphor of running around the playground. See Kawamoto, *Autopoiesis*, 174.
22   Harashima, 'Media approach'.

To take another example, there is an aesthetic sensibility that finds the malfunction or unpredictable movement of the machine interesting. Something like a vital force seems to overflow from the place where the machine deviates from the rules. One might think that the machine, like the living being or nature, is unpredictable and autonomous. However, the two observations allow us to discern the difference between the unpredictability of the mechanical object and that of the living being. Technology has its own unpredictability, but it is different from living contingency. There remains, of course, some incomprehensibility in a system as an object, but that incomprehensibility is due to the limitations of the observing subject, who is a human being. That is different from the incomprehensibility of the living being that comes from its being an informationally closed system. Regarding the aesthetics of imperfection or failure, although that imperfection or failure can be observed as if the vital force is overflowing from deviation, this is the way we see it through material observation; the 'mechanistic worldview'. Through informational observation, such a vital force is not disorder, but rather it reveals its vitality, which is the order of the biological. To see this, is what I call here 'the biological worldview'. With the two modes of observation, material and informational, we can see both the mechanistic and the biological worldviews.

By distinguishing between material and informational observations, we can see the living being not only as a materially open system but also as an informationally closed system, that is, as an autonomous and autopoietic system. The living being has two aspects: mechanistic and biological. In the new cybernetics, the living being is observed as a materially open and informationally closed system. The informational closure is intrinsic to the creativity of the living being. However, without the two modes of observation, the openness and closure are incompatible. In classical cybernetics, or in first- and second-generation systems theories, the living being is observed as an open system. This means that these systems theories observe the living being as an open system both materially and informationally; they observe the living being as a heteronomous system. This is why classical cybernetics is a mechanical systems theory that blurs the distinction between the living being and the machine. If we look at society and ecosystems through this mechanistic worldview, we see people as parts of a machine of society, and nature as a stock of resources to be exploited—in short, a cybernetics of enframing. By contrast, what would society and ecosystems look like in the new cybernetics, in which we see not only the heteronomous aspect of the living system, but also its autonomous autopoietic aspect, through both material and informational observation?

Life information

Among the new cybernetics, Toru Nishigaki's fundamental informatics has explored biological cybernetics with a particular emphasis on the notion of observation.[23] Although I cannot introduce the entire theory here, I would like to refer to two ideas that help us to envision cybernetics for the twenty-first century. The first is Nishigaki's concept of information, which takes into account the difference and relation between the living being and the machine. The second is his systems model, of the human being as an ambiguous system that is autonomous and heteronomous.

First, the concept of information. Let us approach this from a biological perspective in order to delve into the informational observation and the biological worldview. The mathematical concept of information, the probabilistic concept of information as entropy/negentropy in Claude Shannon's communication theory and Wiener's classical cybernetics, are mechanistic concepts of information from material observation. By contrast, the biological concept of information is aimed at grasping more fundamental information from which such mechanistic concepts of information were derived. According to Nishigaki, information is fundamentally 'something that brings about *significance* to a living thing', and it is internally formed through the survival of the living being.[24] This fundamental information is called 'life information'. In fundamental informatics, social information like linguistic signs, and mechanical information like digital data, are all considered as transduced from the life information.

23   Nishigaki, *Fundamental Informatics*, vol. 1, 8–11.
24   Toru Nishigaki, *Seimei to Kikai wo tsunagu chi* (Tokyo: Kyoto University of the Arts and Tohoku University of Art and Design Press Geijutsu Gakusha, 2022). Translated by Toru Nishigaki as *The Wisdom to Bridge the Gap between Lives and Machines: An Introduction to Fundamental Informatics* (2013), https://digital-narcis.org/nishigaki_pdf/introductionToFI1_v1.pdf, 15; original emphasis.

The living being lives in its environmental world constructed by itself as it lives its life. The environmental world is of lived significance to the living being. In other words, everything in the experiential environmental world has its own significance within the teleological nexus of significance to the living being to live. Through living its life, the experiential world of the nexus of significance to itself is constructed. This significance is the fundamental information, life information. The living being, through living, lives in the world of lived significance that it itself constructs as it lives, and on the ground of this world, it takes another step in its life. Therefore, Nishigaki, referring to Gregory Bateson, also defines information as 'a pattern by which a living thing generates patterns'.[25]

This self-referentially, self-generating nature of information is largely described in Bateson's concept of information, as 'a difference that makes a difference'.[26] However, there is one crucial difference between Bateson's concept of information and Nishigaki's: life. Nishigaki's concept of information emphasizes the living being as the observer-constructor. In other words, it is not a subject who observes an object from outside, but a living being who constructs its own world while living within it, for which a difference makes a difference. Life information is significant to a living being, irreplaceable and unique. In addition, the living being is a living being that constructs its own world of significance while living within it. Therefore, information is *a pattern by which a living thing generates patterns*. The phrase *by which a living thing* is a simple expression of the cosmology that forms the background of this concept of information. In short, living life is the ground for in-formation.

Information is fundamentally significance internally formed through living life. Fundamental informatics calls this life information, and classifies three categories of information: life information, social information, and mechanical information. The latter two are generated from life information.[27] Life information acts as primitive affect of vital

25   Ibid., 4, original emphasis.
26   Gregory Bateson, *Steps to an Ecology of Mind: Collected Essays in Anthropology, Psychiatry, Evolution, and Epistemology* (Chicago: University of Chicago Press, 2000).
27   Nishigaki, *Fundamental Informatics*, vol. 1, chap. 1; vol. 2, chap. 1; vol. 3, chap. 3.

activities and has not yet been cognized by consciousness or articulated through language. When people attempt to convey life information to others, they express it through gestures, images, words, and more; a combination of symbols and their associated meanings is generated, and this is referred to as social information. The generation of social information is fundamentally achieved through communication on the scene. Individuals attempt to convey the meaning and value of their own lived life information through their own social efforts. Such gestures, images, and words always involve the individual's embodiment and affect, their lived meaning and value. The symbols and their associated meanings of social information are fundamentally inseparable. Mechanical information is the abstraction of social information, leaving only the symbols. As communication using social information becomes stable, even transmitting only symbols like written text across time and space, can convey a certain degree of meaning. Through abstraction into mechanical information, the inseparable aspects of lived meaning and value in social information become latent and are then re-enacted by the interpreter. For example, even if you cannot read or write Japanese, you might still be able to copy Japanese characters without understanding their meaning, and when people who understand Japanese read those characters, they will be able to make sense from those symbols. Based on the same principle, today's artificial intelligence can perform various tasks in natural language processing (NLP), such as text generation, solely through the manipulation of symbols, without understanding their meaning. The condition that enables such operations is the abstraction of social information into mechanical information, which allows the processing of symbols independently from their lived meaning and value.

Life information, social information, and mechanical information are continuous, but fundamentally, information is produced as life information and then transduced into social information, which is further abstracted into mechanical information. This is in the reverse order of the major approach to symbols and meanings in contemporary artificial intelligence research and robotics. The well-known frame problem and symbol grounding problem ask how we are able to attach meanings to, or generate meanings from, meaningless symbols that are mechanical information. This implies the premise that there are first meaningless symbols, and then meanings are attached to or generated from them. This order of questioning is inverted, from the perspective of the order of transduction of information in fundamental informatics; first there are meanings, and then symbols are transduced from them. This reversal of the order is similar to the reversal of the mechanist and biological perspectives on the patterns of the living being discussed earlier. In fundamental informatics, the mechanical is positioned within the biological system in the form of transduction from life information to mechanical information. The machine and the living being are understood in terms of information from an integrated perspective. This is not identification of the machine and the living being, but rather transduction of life information to mechanical information.

Under the technological condition of classical cybernetics, the information society has increasingly been emphasizing mechanical information only. The academic world is no exception. After the linguistic turn in the twentieth century, various turns have been proposed to overcome its limitations. From the standpoint of fundamental informatics, we would expect an informatic turn, in the sense that it sheds light not only on social and mechanical information, but also on life information. But in fact, what has been happening so far is the opposite; a false informatic turn in the sense of a turn towards mechanical information. This is precisely what Heidegger meant by the completion of Western metaphysics through cybernetics, the end of philosophy, and world domination by Western European civilization. Following Nishigaki, I argue that the task of cybernetics for the twenty-first century is to achieve the real informatic turn toward life information.[28] Among the potential research subjects, we could think of the unconscious, affect, and embodiment, but in a different way from mechanistic approaches. Within the mechanistic development of classical cybernetics, there are many approaches today where the unconscious, affect, and embodiment are researched as forms of information processing. But what I expect from cybernetics for the twenty-first century is research that takes life information into account, rather than focusing exclusively on mechanical information, as is the case in technological universalism.

So far, I have introduced the concept of information in fundamental informatics; 'something that brings about significance to a living thing', and 'a pattern by which a living thing generates patterns'. I would like to go a little further here into the construction of the environmental

28   Toru Nishigaki, *Jouhougakuteki Tenkai* (The informatic turn) (Tokyo: Shunjusha), 2005.

world of the living being as a biological cybernetic system. When we say that information is 'something that brings about significance to a living thing', and the living being lives in its own environmental world of such significance, some might wonder if this is not the same as enframing, since it is cybernetics that confines human beings to a world of useful things. However, biological cybernetics differs from enframing cybernetics in a crucial respect: the observer's point of view. To whom is the useful thing of use? Enframing conceals this question. This is why enframing is totalizing, and why technology is superficially universalizing. To say that something is universally useful, premises an observer observing the whole world as an object from outside as the basis for value judgment. Enframing technology conceals this, providing a loophole for pretending to be a transcendent observer to beings in the world that would never be able to take such a point of view, such as a person, a community, or a machine.

Neocybernetics, which emphasizes the viewpoint of the observer as a living being, does not start from this premise, because from the viewpoint of a living being, it is impossible to observe the whole world from outside that world. Rather, it starts from observing the world as it is observed by an observer living in the world. That is to say, each living being is living in its own environmental world of significance. In each of those worlds, countless other living beings are also living, each constructing its own world, and each living being is living in that world: a pluralistic world. Neocybernetics asks how this is constructed. In this sense, it asks what it is, if not technology, that is constructing my world. This is a question of the human being, of life living itself.

Hierarchical autonomous communication system

The 'self' (自己, *jiko*) of 'self-producing system' (自己産出系, *jikosanshutsukei*) and 'autonomous system' (自律系, *jiritsukei*) is ambiguous in nature. In Japanese, it is known that the word '自' (*ji*) contains both meanings of this ambiguity: 'what was done voluntarily' (みずから, *mizukara*) and 'what has turned out to be' (おのずから, *onozukara*).[29] The Japanese

29   Seiichi Takeuchi, *Flower Petals Fall, but the Flower Endures: The Japanese Philosophy of Transience (New English Edition)*, trans. Japan Publishing Industry Foundation for Culture (JPIC) (Tokyo: JPIC, 2019), 32.

word '自然' (*shizen* or *jinen*), which is now usually used as a translation of the word 'nature', expresses this ambiguity as well, and also means absolute contingency beyond human control. These complex connotations help us understand that the self-producing system, or the autonomous system, is not simple self-identification or self-regulation, but rather superimposition of self and other—an ambiguous system of autopoiesis and allopoiesis, or of the autonomous and the heteronomous—and also that it is contingent. Life is living deep inside myself. I feel that I am living, while life inside myself lives by itself.

In fundamental informatics, the human being—this ambiguous being of autonomy and heteronomy—is described in a systems model: the hierarchical autonomous communication system (HACS).[30] In this light, let us step onto the path of a new cybernetic approach to life-in-formation working deeper inside than technology.

In the HACS model, human beings as living social beings are considered to be autonomous systems, because they are living beings, but they are also considered to be heteronomous systems, because they are living under social norms. This is an antinomy between autonomy and heteronomy. But if we consider the two modes of observation, we can comprehend this ambiguity not as a mere contradiction, but as a description of the same human being from two different observations; human beings are observed as autonomous systems from the perspective of the psychic system, and as heteronomous systems from the perspective of the social system. In this way, we can observe human beings as HACS in which the psychic system and the social system, while both are autonomous, overlap hierarchically and operate correlatively.

Let us consider the hierarchical and autonomous correlative operation of HACS in a more concrete example: a situation in which two people are communicating, that is, two psychic systems and one social system are operating as HACS. The psychic system is an autonomous system, a kind of autopoietic system composed of thoughts that produce thoughts; it can also produce, as by-products of its operation, expressions such as gestures, spoken words, and written words, that is, materials for communication. Now, when a psychic system produces such an expression, it becomes a perturbation for another psychic system. Of course, since the psychic system is autonomous, it does not receive the expression in the same way a machine receives a signal as

30   Nishigaki, *Fundamental Informatics*, vol. 2, chap. 1; vol. 3, chap. 3.

input, but the expression can bring forth some changes in the environment of the system, disturbing its operation; the system continues its autonomous operation while itself compensating for the disturbance, and can produce an expression as a by-product of this operation. This expression then affects the first system as another perturbation, and the first system continues to operate under the disturbance, producing another expression as a by-product of its operation. Thus, communication occurs. Suppose that such communication continues to be produced. At this point, if we focus on this communication production process, we can observe a recursive process in which produced communication produces communication. What we have observed here is an autonomous system that consists in a different phase from the psychic systems: a social system. In the HACS model, the psychic systems as lower systems, and the social system as a higher system, operate hierarchically and autonomously.

When the operation is observed informationally, the lower system is operating as a self-producing autonomous system, but when observed materially, it is producing by-products, a chain of production that results in communication (composed of those by-products). The recursive process of communication production operates as an autonomous system when its operation is observed informationally: this is the higher system. Thus, by observing from multiple viewpoints, we can observe the lower and higher systems operating as HACS.

When we observe the lower system from the perspective of the higher system, we observe the lower system as if it were an allopoietic heteronomous system that produces some materials that serve as components for the higher system. When we observe its operation informationally, the lower system is operating as an autopoietic autonomous system, but since, from the viewpoint of the higher system, the lower system is observed as an object from outside, the autonomous operation of the lower system cannot be observed from the perspective of the higher system. On the other hand, the higher system is itself an autopoietic system, meaning that anything not participating in the network of the communication production process is not a component of the system; no hierarchical relation can be established with any system that does not produce materials for communication. Put differently, being a lower system means that some constraint from the higher system is at work. In the case of human society, this constraint can be morality, or another form of power. Of course, it is possible to change the constraint from the bottom up, since the components of the higher system are produced by the lower systems. But being hierarchical means that there is always already some constraint at work. This asymmetry brings about complex theoretical problems, but needless to say, it has also caused human beings anguish and tragedy.

It is sometimes said that modern technology blurs the distinction between the living being and the machine. From the informational observation, machines in modern technology are nothing but allopoietic heteronomous systems, which should be clearly distinct from the living being. Why does the distinction between the living being and the machine seem so blurred? In light of the HACS model, this is because it is impossible to identify whether a lower system is informationally autonomous or heteronomous, from the viewpoint of its higher system. Modern technological information processing machines are capable of producing materials for communication, which are the components for the social system. From the viewpoint of the social system, such machines are observed to have become members of society and are given the same status as humans. From the viewpoint of the social system, information processing machines are observed as a kind of pseudo-autonomous system or what constitutes, what Mark Hansen calls, 'provisional closure'.[31] In cybernetics for the twenty-first century, how to position such machines that interact with humans and produce materials for social communication, and how to develop and implement them in society while understanding distinctions and relationship with humans, are already important issues.

The lower system of HACS, despite being observed as a heteronomous system by the higher system, is an autonomous system when observed informationally from within the operation of the lower system itself. HACS consists of the correlative operation of the higher and lower autonomous systems. This means that the machine, which is a heteronomous system, cannot be a lower system of HACS. This critical distinction becomes blurred when we observe the lower system only from the viewpoint of the higher system, because from that perspective, we can only observe the lower system as an object of the material and mechanistic observation, from outside. If we consider

31   Mark B. N. Hansen, 'System-Environment Hybrids', in *Emergence and Embodiment*, ed. Bruce Clarke and Mark B. N. Hansen (Durham, NC: Duke University Press, 2009): 113–142.

only the social system, the distinction between the human being and the machine becomes blurred. However, in HACS, where autonomous systems constitute a hierarchy, the living being and the machine are clearly distinct from each other from the informational and biological perspective, and the machine is not positioned as the lower system of HACS. A society in which humans are treated like machines, or machines are treated like living things, is impossible in the cosmology represented in the HACS model.

Then, where is technology, or technics more broadly, positioned in the HACS model? The answer is: the media.[32] In fundamental informatics, the media have two major functions. The first is information processing, storage, conversion, and transmission. This is what is generally referred to as 'media' in media studies. The second is to help the hierarchical and autonomous operation of the higher and lower systems. This is a mechanism for coordinating the successive occurrence of communication.[33] The important point here is that media help the succession of correlative operations of the higher and lower systems as HACS, in other words, it provides empirical norms and knowledge about the values of HACS, for example, what kind of lower system behaviour can be compatible with its correlative operation in the higher system. This is actualized in a form that is accessible to the lower system: selective criteria, legal rules, archives of cases, and so on. It is, so to speak, a trace of the patterns left by the history of the hierarchical and autonomous operation of the higher and lower systems. In this way, HACS will continue to operate self-referentially. Of course, since HACS are autonomous systems, they transform contingently. The values of the higher system and the values of the lower system change at the rhythms of their respective timescales, and the media also change accordingly. Since HACS are autonomous systems, they do not operate according to a given set of rules, and their media do not provide such rules, but just a record of patterns that have been empirically viable through the history of the operation of the HACS. Situated

32   Harashima, 'Media approach'.
33   This notion of media in fundamental informatics developed based on Niklas Luhmann's concept of communication media, especially *Erfolgsmedien* (success media). See Takehiko Daikoku, *'Media' no Tetsugaku* (Philosophy of 'media'), (Tokyo: NTT Publishing, 2006); Nishigaki, *Fundamental Informatics*, vol. 1, chap. 3; vol. 2, chap. 1; vol. 3, chap. 3; Niklas Luhmann, *Die Gesellschaft der Gesellschaft* (Frankfurt: Suhrkamp, 1997), chap. 2.

in an environment that fluctuates contingently, HACS operate not only according to their past knowledge and the data recorded in its media, but also flexibly and heuristically, and the result of its operation is then left as media again.

In short, the media are technics that help HACS continue their hierarchical operation. This means that the media act on the constraint from the higher system to the lower system. The media technics help the hierarchical operation of the HACS, by regulating the constraint. Technics as media affects how the human experience as a social being is constructed. The essence of technics as media is to help the hierarchical operation of HACS by acting on the construction of the environmental world of significance to the system.

Although the social constraint, on which the media act, constrains the thoughts of the psychic systems, it does not construct the worlds of fundamental significance to human beings. Life living itself constructs the world of significance. This means that, although technics as media acts on how the human experience as a social being is constructed, the condition making the construction itself possible, is life. The higher and lower systems, helped by the media, correlatively operating, each transforms autonomously and self-productively, and its dynamic is life-in-formation.

Thus it becomes clear that enframing cybernetics conceals two things. The first is the already mentioned criterion of value judgments, namely the observer observing the higher system. The second is the existence of the lower system. Enframing cybernetics conceals the observation of the autonomous system that constructs the world of significance. After all, the cybernetic system of enframing is a higher system that observes the living being as a heteronomous system, and modern technology is its medium. It lacks the informational observation making sense from the viewpoint of the living being (the lower system). In short, enframing cybernetics conceals the fact that there exists hierarchical autonomy. Hierarchical autonomy makes it obvious that there are two points of view, not one. In this context, we can interpret what Heidegger pointed out about cybernetics and enframing as meaning that the first- and second-generation systems in the paradigm of classical cybernetics are all about enframing. If we try to understand social systems and global ecosystems with a systems theory on the basis solely of informationally open systems, without distinguishing two modes of observation, we end up with enframing. The aforementioned example, the distorted image of mechanistic society, is typical of such understanding of human societies and human beings as social beings only from the viewpoint of the social system. This is why I have emphasized the importance of the two modes of observation, and the importance of the notions of life information and HACS in the new cybernetics.

Cybernetics for the twenty-first century

The critical task for cybernetics for the twenty-first century is to observe an even higher system than social systems, because social systems are constrained by higher global systems. Today, the dominant global system is global capitalism, whose symbolic values are economic growth and technological innovation. Modern technology, which is essentially enframing, is global capitalism's medium, under which the heart of life is being suppressed and under threat of being reduced or even eliminated. To realize other values, different from those of the global system, is the key to cybernetics for the twenty-first century; to realize different global systems that will save the heart of life in crisis. What we should strive for is a global system that respects life. Respect for life here does not mean survival, life support, or immortality from the material and mechanistic point of view; these could even lead to the suppression of the heart of life. The contradictory ideal of realizing the growth of the informational and biological heart through material and mechanistic manipulations would lead to such a consequence. Rather, respect for life here means respecting the values of systems that take care of life-in-formation observed informationally and biologically. It is a way to live as human beings as HACS to realize a correlative hierarchical autonomy among psychic systems, social systems, and a global system that takes as its values respect for life; a way of life in which we can live autonomously and, as it is, fit with the values of the higher system of life. In other words, we will be able to observe the significance of each individual living system observed from the perspective of a cosmic system of life, corresponding to the significance of everything in a world observed from within each individual living system.

Is it possible to bring about such a transformation of a global system, and the correlative transformation of psychic systems through changes in social institutions or technological innovations? This is the wrong way to frame the question. Rather, cybernetics for the twenty-first century is about the gradual growth and salvation of each individual heart, no matter how long it takes. Then the global system will also transform little by little. It may take a tremendous amount of time. It is a long way, but it is a modest way. It can only be undertaken individually; not by following a prescribed way of doing things, but through living one's own life. We must answer our own questions ourselves, because the heart is autonomous, it is self-producing. This is a problem in the realm of life. As an informationally closed system, a living system in neocybernetics, the process of the heart is not something that can be controlled in accordance with mechanical laws, but happens singularly; it is an informationally closed system, not an informationally open system like a machine. Nevertheless, the material and mechanistic realm does have an important role for the process of the heart. We must strive to keep living beings materially alive until the wish is fulfilled. Modern technology has been accused of taking time away from human beings. We can say that this is because the process of the heart takes a tremendous amount of time. Material technics must make this time, and it must be sustainable. I suggest that cybernetics for the twenty-first century should be a technics that can maintain the compatibility of living beings' informational and material aspects, by making physical time for them to make their lived history, and to sustain their life until the correlative transformation is realized.

Technology acts on the construction of the environmental world in which a human being lives as a social being. However, what the new cybernetics, such as fundamental informatics, has argued is that, at a deeper level than technology, life living is the ground for the construction of the world of significance to a living being: life-in-formation. Taking care of this, we will realize that every little thing in the world as it appears is precious and makes life alive: the nature of the self, by itself. Taking care of this heart would be an important step for cybernetics for the twenty-first century. This is a growth. But this is not a calculable growth, like economic growth as a measure for the global capitalist system. This is a growth of the heart. This is not to deny material growth, but to affirm informational growth. Affirming informational observation does not deny material observation, and vice versa. Affirming the material observation does not deny the informational observation. However, we cannot observe the informational when we are observing the material, and we cannot observe the material when we are observing the informational. The two observations must be superimposed. As a reflection on the technological civilization of classical cybernetics, which tend to overemphasize the mechanistic development based on material observation, I suggest, from the standpoint of the new cybernetics, that we should affirm the importance of the biological growth of the heart, based on informational observation; distinguishing between the mechanistic and biological orders, we should value the singularity of life.

This is a step, growth, not in a progress toward a determined destination, but rather in a process of becoming aware of the here and now. Informational observation is the realization that the self is, as it is, self-producing and autonomous. In other words, it helps us remove the constraints that we, as living systems, do not really need to be attached to. This does not mean that we are free from material constraint or power; that is a matter of the material. But regardless of whether we achieve such liberation or not, we realize that living beings are autonomous. If we blur the fundamental distinction between the orders of the material and the informational, it seems as if there is a trade-off between constraint and autonomy; and if we premise that we are not autonomous as long as we are not liberated, then this premise would suppress the autonomy of the heart, of natural life, which everyone is living by itself. Informational observation, observing this autonomy, is a step towards the process. Biological autonomy is not a goal, but a starting point. Informational observation does not make the material world disappear. It does not make the constraints of social and global systems disappear, nor does it enable us to deliberately manipulate them. It just means that we can observe and take care of life-in-formation, which is the dynamic of the social and global systems transforming. It may be small, but it would provide us with the power to live, encouraging us to live together. Cybernetics of the heart, or steering technics for us to survive our passages of life, will help us to make this step.[34]

34   In relation to this concluding paragraph, Yuk Hui suggested in a dialogue with me that it might be possible to interpret in this way the tanka (Japanese short poem) of the Japanese philosopher Kitaro Nishida (1870–1945): '人は人吾は吾なりとにかくに吾行く道を吾は行くなり' (*hito wa hito / ware wa ware nari / tonikaku ni / ware yuku michi wo / ware wa yuku nari*), which could translate to 'People are people, I am I, in any case, I will go the path I go' (Kitaro Nishida, *Nishida Kitaro Kashu* (Kitaro Nishida Poem Collectoin), ed. Kaoru Ueda (Tokyo: Iwanami Shoten, 2009), 46). This tanka, created by Nishida in 1934, is known today for being inscribed on

a monument placed beside a pedestrian path in Kyoto called 'Tetsugaku no michi' (Philosopher's Walk), where he used to take walks while deep in thought. I cannot delve into it here, but I believe that Hui's insight raises an important question, if, as Hui suggests, we interpret that the tanka in relation to the conclusion, '人は人吾は吾' (people are people, I am I), implies not self-centred individualism or egoism, but a state of being where each person is autonomous, and yet '吾行く道を吾は行くなり' (I will go the path I go) also signifies that the path of the other is itself the path I ought to take or hope to take. It is a profound state of mind or disposition that can be deeply appreciated. It not only reminds us of Nishida's concept of 'absolutely contradictory self-identity', but also naturally compels us to think about his unfathomable emotions, his philosophizing from the deep 'sorrow' (悲哀, *hiai*) within the tumultuous journey of life (also refer to note 1). In the context of this essay, there is another important issue that should be highlighted about Nishida. It is a question that constitutes the background for the very topic of cybernetics for the twenty-first century: the question of overcoming modernity. Nishida, who was one of the prominent Japanese thinkers in the first half of the twentieth century, was a pioneer of modern Japanese philosophy and is also regarded as the founder of the well-known (or notorious) Kyoto School. If we, today, endeavour to overcome modernity, it is inevitable that we will have to confront the Kyoto School, who, a century ago, earnestly faced the same question, but ultimately ended up with the serious failure of what Hui referred to as 'metaphysical fascism'. See Hui, *The Question Concerning Technology*.

Reference

Bateson, Gregory. *Steps to an Ecology of Mind: Collected Essays in Anthropology, Psychiatry, Evolution, and Epistemology*. Chicago: University of Chicago Press, 2000.

Clarke, Bruce and Mark B. N. Hansen, eds. *Emergence and Embodiment: New Essays on Second-Order Systems Theory*. Durham, NC: Duke University Press, 2009.

Derrida, Jacques. *Of Grammatology*. Translated by Gayatri Chakravorty Spivak, Baltimore: Johns Hopkins University Press, 2016.

Hansen, Mark B. N. 'System-Environment Hybrids', in *Emergence and Embodiment*, ed. Bruce Clarke and Mark B. N. Hansen, 113–142. Durham, NC: Duke University Press, 2009.

Harashima, Daisuke. 'Kaisouteki jiritsusei no kansatsukijutu wo meguru media approach' (Media approach to observation-description of hierarchical autonomy), in *Kisojouhougaku no Frontier* (The frontier of fundamental informatics), ed. Toru Nishigaki, 137–157. Tokyo: The University of Tokyo Press, 2018.

———. 'Ikirareta imo to kachi no jikokeisei to jiritsusei no guuzen' (Self-formation of lived meaning and contingency of autonomy), in *Autonomy in the Age of Artificial Intelligence*, ed. Shigeo Kawashima, 69–94. Tokyo: Keiso Shobo, 2019.

Heidegger, Martin. *On Time and Being*. Translated by Joan Stambaugh. New York: Harper & Row, 1972.

———. *The Question Concerning Technology and Other Essays*. Translated by William Lovitt. New York: Garland, 1977.

Hui, Yuk. *The Question Concerning Technology in China: An Essay in Cosmotechnics*. Falmouth: Urbanomic, 2016.

———. *Recursivity and Contingency*. London: Rowman & Littlefield, 2019.

Kawamoto, Hideo. *Autopoiesis: Daisan-sedai System* (The third-generation system). Tokyo: Seidosha, 1995.

Luhmann, Niklas. *Social Systems*. Translated by John Bednarz, Jr. with Dirk Baecker. Stanford: Stanford University Press, 1995.

———. *Die Gesellschaft der Gesellschaft*. Frankfurt: Suhrkamp, 1997.

Maturana, Humberto and Francisco J. Varela, *Autopoiesis and Cognition: The Realization of the Living*. Dordrecht: D. Reidel, 1980.

Nishida, Kitaro. *Nishida Kitaro Kashu* (Kitaro Nishida poetry collection). Edited by Kaoru Ueda. Tokyo: Iwanami Shoten, 2009.

Nishigaki, Toru. *Kiso Jouhougaku* (Fundmental informatics) *I, II, III*. Tokyo: NTT Publishing, 2004, 2008, 2021.
———. *Jouhougakuteki Tenkai* (The informatic turn). Tokyo: Shunjusha, 2005.
———. 'Saishukougi: La Mancha no Jouhougakusha' (The last lecture: informatics researcher of La Mancha), memorial lecture, The University of Tokyo, 2013.
———. *Seimei to Kikai wo tsunagu chi*. Tokyo: Kyoto University of the Arts and Tohoku University of Art and Design Press Geijutsu Gakusha, 2022. Translated by Toru Nishigaki as *The Wisdom to Bridge the Gap between Lives and Machines: An Introduction to Fundamental Informatics* (2013), https://digital-narcis.org/nishigaki_pdf/introductionToFI1_v1.pdf.
Ohi, Nami. 'Imi no kaifuku ni yoru soushitsu-taiken no kachi no hanten: shinteki-system no hattatsu-model' (Meanings recovery enables us to survive loss experiences: a model proposal of psychic systems development process). *Shakai Jouhougaku* (Socio-informatics) 8, no. 1 (2019): 49–64.
Takehiko, Daikoku. *'Media' no Tesugaku* (Philosophy of 'media'). Tokyo: NTT Publishing, 2006.
Takeuchi, Seiichi. *'Kanashimi' no Tesugaku* (Philosophy of 'Kanashimi'). Tokyo: NHK Publishing, 2009.
———. *Flower Petals Fall, but the Flower Endures: The Japanese Philosophy of Transience (New English Edition)*. Translated by Japan Publishing Industry Foundation for Culture (JPIC). Tokyo: JPIC, 2019.
von Foerster, Heinz. *Observing Systems*. Seaside, CA: Intersystems, 1981.
———. *Understanding Understanding: Essays on Cybernetics and Cognition*. New York: Springer, 2003.
von Glasersfeld, Ernst. *Radical Constructivism: A Way of Knowing and Learning*. London: Routledge, 1995.
von Uexküll, Jakob. *A Foray into the Worlds of Animals and Humans: With a Theory of Meaning*. Translated by Joseph D. O'Neil. Minneapolis: University of Minnesota Press, 2010.
Wiener, Norbert. *Cybernetics: Or Control and Communication in the Animal and the Machine*. Cambridge, MA: MIT Press, 1948.

Biographies

Brunella Antomarini

teaches aesthetics and contemporary philosophy at John Cabot University, Rome. She has a multidisciplinary education in contemporary epistemology, aesthetics, anthropology and post-humanism. Her current research concerns the analysis of the common functions of the organic body and the retroactive machine through an epistemological convergence of different views, such as pragmatism, cybernetics, and systems theory. Among her books are: *Le macchine nubili* (2020); *Thinking Through Error* (2012); *The Maiden Machine: Philosophy in the Age of the Unborn Woman* (2013); and *Aesthetics in Present Future. The Arts in the Technological Horizon* (co-authored, 2013). She is the editor of Yuk Hui's book *Pensare la Contingenza: La rinascita della filosofia dopo la cibernetica* (Rome, 2022).

and technics in contemporary information societies from the perspective of fundamental informatics and new cybernetics, with a focus on the differences between living beings and machines as systems, to reflect on the modern technological condition and to realize new values based on respect for life. His books include *Critical Words: Media Theory* (2021, in Japanese), *Autonomy in the Age of Artificial Intelligence: Reconstructing the Basic Concept for the Future* (2019, in Japanese), and *Frontiers of Fundamental Informatics: Can Artificial Intelligence Have Its Umwelt?* (2018, in Japanese), and he has published in the journals *Gendai Shiso* and *Eureka*. He is the translator of Yuk Hui's *Recursivity and Contingency* (2022) and co-translator of Tim Ingold's *Being Alive* (2021) in Japanese.

Slava Gerovitch

teaches history of mathematics at MIT. He holds two PhDs; one in philosophy of science (from the Institute for the History of Natural Sciences and Technology, Moscow, and one in history and social study of science and technology (from MIT's Science, Technology and Society programme). He has written extensively on the history of Soviet mathematics, cybernetics, cosmonautics and computing. He is the author of *From Newspeak to Cyberspeak: A History of Soviet Cybernetics* (2002), which won an honourable mention for the Vucinich Book Prize for an outstanding monograph in Russian studies; *Voices of the Soviet Space Program: Cosmonauts, Soldiers, and Engineers Who Took the USSR into Space* (2014); and *Soviet Space Mythologies: Public Images, Private Memories, and the Making of a Cultural Identity* (2015), the winner of the Gardner-Lasser Aerospace History Literature Award and a finalist for the Historia Nova Prize for the best book on Russian intellectual and cultural history.

Yuk Hui

is Professor of Philosophy at Erasmus University Rotterdam where he holds the Chair of Human Conditions, and a professor at the City University of Hong Kong. He wrote his doctoral thesis under Bernard Stiegler at Goldsmiths College, London and obtained his Habilitation in philosophy from Leuphana University, Germany. Hui is the author of several monographs that have been translated into a dozen languages, including *On the Existence of Digital Objects* (2016), *The Question Concerning Technology in China:—An Essay in Cosmotechnics* (2016), *Recursivity and Contingency* (2019), *Art and Cosmotechnics* (2021) and forthcoming *Machine and Sovereignty* (2024). Hui is co-editor of *30 Years after Les Immatériaux: Art, Science and Theory* (2015) and editor of the issue *Philosophy after Automation* (*Philosophy Today*, Vol.65. No.2, 2021), among others. Hui has been the convenor of the Research Network for Philosophy and Technology since 2014 and a juror of the Berggruen Prize for Philosophy and Culture since 2020.

Daisuke Harashima

is a Research Associate of the Future Robotics Organization at Waseda University, Tokyo. He writes and teaches on humanities

N Katherine Hayles

is Distinguished Research Professor of English at the University of California, Los Angeles and the James B. Duke Professor of

Literature Emerita at Duke University, and teaches and writes on the relations of literature, science and technology in the twentieth and twenty-first centuries. She has published eleven books and over a hundred peer-reviewed articles, and her research has been recognized by a Guggenheim Fellowship, two National Endowment for the Humanities Fellowships, a Rockefeller Residential Fellowship at Bellagio, a National Humanities Center Fellowship, and a University of California Presidential Award, among other awards. She is a member of the American Academy of Arts and Sciences. Her books have won numerous awards, including the Rene Wellek Prize for the Best Book in Literary Theory in 1998–99 for *How We Became Posthuman: Virtual Bodies in Cybernetics, Literature, and Informatics*, and the Suzanne Langer Award for Outstanding Scholarship for Writing Machines. She writes on media theory, experimental fiction, literary and cultural theory, science fiction, and contemporary American fiction. She has won two teaching awards, and has held visiting appointments at Princeton, the University of Chicago as the Critical Inquiry Visiting Professor, and at the Institute for Advanced Studies at Durham University, UK, among others. Her most recent book is *Postprint: Books and Becoming Computational* (2021).

Dylan Levi King

is a Tokyo-based independent researcher, writer, and translator, focused on contemporary Chinese culture and philosophy. His most recent translation is *The New Civilization Upon Data: How Big Data Reshapes Human Civilization, Business and the Personal World* by Tu Zipei (2022). His writing has appeared in Palladium, the Spectator, and Chinese Literature Today.

Michał Krzykawski

is Associate Professor in Philosophy and Head of the Centre for Critical Technology Studies at the University of Silesia, Katowice, Poland. His research revolves around continental philosophy of science and technology, critical theory, and political economy. He is particularly interested in a dialogue between philosophical

thinking, technology and science in the context of epistemological, psychosocial, and ecological issues related to the current digital transformation. He is the author of *The Other and the Common: Thirty-Five Years of French Philosophy* (2017, in Polish) and co-author of *Bifurcate: There Is no Alternative*, edited by Bernard Stiegler with the Internation Collective (2021).

David Maulén de los Reyes

teaches history of technology at the Metropolitan Technological University (UTEM) and Universidad Adolfo Ibáñez (UAI), Chile. He has written about the relationships between art, science and technology in Chile and Latin America within the processes of social change, developing a specific methodology of the sociology of symbolic production for the retrospective study of project disciplines such as design, architecture, urban planning and engineering. Curatorial projects include: the third biennial of the National Museum of Fine Arts (MNBA), 'The Situation of Chilean Contemporary Art'; the project for the new Gabriela Mistral cultural centre; visualization of information 'Genealogical Trajectories of Buildings for the 3rd United Nations Conference on Trade and Development UNCTAD III'; and regional curator for the project 'Everyone is a Bauhaus: Past and future of a concept', at ZKM, Karlsruhe. He has contributed to the platform 'Is Modernity Our Antiquity?' at Documenta 12 in Kassel. He was co-editor of the special issue on cybernetics in Latin America of the AI & Society journal, research that he continues to develop.

Andrew Pickering

is Professor Emeritus of Sociology and Philosophy at University of Exeter, UK. He has held fellowships at the Institute for Advanced Study at Princeton and the Stanford Center for Advanced Study in the Behavioral Sciences, and universities including MIT, Princeton, and Durham. He is a leading figure in science and technology studies and has published widely on the history, sociology and philosophy of science, technology and mathematics. His writings have been translated into many languages, including Chinese translations of his books *Constructing Quarks: A Sociological History of Particle Physics* (1984), *Science as Practice and Culture* (1992), *and The Mangle of Practice: Time, Agency and Science* (1995). *His most recent book is The Cybernetic Brain: Sketches of Another Future* (2010). He is now working on cybernetic relations with nature and cybernetic art.

Dorion Sagan

is a celebrated writer, ecological philosopher, and author or co-author of twenty-five books, translated into fifteen languages. As an ecological theorist he has been at the forefront of bringing our growing understanding of symbiosis as a major force in evolution into the intellectual mainstream, in both science and the humanities, and rethinking the human body as a 'multispecies organism'. With Carl Sagan and Lynn Margulis, his parents, he is co-author of the entries for both 'Life' and 'Extraterrestrial Life' in the Encyclopedia Britannica.

Mathieu Triclot

teaches philosophy at the University of Technology of Belfort-Montbéliard, France. His research belongs to the French tradition of 'philosophy of technical milieux' (Simondon, Beaune, Stiegler). His first book, *Le moment cybernétique* (2008), is a history of American cybernetics and the invention of the notion of information. Since the publication of *Philosophie des jeux vidéo* (2011), he has participated in the development of game studies in the French-speaking world, notably by defending the perspective of play studies, centred on the phenomenological analysis of the regimes of experience with the computing machine. He has participated in numerous research projects in the field and is now working on the problems of a 'techno-aesthetic' and the analogies between games and music or dance, looking in particular at the relationship between gesture, computer programme and image. More recently, his research has focused on the role that the notion of 'technical milieux' can play in the context of design, and the reform of engineering training.

Special thanks to
Media Lab of Guangdong Times Museum and M Art Foundation